Lifestyle Journalism

Lifestyle journalism has experienced enormous growth in the media over the past two decades, but scholars in the fields of journalism and communication studies have so far paid relatively little attention to a field that is still sometimes seen as 'not real journalism'. There is now an urgent need for in-depth exploration and contextualisation of this field, with its increasing relevance for 21st century consumer cultures.

For the first time, this book presents a wide range of studies which have engaged with the field of lifestyle journalism in order to outline the various political, economic, social and cultural tensions within it. Taking a comparative view, the collection includes studies covering four continents, including countries such as Australia, China, Norway, Denmark, Singapore, the UK and the USA. While keeping the broader lifestyle field in mind, the chapters focus on a variety of sub-fields such as travel, music, food, health, fashion and personal technology journalism. This volume provides a fascinating account of the different facets of lifestyle journalism, and charts the way forward for a more sustained analysis of the field.

This book was originally published as a special issue of *Journalism Practice*.

Folker Hanusch is a former journalist and now Senior Lecturer in Journalism at the University of the Sunshine Coast, Australia. He has published widely on topics such as lifestyle, particularly travel, journalism, journalists' professional views, comparative journalism studies, indigenous journalism and news media representations of death and dying.

Journalism Studies: Theory and Practice
Series editor: Bob Franklin, Cardiff School of Journalism, Media and Cultural Studies, Cardiff University, UK

The journal *Journalism Studies* was established at the turn of the new millennium by Bob Franklin. It was launched in the context of a burgeoning interest in the scholarly study of journalism and an expansive global community of journalism scholars and researchers. The ambition was to provide a forum for the critical discussion and study of journalism as a subject of intellectual inquiry but also an arena of professional practice. Previously, the study of journalism in the UK and much of Europe was a fairly marginal branch of the larger disciplines of media, communication and cultural studies; only a handful of Universities offered degree programmes in the subject. *Journalism Studies* has flourished and succeeded in providing the intended public space for discussion of research on key issues within the field, to the point where in 2007 a sister journal, *Journalism Practice,* was launched to enable an enhanced focus on practice-based issues, as well as foregrounding studies of journalism education, training and professional concerns. Both journals are among the leading ranked journals within the field and publish six issues annually, in electronic and print formats. More recently, 2013 witnessed the launch of a further companion journal *Digital Journalism* to provide a site for scholarly discussion, analysis and responses to the wide ranging implications of digital technologies for the practice and study of journalism. From the outset, the publication of themed issues has been a commitment for all journals. Their purpose is first, to focus on highly significant or neglected areas of the field; second, to facilitate discussion and analysis of important and topical policy issues; and third, to offer readers an especially high quality and closely focused set of essays, analyses and discussions.

The *Journalism Studies: Theory and Practice* book series draws on a wide range of these themed issues from all journals and thereby extends the critical and public forum provided by them. The Editor of the journals works closely with guest editors to ensure that the books achieve relevance for readers and the highest standards of research rigour and academic excellence. The series makes a significant contribution to the field of journalism studies by inviting distinguished scholars, academics and journalism practitioners to discuss and debate the central concerns within the field. It also reaches a wider readership of scholars, students and practitioners across the social sciences, humanities and communication arts, encouraging them to engage critically with, but also to interrogate, the specialist scholarly studies of journalism which this series provides.

Available titles in the series:

Mapping the Magazine: Comparative Studies in Magazine Journalism
Edited by Tim Holmes

The Future of Newspapers
Edited by Bob Franklin

Language and Journalism
Edited by John Richardson

The Future of Journalism
Edited by Bob Franklin

Exploration in Global Media Ethics
Edited by Muhammad Ayish and Shakuntala Rao

Foreign Correspondence
Edited by John Maxwell Hamilton and Regina G. Lawrence

How Journalism Uses History
Edited by Martin Conboy

Lifestyle Journalism
Edited by Folker Hanusch

Environmental Journalism
Edited by Henrik Bødker and Irene Neverla

Online Reporting of Elections
Edited by Einar Thorsen

The Future of Journalism: Developments and Debates
Edited by Bob Franklin

Lifestyle Journalism

Edited by
Folker Hanusch

Routledge
Taylor & Francis Group

LONDON AND NEW YORK

First published 2013
by Routledge
2 Park Square, Milton Park, Abingdon, Oxon, OX14 4RN

Simultaneously published in the USA and Canada
by Routledge
711 Third Avenue, New York, NY 10017

Routledge is an imprint of the Taylor & Francis Group, an informa business

This book is a reproduction of *Journalism Practice*, volume 6, issue 1. The Publisher requests to those authors who may be citing this book to state, also, the bibliographical details of the special issue on which the book was based.

British Library Cataloguing in Publication Data
A catalogue record for this book is available from the British Library

ISBN13: 978-0-415-82752-2

Typeset in Helvetica
by Taylor & Francis Books

Publisher's Note
The publisher would like to make readers aware that the chapters in this book may be referred to as articles as they are identical to the articles published in the special issue. The publisher accepts responsibility for any inconsistencies that may have arisen in the course of preparing this volume for print.

Contents

Citation Information   ix
Notes on Contributors   xi

Preface
Bob Franklin   xiii

1. Broadening the Focus: The case for lifestyle journalism as a field of
   scholarly inquiry
   Folker Hanusch   1

2. Lifestyle Journalism as Popular Journalism: Strategies for evaluating
   its public role
   Elfriede Fürsich   11

3. Lifestyle Journalism: Blurring boundaries
   Nete Nørgaard Kristensen and Unni From   25

4. The Devil May Care: Travel journalism, cosmopolitan concern, politics
   and the brand
   Lyn McGaurr   41

5. Bread and Circuses: Food meets politics in the Singapore media
   Andrew Duffy and Yang Yuhong Ashley   58

6. Health and Lifestyle to Serve the Public: A case study of a cross-media
   programme series from the Norwegian Broadcasting Corporation
   Roel Puijk   74

7. Hypertextuality and Remediation in the Fashion Media: The case of
   fashion blogs
   Agnès Rocamora   91

8. Service Journalism as Community Experience: Personal technology
   and personal finance at *The New York Times*
   Nikki Usher   106

9. A New Generation of Lifestyle Magazine Journalism in China: The
   professional approach
   Shuang Li   121

Index   137

Citation Information

The chapters in this book were originally published in *Journalism Practice*, volume 6, issue 1 (February 2012). When citing this material, please use the original page numbering for each article, as follows:

Preface
Original title in journal special issue: EDITORIAL NOTE
Bob Franklin
Journalism Practice, volume 6, issue 1 (February 2012) pp. 1

Chapter 1
Broadening the Focus: The case for lifestyle journalism as a field of scholarly inquiry
Folker Hanusch
Journalism Practice, volume 6, issue 1 (February 2012) pp. 2-11

Chapter 2
Lifestyle Journalism as Popular Journalism: Strategies for evaluating its public role
Elfriede Fürsich
Journalism Practice, volume 6, issue 1 (February 2012) pp. 12-25

Chapter 3
Lifestyle Journalism: Blurring boundaries
Nete Nørgaard Kristensen and Unni From
Journalism Practice, volume 6, issue 1 (February 2012) pp. 26-41

Chapter 4
The Devil May Care: Travel journalism, cosmopolitan concern, politics and the brand
Lyn McGaurr
Journalism Practice, volume 6, issue 1 (February 2012) pp. 42-58

Chapter 5
Bread and Circuses: Food meets politics in the Singapore media
Andrew Duffy and Yang Yuhong Ashley
Journalism Practice, volume 6, issue 1 (February 2012) pp. 59-74

Chapter 6
Health and Lifestyle to Serve the Public: A case study of a cross-media programme series from the Norwegian Broadcasting Corporation
Roel Puijk
Journalism Practice, volume 6, issue 1 (February 2012) pp. 75-91

Chapter 7
Hypertextuality and Remediation in the Fashion Media: The case of fashion blogs
Agnès Rocamora
Journalism Practice, volume 6, issue 1 (February 2012) pp. 92-106

Chapter 8
Service Journalism as Community Experience: Personal technology and personal finance at The New York Times
Nikki Usher
Journalism Practice, volume 6, issue 1 (February 2012) pp. 107-121

Chapter 9
A New Generation of Lifestyle Magazine Journalism in China: The professional approach
Shuang Li
Journalism Practice, volume 6, issue 1 (February 2012) pp. 122-137

Notes on Contributors

Andrew Duffy is a former magazine and newspaper writer and editor, and is currently a senior lecturer in journalism at the Wee Kim Wee School of Communication and Information at Nanyang Technological University, Singapore. His research interests include young journalists' use of the Internet, formation of trust in user-generated reviews online, as well as the power of travel writing and other 'soft' journalism as an indicator of identity, culture and society.

Unni From, PhD, is Associate Professor in the Department of Information and Media Studies at Aarhus University, Denmark. She has published books and articles on television drama, soap operas, audience studies, journalism on consumerism, lifestyle and culture.

Elfriede Fürsich, PhD, is Research Associate Professor of Communication at Boston College, USA. She specializes in issues of media, globalization, and mobility. She has investigated the impact of globalization on media ranging from travel shows and music reviews to business journalism and African Internet sites. She is currently a Visiting Professor at Freie Universität Berlin, Germany.

Folker Hanusch is a former journalist and now Senior Lecturer in Journalism at the University of the Sunshine Coast, Australia. He has published widely on topics such as lifestyle, particularly travel, journalism, journalists' professional views, comparative journalism studies, indigenous journalism and news media representations of death and dying.

Nete Nørgaard Kristensen, PhD, is Associate Professor in the Department of Media, Cognition and Communication at the University of Copenhagen, Denmark. She has published books and articles on journalism-source-relations, strategic communication, journalism as profession, media coverage of war, political communication, cultural journalism, and amateur visuals in the news.

Shuang Li, PhD, is a researcher and columnist based in London, UK. A former newspaper and magazine journalist in Beijing, China, she is interested in the transition of journalism, international media comparison and the impact of social media.

Lyn McGaurr has worked as a journalist, writer, editor and public relations practitioner. She has a first-class honours degree in journalism and is completing a journalism PhD at the University of Tasmania. In addition to travel journalism and place branding, her research interests include cosmopolitanism, and media representations of environmental conflict and risk.

Roel Puijk is Professor of Film and Television Studies at Lillehammer University College, Norway. He leads the research programme "Television in a digital environment" (see tide. hil.no), financed by The Research Council of Norway, of which the article in this issue also is a result. His main publications are in the field of ethnographic studies of factual television production. In addition he has conducted research on media coverage of the Olympic Games and other media events. In both fields he has expanded the scope of his research by including the use of new media and the interaction between these media.

Dr. Agnès Rocamora is a Reader in Social and Cultural Studies at the London College of Fashion, University of the Arts London, UK. She is the author of *Fashioning the City: Paris, Fashion and the Media* (2009). Her writing on the field of fashion, on the fashion media and on fashion blogging has appeared in various journals, including *Fashion Theory, Sociology,* and the *Journal of Consumer Culture*. She is a contributor to *Fashion's World Cities* (ed. by C. Breward and D. Gilbert, 2006) and *Fashion as Photograph* (ed. by E. Shinkle, 2008) and is currently developing her work on fashion and new media.

Nikki Usher is an Assistant Professor at the School of Media and Public Affairs at George Washington University, USA. Her work focuses on the intersection of new media, journalism, and technology. She is specifically interested in news production, and has looked at major mainstream media outlets around the world they transition for the digital age, including *The New York Times*, Al Jazeera, the BBC, National Public Radio and the Christian Science Monitor, among a growing list. You can find her work at www.nikkiusher.com or look for her on twitter at @nikkiusher.

Yang Yuhong Ashley is a recent graduate from the Sociology Department of the School of Humanities and Social Sciences at Nanyang Technological University, Singapore.

PREFACE

I am delighted to draft a brief introductory note to this special issue of *Journalism Practice* which focuses on lifestyle journalism and its prolific growth across recent decades and across all media platforms. Lifestyle or service journalism has occasionally been the subject of criticism—if not opprobrium—by some journalists and scholars, reflecting its emphasis on "soft news" and its alleged too proximate connection with the market and public relations. The editorial concerns of lifestyle journalism are extraordinarily wide and embrace subjects from gardening and health to DIY and cookery, as the essays included in this special issue confirm. This breadth of editorial concerns raises definitional problems for scholars of lifestyle journalism. Guest editor Dr Folker Hanusch prepares the ground for subsequent essays by offering the following account. Lifestyle journalism, he suggests, is

> a distinct journalistic field that primarily addresses its audiences as consumers, providing them with factual information and advice, often in entertaining ways, about goods and services they can use in their daily lives. Examples of lifestyle journalism include such fields as travel, fashion, style, health, fitness, wellness, entertainment, leisure, lifestyle, food, music, arts, gardening and living. These may constitute individual sections in newspapers, entire magazines, programs on radio or television, or even dedicated websites.

A key ambition for this collection is to help to redress the relative scholarly neglect of lifestyle journalism or "news you can use", but also to suggest that we need to be more open to an understanding of journalism which extends beyond a consideration of just "hard" news and watchdog journalism. Consequently, the studies published in this issue try to conceptualise and define the field but also explore lifestyle journalism by focusing on travel, food, fashion blogs, music, financial advice and personal technology in a range of national contexts including Australia, China, Denmark, Norway, Singapore, the United Kingdom and the United States. I believe the research presented here constitutes an important body of work which will become essential reading for students of lifestyle journalism.

I am, as ever, indebted to the manuscript reviewers Professor Sammye Johnson, the Carlos Augustus de Lozano Chair in Journalism at Trinity University, San Antonio, USA and Professor Tim Luckhurst, who heads the Centre for Journalism and the News Industry at the University of Kent, UK, for their generosity in giving their time and attention to this collection of essays and offering authors such invaluable advice. I am very grateful to them and pleased to have this opportunity to thank them very publicly for their assistance with this special issue of *Journalism Practice.*

BOB FRANKLIN
Editor

BROADENING THE FOCUS
The case for lifestyle journalism as a field of scholarly inquiry

Folker Hanusch

This introduction to the special issue outlines the case for an increased focus on studying lifestyle journalism, an area of journalism which, despite its rapid rise over recent decades, has not received much attention from scholars in journalism studies. Criticised for being antithetical to public interest and watchdog notions of journalism, lifestyle journalism is still ridiculed by some as being unworthy of being associated with the term journalism. However, in outlining the field's development and a critique of definitions of journalism, this paper argues that there are a number of good reasons for broadening the focus. In fact, lifestyle journalism—here defined as a distinct journalistic field that primarily addresses its audiences as consumers, providing them with factual information and advice, often in entertaining ways, about goods and services they can use in their daily lives—has much to offer for scholarly inquiry and is of increasing relevance for society.

Introduction

Recent decades have seen an apparently rapid rise in media content that falls outside what many have traditionally regarded as "good" journalism. Increasingly, it seems, newspapers, magazines, radio, television and the Internet are preoccupied with what is generally referred to as soft news, rather than the hard, political news which many commentators and scholars would like to see journalists producing. Soft news, which comes in a variety of shapes and forms, is typically seen by them as an indication of an ongoing tabloidisation of the news media, and as such an undesirable development which, in their view, runs counter to idealised notions of what journalism should be and do. Much of this softer journalistic content has come to be known as lifestyle journalism, the part of journalism that primarily focuses on audiences as consumers, providing them with factual information and advice, often in entertaining ways, about goods and services they can use in their daily lives.

The rise of lifestyle journalism can be traced back as far as the 1950s and 1960s and the emergence of consumer culture, when newspapers in many developed countries began to establish dedicated sections to areas that traditionally lay outside the main focus of the first few pages, including areas such as travel, food and health. Cole (2005) believes that this exponential increase in journalism content in the mainstream media was due to technological innovations which allowed newspapers to increase dramatically the number of pages they published daily. He argues that, because there was not enough news to fill papers that were 10 times bigger than previously, softer forms of journalism, such as "health and fitness, food and drink, fashion, property and home improvement, children and education, computers and gaming, gardening and relationships" increasingly entered the fold (Cole, 2005, p. 33). As the number of television channels grew with the arrival of cable and satellite television in many developed countries, airtime had to similarly be filled with content, leading to the establishment, over time, of entire channels devoted to soft news content. The US-based Discovery Channel with its variety of programs and networks on health, cooking, travel and other areas is just one case in point. In fact, the field has become so important to news organisations that a few years ago the news agency Reuters established a wire service devoted specifically to lifestyle content, which includes "entertainment, leisure, lifestyle, food, music, arts, human interest and health stories" (Brook, 2006). Today, even venerable journalistic institutions such as the BBC and the *New York Times*, which have long been synonymous with hard-news reporting and are regarded as bastions of the best that journalism has to offer, have begun to include extensive programming or sections on lifestyle content.

What is Lifestyle Journalism?

Because relatively little research on lifestyle journalism as a distinct journalistic field exists, in trying to define it, it is useful to go back to traditional definitions of what journalism is, in order to better situate the field. Doing so will also provide us with some insight into why this particular journalistic sub-field has been discredited by journalists and scholars alike. As Zelizer (2004) has shown, there are a number of definitions of journalism, which have at various times been influenced by the agendas of those that have tried to define the term. She has pointed out that scholars have explained journalism through five definitional sets which are not necessarily mutually exclusive. Thus, journalism can be seen "as professionalism, as an institution, as a text, as people, and as a set of practices" (Zelizer, 2004, p. 3). Schudson (2003, p. 11) writes that "journalism is the business or practice of producing and disseminating information about contemporary affairs of general public interest and importance". While he warns about normative definitions of journalism and acknowledges that there are other types of journalistic practice, Schudson nevertheless focuses on journalism that relates to political affairs, because it is "that part of journalism that makes the strongest claim to public importance" (2003, p. 15). This focus on journalism's relationship with politics surrounds much of the existing academic work on journalism, and, as Zelizer (2011) notes, there has long been a normative focus on this link. A result of the attention given to the political has been that journalism which is market-oriented, privileging soft over hard news, is seen as almost unworthy of the term journalism. Franklin, for example, has lamented the fact that "the task of journalism has become merely to deliver and serve up what the customer wants; rather like a deep-pan pizza" (1997, p. 5).

Journalism that focuses on areas of societies outside the political domain and which has a closer connection to the economic field than supporters of an entirely independent watchdog role of the media would like, has thus often been held in contempt—an attitude that researchers in fields such as sports journalism—sometimes described as the "toy department of the media"—have also noted (Rowe, 2007, p. 385). This relative neglect of market-driven journalism such as lifestyle journalism has resulted in there being comparatively little knowledge about its structures, processes of production, content and effects it may have on audiences. Journalism outside the normative ideal has thus "become denigrated, relativized, and reduced in value alongside aspirations for something better" (Zelizer, 2011, p. 9).

However, despite the abundance of normative definitions of journalism, there are other conceptualisations which might be more useful and inclusive of types of journalism that fall outside prescriptive expectations. Definitions put forward by scholars from the field of cultural studies have generally been much more accepting of the study of journalism on the margins. For example, McNair (1998, p. 9) sees journalism as "an account of the existing real world as appropriated by the journalist and processed in accordance with the particular requirements of the journalistic medium through which it will be disseminated to some section of the public". Using such a broad and relatively value-free definition at least provides us with a more open interpretation for a large variety of types of journalism. There is little judgment in such a definition that would privilege political or public-interest reporting over journalism that, for example, aims primarily to entertain but is still based in fact. Further, the focus on the "existing real world" is an important marker when referring to journalism, in order to differentiate it from fictional accounts. In trying to define travel journalism, Fürsich and Kavoori (2001) applied a similar notion by Hartley (1996)—whose central defining aspect was that journalism purports to be true—to differentiate between travel journalists and travel writers.

Yet, while cultural studies-based definitions and conceptualisations have certainly broadened the study of journalism to include those practices on the margins, one can argue that a reverse narrowing has occurred, in that such an approach has quite often focused on only the odd types of journalism and the media attracting attention from scholars, while market-driven journalism within established journalistic institutions that also focus on hard news has been somewhat neglected. Or, as Zelizer (2011, p. 10) puts it, in such research "the *New York Times* and the BBC do not merit as much attention as does Comedy Central or reality television" (Zelizer, 2011, p. 10).

Nevertheless, a broader, less normative view or definition of journalism is needed in order to encompass other forms of journalism outside the mainstream, and to arrive at a working definition of what lifestyle journalism is. A cursory examination of the academic use of the term "lifestyle journalism" shows that it is being applied in a variety of contexts, albeit often only in passing and with somewhat murky edges in terms of what it includes. The proximity of lifestyle journalism to the economic field is a recurring theme, particularly in work that sees such journalism as inferior to "real" journalism, as if political journalism was never a victim to economic influences. That such criticism is erroneous and perhaps somewhat glorifies a kind of journalism that exists more as an idealised concept than in reality is a theme I will return to later.

The strong market-orientation of lifestyle journalism is certainly a defining aspect of the field. A further component is the fact that much of lifestyle journalism provides "news you can use", that is, news which audiences can apply in their own lives. This might include stories about holiday destinations which provide practical advice about places to stay, a drive test of a new car model, or a column about how to lead a healthier life. In this context, lifestyle journalism has much in common with—and may in fact be hard to distinguish from—service journalism, which has been described as "the way the news media provide their audiences with information, advice and help about the problems of everyday life" (Eide and Knight, 1999, p. 525). Further, as Hanitzsch (2007) has noted in relation to market-driven journalism more generally, "the materialization of infotainment news and lifestyle journalism exemplifies [the] trend toward a blending of information with advice and guidance as well as with entertainment and relaxation". In her article in this issue, Elfriede Fürsich identifies three constituting dimensions of the field of lifestyle journalism: providing advice, a review function, and commercialisation. In a study of Australian travel journalists' professional views (Hanusch, 2011b), I found evidence for five distinct dimensions through which journalists in this sub-field of lifestyle journalism see themselves: as cultural mediators, critics, entertainers, information providers and travellers. The theme of market orientation was expressed in the entertainer and information provider dimensions, while motivational aspects were expressed in the critics and travellers dimensions. These four dimensions provide some useful approaches for studying lifestyle journalism at large, as they can be applied in other fields as well.

Bearing the above conceptualisations in mind, we can define lifestyle journalism as a distinct journalistic field that primarily addresses its audiences as consumers, providing them with factual information and advice, often in entertaining ways, about goods and services they can use in their daily lives. Examples of lifestyle journalism include such fields as travel, fashion, style, health, fitness, wellness, entertainment, leisure, lifestyle, food, music, arts, personal technology, gardening and living. These may constitute individual sections in newspapers, entire magazines, programs on radio or television, or even dedicated websites. As the articles in this special issue demonstrate, lifestyle journalism is affected in similar ways to other types of journalism by wider developments, such as the rise of participatory journalism.

Why Lifestyle Journalism Needs to be Studied

As I have noted previously, lifestyle journalism is regularly criticised by journalists—particularly those who concentrate on hard news—who discount its practice as being aligned too closely with market-driven demands and, particularly, the public relations industry. As a result, lifestyle journalism is seen as a frivolous pursuit or a guilty pleasure, barely worthy of the term journalism. This view also extends to the academic community, which has rarely taken the field seriously, despite the obvious importance lifestyle journalism plays in terms of its prominence in media output and consumption in the twenty-first century. When lifestyle journalism is discussed at all, it is most often in terms of the view that it is dumbing down and detracts from serious journalism. Interestingly, the term lifestyle journalism is not even included in Franklin et al.'s (2005) volume on key concepts in journalism studies, nor are any of its variants, such as service journalism. Nevertheless, the terms infotainment and market-driven journalism appear, albeit generally in a context of such journalism contributing to a "dumbing down" of audiences. There has been some attention to the topic predominantly from a cultural studies perspective, which has engaged with the meanings produced by such journalism on the margins. Most notably, Hartley (2000) has repeatedly argued that the softer side of the media, such as lifestyle and consumer journalism, could actually have a beneficial impact on audiences who are increasingly tired of traditional hard news formats. Hartley (2000, p. 40) believes that such practices are "the ones who extend the reach of media, who teach audiences the pleasures of staying tuned, who popularize knowledge". In this vein, he sees enormous potential for such journalistic endeavours to contribute to the public sphere, albeit in perhaps different ways than traditional mainstream journalism.

Nevertheless, while individual areas such as travel (Fürsich, 2002; Hanusch, 2010, Hanusch, 2011a, 2011b; McGaurr, 2010; Santos, 2004, 2006) have received some attention over the past decade, there exist few comprehensive approaches examining the field of lifestyle journalism in its entirety, with attention to its structures, conditions of production, its messages as well as its meanings in an increasingly globalised, consumption-driven world. What is further needed is a scholarly debate about the impact that lifestyle journalism is having on traditional concepts and understandings of journalism. To what extent does lifestyle journalism challenge established views of what journalism is or what it should be about?

Commercialism has always been an integral component of journalism, despite normative arguments that see an historical period during which journalism was supposedly perfect. Schudson (1995, p. 203) has argued against the "retrospective wishful thinking" that has occurred from time to time when scholars have asserted the existence of a past golden age of journalism. That news does not just include political news or news of public importance is evident from the earliest forerunners of today's newspapers. The *acta diurnal populi Romani*—hand-written newssheets displayed in public places and containing mostly government announcements and official ceremonies as well as a record of births, deaths and marriages—did have official news as their primary objective. But Giffard (1975, p. 107) notes that the *acta* was also full of accounts of wars, as well as "earthquakes, eclipses, famines and prodigies". Later, the *acta* also included news of crimes and divorce, and increasingly news about social life and, as Stephens (2007, p. 57) reports, a large number of human-interest stories: "Pliny the Elder attributes to the *acta* . . . the story of the execution of a man whose dog simply would not leave his dead master's side, even going so far as to follow his master's corpse into the Tiber River in an effort to keep it afloat." The criticism that is often levelled at a perceived dumbing down in today's media (which assumes that news media provided only intelligent commentary during earlier times) was evident even during Roman times, with statesmen like Cicero heavily objecting to the reports of gladiators, burglaries and adjourned trials, which he described as "tittle-tattle". As Stephens (2007, p. 55) points out, "people have been following such stories, and high-minded people like Cicero have been complaining about them, for millennia".

Johann Carolus, credited as publishing the world's first newspaper, *Relation*, in 1605, is said to have had no journalistic motives for changing his production of handwritten newssheets to the new technology of mass printing. Commercial aspects were the primary objective. "All he was interested in, as a modest entrepreneur, was rationalizing the running of the business and making it more efficient—'gaining time', because 'the copying has been slow'" (Weber, 2006, p. 392). From the first days of regular newspapers, political news was, along with numerous sensationalised and "soft" stories, only a part of the daily news staple. Similarly, commercial motives were primarily responsible for the introduction of women's pages and women's magazines and a slow increase in the number of female journalists in the late nineteenth and early twentieth century. For example, Kitch (2002, p. 88) has argued that the increasing visibility of female journalists during the course of the twentieth century signalled a "growing importance of female newspaper readers during an era when rising literacy, a growing middle class and industrialisation changed the pattern of women's lives". Whitt (2008) also points out that the expansion in women's pages in newspapers during the 1950s and 1960s can be traced back to an attempt to attract female readers in order to open new markets. Eide and

Knight (1999) also see the development of mass consumption in the 1950s as a pre-condition for the rise of service journalism in Norway.

The rise of a consumer culture in the West, in line with increased amounts of individual leisure time, has obviously led to a demand for information about how to best spend the free time. This has allowed news media to attract new markets for audiences and, respectively, advertisers. Lifestyle journalism benefits from advertisers' support and eases financial costs on news outlets, thus rendering this type of journalism more profitable and more easily supportable from a management perspective. Very few publications are able to finance all the trips required for a 20-page travel section, or pay for all the gadgets their journalists should review for readers. Of course, this has ethical implications, and it will be important for future studies to investigate these more in-depth. So far, there are only general assumptions that lifestyle journalists are in the pockets of advertisers and are inherently unethical. As recent evidence on travel journalists, however, demonstrates, this group actually tries to work very hard to be ethical and truthful in their assessments of destinations and travel providers (Hanusch, 2011b). It is thus crucial that journalism scholars take up the challenge and give serious attention to studying lifestyle journalism in order to shed new light on how this phenomenon may be changing or reformulating central tenets of journalism itself, as well as the effect this may have on audiences.

An Agenda for Studying Lifestyle Journalism

Why then has lifestyle journalism been so neglected in past research? One reason perhaps lies in a popularly-held view that unserious journalism cannot be deserving of serious attention. Types of journalism that do not conform to the idealist journalistic notions of critical watchdog journalism have thus been relegated to the margins of academic inquiry. Yet, to understand journalism in its entirety, it is important to take a holistic view of the field, rather than a narrow one that is guided by normative expectations of what journalism is or should be. As the articles in this issue demonstrate, lifestyle journalism is not necessarily uncritical by definition, and it can have quite serious implications on aspects such as national identity. It is thus certainly deserving of further study. Hence, much as comparative journalism research across cultures allows us to better understand one's own culture of journalism and generalise theories and findings (Hanitzsch, 2009), so does comparative research across different journalistic sub-fields—both within and across cultures—enable us to come to a more complete understanding of the various orientations, structures, tensions and opportunities for journalism as a whole. This is crucial in order to move away from narrow foci on particular types of journalism, the theories of which may not be easily applicable to other journalistic fields.

The collection of articles about lifestyle journalism in this special issue provides some unique insights into the role that lifestyle journalism plays around the world, and it offers a useful starting point for renewed efforts at comprehensive analyses of a journalistic field that is distinguished from other types of journalism by its focus on consumption, entertainment and advice. The studies presented in this issue cover a variety of types of lifestyle journalism, such as travel, music, food, fashion and personal technology, as well as broader analyses of the field itself. In the spirit of cross-cultural comparative research, an increasingly important component of journalism studies in a globalised world, studies cover four continents, including countries such as Australia, China, Denmark, Norway, Singapore, the United Kingdom and the United States. This was a conscious decision, in order to highlight the ways in which lifestyle journalism matters around the world, regardless of the media system in which it operates.

In opening the issue, Elfriede Fürsich demonstrates convincingly the ways in which lifestyle journalism has a public relevance and democratic potential that it would be foolish to neglect. While she does acknowledge that this may not be the case for every type of lifestyle journalism or in every case, her analysis of travel and music journalism highlights specific instances where this journalistic field can have an impact. Lifestyle journalism as a field is also the focus of the article by Nete Nørgaard Kristensen and Unni From, who present a longitudinal analysis of lifestyle and cultural journalism in the Danish press during the twentieth century. Combined with interviews with Danish journalists, they are able to identify a blurring of boundaries between what used to be relatively distinct fields. They find that the coverage of lifestyle is expanding and cultural, consumer and lifestyle journalism are becoming increasingly inseparable, a process that also creates difficulties for journalists in deciding about news. Seen in the light of an ongoing mediatisation in society, Kristensen and From provide important starting points for further cross-cultural studies that could investigate this phenomenon.

The following articles present studies of individual fields within lifestyle journalism, focusing on travel journalism, food, health reporting, fashion and personal technology, which nevertheless should demonstrate to the astute reader a range of important connections across sub-fields to show the importance of lifestyle journalism itself. Lyn McGaurr continues her work on travel journalism and the Australian island state of Tasmania. Tasmania presents a unique case for analysis because of its modern-day branding as an eco-destination, while it has been the site of a range of internal environmental conflicts and resulting negative publicity. Examining the relationship between travel journalism and tourism branding, McGaurr finds evidence that travel journalists can and do sometimes subvert traditional conventions and expectations which would have them write only positive stories. Much like Fürsich in her analysis, she demonstrates that travel journalism does have public relevance and can potentially play a political role. The political role of lifestyle journalism is also evident in Andrew Duffy and Yang Yuhong Ashley's paper on the politics of food in Singapore, a nation that prides itself in its multiculturalism and resulting cosmopolitan array of food. In a fascinating account of the ways in which the topic of food is used in food writing, as well as in general reporting, they demonstrate the importance such stories can play in developing and maintaining notions of national identity. Thus, lifestyle journalism's role in discourses of identity is a crucial consideration for future studies in this area.

Lifestyle journalism's close link with media commercialisation means there may be a tendency to locate such types of journalism within commercial media, but of course the changes in the media environment that have occurred over the past few decades have meant that public broadcasters have not been immune from trends toward market-driven journalism. In an in-depth case study of the Norwegian public broadcaster NRK's health program *Puls*, Roel Puijk finds further evidence for an increased focus on lifestyle and advice in the television program. In doing so, even public broadcasters are attempting to further bind their audiences to their organisation in order to remain relevant in a competitive market environment. The program's accompanying Internet site has over time become more autonomous and, interestingly, became more focused on facts and information while the television program focused more on entertainment.

The online environment's impact on lifestyle journalism is also the focus of the next two articles. First, Agnès Rocamora highlights the ways in which participatory journalism is increasingly affecting fashion journalism. She argues that fashion blogs have become a central platform for providing fashion news, and have had a democratising effect on fashion journalism in that labels, which in the past may not have received much attention from media organisations, are now more present in online fashion journalism. Using a number of examples, Rocamora identifies a process of co-dependence and influence among fashion blogs and traditional fashion journalism that are redefining the field. The next paper also focuses on the online environment, but this time on the ways in which a traditional news organisation, the *New York Times*, has adopted online in its personal technology and personal finance sections. In an in-depth case study including a number of interviews with journalists at the news organisation, Nikki Usher shows that even such heavily consumer-focused content is subject to the high standards of a newspaper like the *New York Times*. This is an indication once again that lifestyle journalists take their jobs very seriously and do not merely uncritically shovel public relations material directly into their content as some critics would argue. Importantly, Usher argues that through their reporting, journalists are able to create a sense of community with their audience. Finally, Shuang Li shifts our focus to suggest that lifestyle journalism and matters of consumption are important also in societies which have limited press freedom. Her study of Chinese magazine journalists shows a move towards professionalisation where journalists are attempting to preserve their traditional journalistic ideals such as editorial autonomy and a commitment to serving the public. In doing so, these journalists are trying to maintain their relevance as journalists first and foremost.

Conclusion

As this—albeit limited and brief—overview of the field of lifestyle journalism has shown, it is crucial that the study of lifestyle journalism—in fact, the study of journalism at large—strikes a balance between various competing conceptualisations and even goes so far as trying to reconcile them. Journalism research should therefore aim to explore the ways in which journalism that operates supposedly on the margins may in fact also be a critical influence on other journalistic fields. The papers included in this special issue demonstrate the potential benefit such work can bring for journalism studies as a field. Contrary to popular expectations and judging from the content of academic journals, the call for papers for this issue showed that quite a large number of scholars are already undertaking important work in the field. It is crucial these studies are given an outlet, and I hope that this issue can be a first stage of this process. Much more needs to be done in order to move lifestyle journalism studies to the mainstream, of course. Studies need to engage with the conditions of production, messages and reception of lifestyle journalism in all its shapes and forms. Cross-cultural approaches are crucial in this context. While the studies presented here are from across the world, they are still studies from within countries; and future approaches need to adopt truly comparative approaches across countries and media systems. In doing so, we need to maintain lifestyle journalism as a sub-field of the wider journalistic field in order to provide a better understanding of journalism at large. I hope the articles in this special issue will go some way to sparking renewed interest in taking the study of lifestyle journalism seriously, inspiring further research.

REFERENCES

BROOK, STEPHEN (2006) "Reuters Moves into Lifestyle Journalism", *The Guardian*, 1 June, http://www.guardian.co.uk/media/2006/jun/01/reuters.pressandpublishing, accessed 18 March 2011.

COLE, PETER (2005) "The Structure of the Print Industry", in: Richard Keeble (Ed.), *Print Journalism: a critical introduction*, Abingdon: Routledge, pp. 21–38.

EIDE, MARTIN and KNIGHT, GRAHAM (1999) "Public/Private Service. Service journalism and the problems of everyday life", *European Journal of Communication* 14(4), pp. 525–47.

FRANKLIN, BOB (1997) *Newszak and News Media*, London: Arnold.

FRANKLIN, BOB, HAMER, MARTIN, HANNA, MARK, KINSEY, MARIE and RICHARDSON, JOHN E. (2005) *Key Concepts in Journalism Studies*, London: Sage.

FÜRSICH, ELFRIEDE (2002) "Packaging Culture: the potential and limitations of travel programs on global television", *Communication Quarterly* 50(2), pp. 204–26.

FÜRSICH, ELFRIEDE and KAVOORI, ANANDAM P. (2001) "Mapping a Critical Framework for the Study of Travel Journalism", *International Journal of Cultural Studies* 4(2), pp. 149–71.

GIFFARD, C. ANTHONY (1975) "Ancient Rome's Daily Gazette", *Journalism History* 2(4), pp. 106–9–132.

HANITZSCH, THOMAS (2007) "Deconstructing Journalism Culture: toward a universal theory", *Communication Theory* 17(4), pp. 367–85.

HANITZSCH, THOMAS (2009) "Comparative Journalism Studies", in: Karin Wahl-Jorgensen and Thomas Hanitzsch (Eds), *The Handbook of Journalism Studies*, New York: Routledge, pp. 413–27.

HANUSCH, FOLKER (2010) "The Dimensions of Travel Journalism: exploring new fields for journalism research beyond the news", *Journalism Studies* 11(1), pp. 68–82.

HANUSCH, FOLKER (2011a) "Representations of Foreign Places Outside the News: an analysis of Australian newspaper travel sections", *Media International Australia* 138, pp. 21–35.

HANUSCH, FOLKER (2011b) "A Profile of Australian Travel Journalists' Professional Views and Ethical Standards", *Journalism*, DOI: 10.1177/1464884911398338.

HARTLEY, JOHN (1996) *Popular Reality: journalism, modernity, popular culture*, London: Arnold.

HARTLEY, JOHN (2000) "Communicative Democracy in a Redactional Society: the future of journalism studies", *Journalism Studies* 1(1), pp. 39–48.

KITCH, CAROLYN (2002) "Women in Journalism", in: William D. Sloan and Lisa M. Parcell (Eds), *American Journalism: history, principles, practices*, Jefferson, NC: McFarland & Company, pp. 87–96.

MCGAURR, LYN (2010) "Travel Journalism and Environmental Conflict: a cosmopolitan perspective", *Journalism Studies* 11(1), pp. 50–67.

MCNAIR, BRIAN (1998) *The Sociology of Journalism*, London: Arnold.

ROWE, DAVID (2007) "Sports Journalism: still the 'toy department' of the news media?", *Journalism* 8(4), pp. 385–405.

SANTOS, CARLA ALMEIDA (2004) "Framing Portugal: representational dynamics", *Annals of Tourism Research* 31(1), pp. 122–38.

SANTOS, CARLA ALMEIDA (2006) "Cultural Politics in Contemporary Travel Writing", *Annals of Tourism Research* 33(3), pp. 624–44.

SCHUDSON, MICHAEL (1995) *The Power of News*, Cambridge, MA: Harvard University Press.

SCHUDSON, MICHAEL (2003) *The Sociology of News*, New York: W. W. Norton.

STEPHENS, MITCHELL (2007) *A History of News*, 3rd edn, New York: Oxford University Press.

WEBER, JOHANNES (2006) "Strassburg, 1605: the origins of the newspaper in Europe", *German History* 24(3), pp. 387–412.

WHITT, JAN (2008) *Women in American Journalism: a new history*, Champaign: University of Illinois Press.

ZELIZER, BARBIE (2004) *Taking Journalism Seriously*, Thousand Oaks, CA: Sage.

ZELIZER, BARBIE (2011) "Journalism in the Service of Communication", *Journal of Communication* 61(1), pp. 1–21.

LIFESTYLE JOURNALISM AS POPULAR JOURNALISM
Strategies for evaluating its public role

Elfriede Fürsich

This essay argues that lifestyle journalism, which is often considered trivial, should be analyzed for its public potential. I delineate how lifestyle journalism's dimensions of review, advice, and commercialism can be transformed into strategies for research that probe the social, cultural and economic context of this media output. Then I discuss how its discourse is worth analyzing for its ideological connection. John Fiske's ideas on "popular news" and Irene Costera Meijer's concept of "public quality" are presented as guidelines for interrogating the public relevance of this type of journalism. Findings from studies on the globalization discourse in travel journalism and music journalism are used to exemplify this research framework.

Introduction

Lifestyle journalism has been relegated to the backburner of journalism studies. Its close connection to commercial interests is often cited to belittle other potentially positive dimensions of this type of journalism. This essay argues that even this seemingly trivial journalism can be evaluated for its political and civic potential. I first explain how the journalistic dimensions of review, advice and commercialism can be transformed into approaches for journalism research that probe social and cultural aspects of lifestyle journalism. Then I discuss the public role this journalism can play and how its discourse is worth analyzing for its ideological dimensions. By using John Fiske's (1989) idea of "popular news" and Irene Costera Meijer's concept of "public quality" (2001), I outline how concepts such as "relevancy" and "productivity" can be used to investigate lifestyle journalism.

Using examples from studies on travel and music journalism, I highlight under which circumstances lifestyle journalism can become an interlocutor of public relevance. In particular, I explain why and how scholars should look beyond international news to lifestyle journalism to investigate the role of the media in explaining various cultural aspects of globalization to its audiences.

Dimensions of Lifestyle Journalism

For decades we have experienced an increasing "softening" and tabloidization of journalism away from the hard news tradition to more consumer-driven formats that blur the boundaries between information and entertainment. Besides the impact of digitalization and technological convergence and its related breakdown of established business models, it is the growing demand for popular journalism such as human interest stories and infotainment formats that experts name when they lament the end of journalism. Nevertheless, a significant group of journalism scholars has made the case for a more differentiated assessment of popular journalism. These scholars (e.g., Bird, 1992; Dahlgren and Sparks, 1992; Costera Meijer, 2001; Fiske, 1989, 1992; Hartley, 1999) have emphasized the democratic and even empowering potential of journalism that is produced outside the traditional hard news discourse such as in talk shows or tabloid newspapers.

While lifestyle journalism tends to fall into the category of the popular, it is more difficult to pinpoint what exactly distinguishes lifestyle journalism. This type of journalism is produced under various labels such as travel, entertainment, leisure, lifestyle, food, music, arts and gardening (Hanusch, 2012). Other terms that are used are "service" or "consumer journalism" because of its direct address of readers, viewers or users as individuals who make consumer decisions. Some employ the concept of "nonfiction entertainment" (e.g., Fürsich, 2003). That term, which is derived from the book industry, seems to be preferred by media industry executives but removes this content even further from the traditional realm of journalism.

While it makes sense to open the concept of journalism to non-traditional popular forms, it adds analytical clarity to differentiate further a separate category of lifestyle for a type of journalism that is distinguished by the dimensions of review, advice and consumerism. Discussing these dimensions helps to develop strategies for further research.

Reviewing as Social Negotiation

Many areas of lifestyle journalism such as travel, food, music or other arts journalism are created by people who do not just inform an audience about an event or a product but mainly evaluate and criticize. While normative concepts of traditional journalism emphasize critique as well—as watchdog role directed against government and other institutions of power—the critical function of lifestyle journalism refers to providing judgments of taste. This aspect seems to reinforce the private and individualistic predisposition of lifestyle journalism. But at least since Bourdieu (1984) it is clear that questions of taste resonate with wider issues such as class, social mobility, and identity. This relationship opens a first strategy for analyzing lifestyle journalism. Lifestyle journalists as arbiter of "taste cultures" (Bourdieu, 1984; also Gans, 1974) are part of the social negotiation of status and power. These types of journalists are what Bourdieu would call "cultural intermediaries", they mediate between elite and mass culture by negotiating the establishment of status positions. The field's—often criticized—closeness to commercial interests makes lifestyle journalists part of an "increasingly important group of workers who play an active role in promoting consumption through attaching to products and services, particular meanings and 'lifestyles' with which consumers can identify" (du Gay et al., 1997, p. 62).

A central concern for media sociologists and journalism researchers is to evaluate how lifestyle journalists contribute to the reaffirmation of established class structures. Or is there a possibility that their connections to new cultural trends open up spaces for renegotiation of class and status boundaries? This research would move beyond the commercialized lifestyle clustering of market researchers and investigate on concrete cases the social and cultural dimensions of creating social stratification with particular attention to media's role in this process.

Advice as Problem Solving

Another typical dimension of lifestyle journalism is the propensity to provide direct guidance to its readers or viewers. The German communication scholars Hömberg and Neuberger (1994, 1995) offer a detailed engagement with journalism whose main task it is to provide advice (*Ratgeber-Journalismus*). They argued that it is important to distinguish this type of journalism which is found in all types of media and within various beats or geographical reach (such as local, national) by its main function of guidance or advice. According to them, the advice function plays out in five dimensions: first, this type of journalism's main task can be understood as offering information to solve problems: journalists first define problems as important and then offer problem solutions. This function presents an important contribution to reducing complexity and offering meaning in increasingly complex societies (Neuberger, 1996). Second, advice journalism as an institution that caters to large audiences favors problems that are in the realm of the mainstream; i.e. a large number of people are potentially affected by the problem. For instance, health journalism fulfills this dimension since "every recipient is a potential patient" (Hömberg, 2009, p. 8). Third, the audience addressed consists of non-experts. In complex societies most people are specialists of only a few topics and need experts to explain the rest. The fourth criterion speaks to a distinction that others also emphasize for popular versus news journalism (e.g., Costera Meijer, 2001). While news journalism is characterized by collective problem definition and solutions, advice journalism focuses on problems on a personal level that can be solved by individuals. Lastly, Hömberg and Neuberger offered as another distinctive factor the active stance of these journalists towards problem definition and solution. These journalists prefer a direct connection to their audiences by taking on the recipients' perspective and by giving clear value judgments.

Neuberger and Hömberg also presented a helpful typology of advice journalism connected to the relationship between journalists, experts, and recipients (Hömberg, 2009). This typology can easily be adapted to lifestyle journalism in general. As the first type, journalists define the problems and select elite experts for advice. Examples here may be psychological pieces in women's magazines. The second type of journalism picks audiences' problems but recruits journalists or experts to offer solutions (such as advice columns with reader queries in teen magazines). The third type has journalists select problems but invite affected persons from the audience to present a problem solution. The use of confessionals in TV talk shows comes to mind. The fourth type has audiences or affected parties define problems and offer solutions. Journalists step back as mediators of a community of lay experts. Certain types of Internet forums on consumer issues are an example here.

Neuberger and Hömberg argued that given the range and functions of these types of journalistic advice, its societal impact is inherently constrained: "Advice journalism addresses those types of problems that affect a relatively large number of recipients and whose likelihood of occurrence is high. This type of journalism offers self-help strategies for a predominantly lay audience" (Hömberg, 2009, p. 8, own translation). Thus, they considered advice journalism's benefit for society as rather limited. In particular, Hömberg worried that the media might set up a wrong set of expectations when they claim to be able to solve problems. At best, he argued, their professional role of journalists is that of mediators "who manage public discourse on contemporary social issues at times of a declining consensus on values . . . and a rising flood of information" (Hömberg, 2009, p. 18, own translation).

In a recently published dissertation, Eickelkamp (2011) developed a complex functional categorization of what he called service journalism ("*Nutzwertjournalismus*"). He further extended Neuberger and Hömberg's functional spectrum. For example, he also highlighted the potential for appeal and warning functions that this journalism can provide leading to a potential civic role of surveillance and consumer protection.

An analysis of advice or service journalism beyond functional analysis can result in further insights. After all, the agenda-setting ability to propose problems as important and significant is a crucial competency in a mediated world of ephemeral news and issue cycles. This position of power needs to be examined with regard to the relationship of seemingly "private" problems and their possible civic impact. An example would be a historic analysis of food and health journalism in relation to the rise of the ecological and green movement.

Journalism researchers who understand lifestyle journalism as popular journalism and accept a potentially creative potential of the popular avoid the risk of falling back into outdated political concepts. This type of research can help destabilize traditional models that position a rational public sphere (where democracy is enacted) *vis-à-vis* an irrational private sphere (without civic impact).

Consumerism and the New Economy

Lifestyle journalists' problematically-close connection to commercial influences is an important criticism against the profession. For example, the poor state of travel journalism and its dependency on free trips and giveaways is the topic of many critical articles in journalism reviews since the launch of travel sections in newspapers in the 1970s. In 1994, for example, Alexander Eliot complained:

> The materialistic tilt of today's travel journalism is evident; so is its breathlessly upbeat tone. Slickness beats intellect. Polish supplants passion. There's not much variety of viewpoint, very little genuine feeling, and almost no critical acumen around. To be blunt, the distinctions drawn between "editorial" and "advertorial" content appear all but invisible. (Eliot, 1994, p. 56)

From an objective journalism perspective these professional blunders can only be avoided by elevating this type of journalism towards the traditional professional news practices: objectivity ("variety of viewpoint"), ethics (to disclose openly who paid journalists, as does Eliot, 1994), authenticity ("genuine feeling"), and a rational and critical perspective ("intellect"). While these suggestions are valid, they may overestimate the independence of traditional news journalism and its many undisclosed contingencies. The critique also seems less biting now as the financial troubles of the media industry along with new technology and hyper-marketing techniques have caused even traditional journalistic sections to become interwoven with product placement, direct marketing, and "plugs" launched by the public relations and marketing industry.

What does this mean for the analysis of lifestyle journalism? Far from accepting direct commercial influence on journalistic work one can analyze lifestyle journalism for its connection to the current unique historic socio-political situation. The present condition has been described by sociologists as one in which the forces of neoliberal economic globalization and a "new" economy create a society of extreme individualism and uncertainty while demanding intensified flexibility and mobility of people and goods (e.g., Beck, 2008; Sennett, 2006). Formerly distinctive spheres of the private, the public and the commercial are blurring (Featherstone, 2007). In this "liquid modernity" as Zygmunt Bauman (2000) famously termed the era, traditional institutions lose their grip on establishing norms and values, while distinctions between consumption and citizenship become questioned as even political attitudes become lifestyle decisions. The journalism scholar Mark Deuze observed that in these times, "consumer culture and civic engagement seem to be interconnected and co-creative rather than opposing value systems, and as such function to make the daily remix of work, life, and play just a little bit easier" (2009, p. 21). For Deuze or Hartley (1996), one of the central reasons for the crisis in journalism is the field's inability to break its ties to modernity, with its propensity to categorization and reliance on fixed institutions to report on and to criticize. Deuze proposed a form of "liquid journalism" that embraces the "unparalleled degree of human agency and user control in our lived experience of mediated reality" (2009, p. 26). His idea which is geared towards Internet and mobile journalism is also relevant for the analysis of lifestyle journalism. Scholars can evaluate how this type of journalism (also historically) negotiates social change. The question is how the discourses and practices of lifestyle journalism narrate and relate to the changing socio-political situations; and which social, cultural and even psychological scripts are offered to audiences to cope with these concerns.

Moreover, these new economic contingencies do not just relate to the content and audiences but also to the producers of lifestyle journalism. Often, they belong to the "flexible" workforce as the typical corollary of the new economy. They are employed as interns, part-timers or freelancers without benefits and employment guarantees and lack the institutional support of traditional media enterprises. Also, while the Internet offers new professional avenues for lifestyle journalists, their profession is challenged by so-called "content mills" that use crowd-sourcing, repurposing of free online content, optimization of search engine results and underpaid freelancers to generate nonfiction content (Gillette, 2011). These types of precarious work situations are increasingly typical for the media and cultural industries (Hesmondhalgh and Baker 2010; McGuigan 2010). Analyzing lifestyle journalists as part of this workforce can further illuminate the complexity of cultural production in a society of uncertainty.

The Ideology and Politics of Lifestyle Journalism

The previous dimensions established lifestyle journalism as a text and a practice that can be analyzed for its connection to the ongoing cultural, social and economic situation. As with any media analysis, cultural-critical researchers can further inquire into the ideological dimensions of the discourse established in lifestyle journalism. This research evaluates how complex the offered perspectives in media discourses are, i.e., how open or closed the established representations are. Especially interesting for journalism scholars is the question of whether the discourse in lifestyle journalism offers emerging concepts of reality and a wider spectrum of representations and life(style) concepts. Cultural scholars will analyze if the generated text is hegemonic or empowering. The possibilities reach from the obvious to the intricate. To give a few examples: fashion journalism can be analyzed for its discourse on gender (e.g., Weber, 2009), but so can food shows (male cook versus female cook). Food journalism can also be examined for its discourse on global culture with an interrogation of concepts such as authentic, exotic or hybrid. Gardening shows are candidates for gender analysis and they tie into discourses on science as well as space/home/*Heimat*. Living and home improvement shows are an obvious connection here but also speak to issues of gender and class; as do music, film, and art reviewers. The basic idea of these discursive interrogations is that media texts are always produced against the background of a specific structure of feeling; therefore, especially analyses within a longer timeframe are a promising avenue, if lacking so far.

Yet, while studies using lifestyle journalism as media texts are exciting terrain for cultural-critical media scholars in their project to examine the negotiation of ideologies in relation to lived experiences, other journalism scholars may not find their specific role in this research endeavor. As specialists on the possibilities and obstacles to public deliberation and a democratic public sphere they may not directly draw a connection to cultural discourses. Common for journalism scholarship, however, is that it is often based on a duality between media that are important for an informed citizenry and popular media which frivolously focus on individual pleasure and consumption. The assumptions of this binary have been challenged in detail. This approach privileges a problematic traditional "rational" model of citizenship. Instead, the ideal of an informed citizenry as a basis for democracy has been questioned. Also, there has been a significant extension of the idea of citizenship beyond the rational, legal, and state-connected aspects to social, symbolic, and interactive/negotiated aspects under the concepts of "cultural citizenship" (e.g., Hermes, 1998) or "Do-It-Yourself citizenship" (e.g., Hartley, 1999). The media play a significant role in the interactive and individual process of accessing symbolic resources of national identity and citizenship. It is less pertinent if the information is delivered in a traditional rational news discourse or in other popular formats (Klaus and Lünenborg, 2004). The extension of the concept of citizenship allows journalism scholars to investigate traditional as much as popular journalism (and the various mixed forms) concerning its public or civic role. The concepts presented in the next section are intended as helpful conceptual guidelines for this research.

Relevance, Productivity, and Public Quality

John Fiske (1989) was one of the first to engage with the idea of the popular in connection with news and journalism by advocating popular news. His remarks were directed towards television news but can be applied to other forms of journalism as well. Fiske lamented the flawed dichotomy that promoted education and social responsibility on the side of traditional news and relegated emotionality and pleasure to trivial popular taste. According to Fiske, traditional TV news failed to engage the audience in meaningful ways by producing semiotically closed texts. Instead, he suggested the two categories of "productivity" and "relevance" as strategies to overcome the problems of traditional news. For a news program to be productive it should display "a high level of formal openness" and an "internal interrogatory" form, which, similar to quiz shows, sports or game shows, encourage "heightened interest and discussion" and viewer engagement. Relevance could be established through selection and narration of topics in relation to the audience. He advocated forms in which "the experiences of the viewer's life are matched to those represented in the text ... it is not just the selection of stories, but the manner of their re-telling that determines their relevance" (Fiske, 1989, p. 190). By integrating production strategies of popular television formats such as multiple perspectives (versus objectivity) and an unresolved narrative structure (versus narrative closure) he hoped this type of popular news would "undermine social hierarchies", "provoke discussion" and "make them matter".

Irene Costera Meijer moved even further beyond the duality between traditional versus popular journalism. She challenged the very duality (see Costera Meijer, 2001, p. 190, Table 1) of positioning quality journalism as public, rational, content-driven, and with a professional position of "detachment and independence in contrast to the popular journalism as private, emotional, impact-driven and a professional position of proximity and involvement" (2001, p. 190). Based on her work on talk shows and normative quality guidelines for public television in the Netherlands (see Costera Meijer, 2001, 2003, 2005), she developed a third category of journalistic standard which she termed "public quality" (2001).

Costera Meijer's concept of "public quality" connects to lifestyle journalism studies in two ways. The idea introduces a normative but specific category that allows scholars to judge journalism beyond its obvious role as a textual clue to general culture. Moreover, it reconnects this type of cultural journalism analysis to a public or democratic idea of the public sphere. Costera Meijer pointed out that traditional models of journalism are often based on gendered and ethnicized concepts of citizenship that leave out non-white and female audiences: "Current journalism fails to acknowledge fully the significance of people's immediate world: their family, friendships, neighbourhood, town, or country" (2001, p. 198). Integrating more seemingly private and popular moments in coverage, however, does not mean simplifying the coverage, because "opting for public-oriented journalism means that people are not addressed as passive consumers of the entertain-ment industry (who would appreciate news only if it is entertaining) but as potentially active citizens who value information that they can utilise in both their personal and social life" (Costera Meijer, 2001, p. 194).

While Costera Meijer (similar to Fiske) developed her new concepts to overcome deficiencies of traditional news formats, her suggestions also apply to the critical evaluation of lifestyle journalism and its potential for supporting a democratic public sphere. In fact, several of her quality dimensions are already part of some lifestyle journalism. For example, Costera Meijer identified as public quality the ability to "instill a sense of common experience and a basis for social cohesion by not excluding systematically the experiences of particular social groups", as well as "the use of ordinary people's experience along with experts", and the capacity for "turning complex social discussions and issues into issues with clear options" (2001, p. 201). However, it will be up to scholars to analyze to what extent specific examples of lifestyle journalism reach the public quality that Costera Meijer advocates which allows for empathy and dialogue instead of rivalry of opinions. Schudson acknowledged the fine line between narcissistic consumer journalism and journalism that instills authentic "social empathy" (2008, p. 17), which he sees as one of the main purposes of journalism:

> True, covering medicine and education and religion—topics through which we may learn about and acquire empathy for people different from ourselves—blurs into coverage of dieting, restaurants, cars, celebrities, and other fluffy topics of a self absorbed society and can be a distraction from public life rather than an expansion of it. Still, all of these topics are potentially doors into public life. (Schudson, 2008, p. 20)

The question for researchers of lifestyle journalism will be what concepts of "public life" are established and positively sanctioned in the coverage and what aspects are left behind. This question hopefully triggers more holistic investigations of the power of media to define issues that are deemed worthy of public and popular discussion and on whose voices and viewpoints are publicized and silenced in these debates. The main goal of any type of journalism with a public quality ultimately would be to empower all audiences to live and act in a democratic system.

The central intention so far has been to make a case that lifestyle journalism should be investigated not as an aberration of "real" journalism but for its own value. The dimensions of review, advice and commercialism activate a unique combination of distinguishing professional values and routines with consequences on how topics are approached and presented, how experts are chosen and how audiences are understood and integrated. By examining various forms of lifestyle journalism, researchers can help challenge problematic binaries such as public/private, altruistic/hedonistic, rational/irrational or civic/personal that tend to inform discussions on the public sphere. This work can also help break outdated concepts of citizenship by illuminating a site that potentially engages people as cultural citizen. By investigating lifestyle journalism as a specific profession and a unique discourse at a particular time, scholars can explain underlying ideologies and cultural assumptions that guide how we cope with contemporary social, political and economic change. When abandoning the duality between news journalism and popular journalism for a more integral concept of "public quality", research on lifestyle journalism can develop more complex models of how issues of public concern are established and negotiated in the media. Lifestyle journalism as a profession and media content, then, can be explained as a symptom and a symbol for the ongoing shifting public sphere in times of liquid modernity.

Analyzing the Global Sensibility of Lifestyle Journalism

Using some examples from my own research I want to explain how some of these concepts can play out in the analysis of lifestyle journalism. The driving incentive of my studies was to look beyond international news journalism to understand the role of the media in explaining globalization to its audiences. I started my research with the premise that the complexities of the ongoing intensified phase of globalization have posed a challenge to media and journalists. Traditional-comparative and critical-cultural journalism scholars have argued that traditional news journalism often fails to cover the complexities of international relations: journalism developed along a modernist framework and played an important role in discursively creating the nation state (Anderson, 1983; Gans, 1979). However, much journalism research has established that this integrative function often developed against a crude depiction of others. Classic studies found that news factors such as "proximity", conflict" or "focus on elite nations" (Galtung and Ruge 1965) or the news value "ethnocentrism" (Gans, 1979) were significant thresholds that hindered a fair representation of others.

Especially Western reporting of the developing world is almost exclusively triggered by crises, catastrophes and natural disasters—thereby re-emphasizing an image of the developing world as a chaotic place beyond relief and in constant need of support by the West while probably prompting audience apathy (Moeller, 1999). Other limiting factors of foreign reporting are its closeness to political elites (Bennett, 1991), its reliance on binary frames such as Cold War or Anti-Terrorism (e.g., Entman, 2004), and lingering orientalist language and discourses.

Overall, in this post-nation world, news journalism at this point seems ill-equipped for the challenges of covering contemporary globalization, especially the impact of globalization on social and cultural change. The post-Cold War world has not resulted in new types of humanitarian journalism, as was hoped. Moreover, traditional international journalism has been in decline for quite some time, and these cutbacks have intensified further during the current economic crisis in the traditional media industry. Arguably, traditional news has become significantly less important for providing its audiences a "window to the world". This situation justified my approach to paying attention to other media forms that create a discourse of globalization and the Other.

Besides movies, fictional television, and video games, popular journalism is another important site where audiences learn about the world. My studies explored the ideological potential of global travel programs and US music reviews to communicate the cultural complexities of globalization to its audiences. This essay summarizes findings from two streams of research: an examination of travel journalism on television including an analysis of three internationally successful travel shows (Fürsich, 2002a, 2002b; Fürsich and Kavoori, 2001), and a recent study that examined in a textual analysis the coverage of world music in the US popular press during the past 30 years (Fürsich and Avant-Mier, 2009). While travel and music journalism operate on the fringes of traditional journalism, their international outlook and cultural position make them interesting case studies.

In my analysis of travel journalism, I was interested in moving beyond national media outlets to explore a type of non-fiction content that is produced for global audiences. This led me to investigate media production on a global level, starting with my study of Discovery Communication International and its cable outlet Travel Channel by examining the informative potential of travel programs produced for global television. I analyzed three then internationally popular travel shows called *Lonely Planet*, *Travelers*, and *Rough Guide*. The studies included the actual shows but also material (such as business reports or reviews) that allowed tracing the circumstances of production of these shows. By contextualizing the shows' content within their economic conditions of global production and distribution I hoped to demonstrate the potential and limitations of this type of programming for representing Others.

My premise was that since these shows had to appeal to a diverse international audience (Discovery operates in more than 150 countries), these shows had to circumvent stereotypical representations of Others and avoid the problematic "Othering" strategies of traditional television news journalism, especially its reliance on narrow, nation-bound differentiation. Also, the positive topic of the shows could help avoid the typical selection of traditional foreign reporting that concentrates on crises and catastrophe. Because these shows focused on travel, they could exemplify the complex representation work on either side of the tourism exchange; thus, they could challenge the often-criticized cultural dichotomies in media representations of the Other.

My research found that a central idea of travel journalism is also its problem: the narrative is predominantly structured by the search for difference as the ultimate motivation of tourism in general. This drive results in a perpetual replay of manufacturing, celebrating and exoticizing difference. A main journalistic strategy is to essentialize other cultural groups. At best, these shows presented a sense of multicultural understanding. In the worst cases, this strategy left locals (as tourism workers and interviewed "representa-tives" of a country) only as essentialized types: nameless, voiceless or poorly translated. The shows' lifestyle narratives, which stressed individual pleasure and personalized travel, mostly neglected broader political, social and economic problems of contemporary tourism and international relations in general. As programs that have to be sold across borders they often presented a sanitized or static idea of cultural exchange, devoid of political context.

Notably, however, the show *Rough Guide* overcame this problematic discourse by using dimensions of "public quality". This show employed strategies such as allowing for diverse perspectives and addressing audiences not just as pleasure-seeking individuals but as people interested in the living conditions of others across the world. Interestingly, this show used the most innovative format and an irreverent-playful postmodern aesthetic. That means the show was the furthest removed from the production standards of traditional TV journalism or documentary work. Its non-traditional production values correlated positively with its public quality (*Rough Guide* was originally a BBC2 show that lasted much longer on UK television than on the global distributor Discovery). The analysis confirms Costera Meijer's concept of public quality. Within televised travel journalism I found very different approaches towards presenting content, establishing Others and discerning the audience. Not travel journalism *per se* (as lifestyle genre) but the selective use of specific professional strategies, narrative elements and aesthetic decisions can explain if content accomplishes public quality.

The discourse of music reviewers presented a different type of lifestyle journalism. For our study (Fürsich and Avant-Mier, 2009) we analyzed only material that was published in the United States. Similar to travel journalism, the basic idea was that music reviews as a positive discourse could overcome the pitfalls of traditional news journalism. We examined the reviews published on the genre "world music" from its creation in the late 1970s into the mid-2000s. The sample comprised 350 articles including music reviews and informational articles in general newspapers such as the *New York Times*, the *Boston Globe*, or *Los Angeles Times*; general and trade magazines such as *Village Voice*, *Billboard*, and *Rolling Stone*; and other, smaller music magazines. Issues of representing the Other were important, as was in a broader sense the discourse on globalization along the dimensions of cultural exchange, authenticity and hybridity during times of change. We found that during the last 30 years music reviewers faced a time of significant change in the music industry and in cultural production that became entangled in the complexities of cultural globalization. While much of the coverage examined seemed to tie into dominant ideological positions on the West versus "the rest" relationship, we also noticed how, in the struggle over defining the role and place of world music, reviewers continually if slowly worked towards an acknowledgement of a new cultural sensibility.

We found three distinctive phases in which this discourse played out. First, journalists wrote their reviews within the typical modernist framework by categorizing the world music genre and highlighting often didactically the authenticity and pedigree of various music acts. Just as travel journalists or food journalists, the music reviewers mainly established authenticity and patrolled the limits of ethnic purity. This phase was followed by a short phase of re-definition of the genre (triggered by changes in the music market which moved from non-Western artists to diaspora productions). In the third ongoing phase, hybrid global cultural production for the reviewers moved from being non-authentic to "hip". Our analysis illustrated how this change in argumentation was slow and weary and often in contrast to the modernist ideology that remained prevalent in a great deal of music reviews.

Music journalism as lifestyle journalism allowed for a gradual acceptance of a specific new hybrid music genre. This journalism negotiated an emerging attitude not just toward artistic production, but also toward audiences and geopolitical norms, such as the position of the nation state and the understanding of the Other.

Did these reviews make the complicated discourse of the unfolding globalization "relevant" and "productive" to its readers? Without minimizing many problematic and stereotypical representations that we found in these world music reviews, the most exciting moments in these articles displayed different approaches of representing global Others. This move necessitated a significant shift not only in underlying ideological assumptions but in professional routines. For example, our analysis found an increasing integration of world musicians' opinions (in direct quotes or interviews) while in the early phase journalists generally only wrote "about" the musicians. Moreover, the shift required that world music artists were more personalized and evaluated for their specific musical skills, not their exotic otherness and non-rational, "magical" characteristics which dominated early reviews. Especially right after 9/11, some reviews were even used to provide a perspective on the necessity of cultural openness of non-US musicians "from the outside in"—a distinctive break with the ethnocentric news values of international reporting.

While the business model of the investigated travel shows as global television brands hindered their public engagement, the music reviews' connection to the music industry, we would argue, did not necessarily obstruct the discursive change. Music journalism was able to break the modernity discourse of traditional journalism that it held through the first phase of world music reviewing. This modernity discourse emphasized categorization and detachment and routinely led to a belittling of Others as exotic. The closeness to the music industry, however, demanded from reviewers not to ignore major new cultural trends. While they struggled with the new complexity of world music as a hybrid genre, they could not ignore the biggest selling acts—even if those did not fulfill the authenticity criteria established in earlier reviews. Similarly, the fact the younger audiences around the world impartially adopted the music as an everyday music choice needed to be explained. The reviewers had to stay close to their audiences' tastes and the industry's sales to remain credible. This evaluation led us to the finding that this type of lifestyle journalism extended the dominant discourse on globalization not *despite* but *because* it remains close to commercial culture.

World music reviews were "productive" when they engaged their audience in a discussion. As with any cultural reviews, their opinionated stance asks readers to take a position as well. The pleasure of reading world music reviews is derived from a strong expertise in the area presented—"previously existing knowledges" (Fiske, 1989, p. 192) developed by fans of the genre. The "popular" expertise of the critics (isn't every music fan a possible critic?) positions the critics' voices fairly openly amongst the audience, maybe even blurring social hierarchies.

Moreover, these reviews are connected to another—physical—dimension for engaging with global development through listening to music that challenges Western ears. When following this genre and music reviews, audiences are invited to consider central issues of globalization such as unequal access to cultural production, the commercialization of the public sphere, geopolitical transformations, economic inequalities, racism, migration, and diaspora. These reviews begin to make globalization relevant to its readers. The transformation to actual political action is another step, of course. Yet the analyzed 30 years of lifestyle journalism presented an arena that over time raised important questions about globalization.

Conclusion

Our studies found that the position of music and travel journalism as popular lifestyle journalism could activate but also impede the negotiation of ongoing global cultural change. The analyzed travel shows often seemed to be trapped in a problematic strategy of searching for difference and exoticizing others. Music reviewers of world music only hesitantly gave up on static, national concepts of culture and often only reluctantly accepted global culture as a dynamic, hybrid and transnational process. Nevertheless, there are moments in this journalism that indicated a shift in ideological assumptions: the gradual dissolution of traditional dichotomies and the integration of more dynamic and hybrid ideas of cultural change and international relations. At their "public" moments, these types of journalism created a relevant and productive discourse on globalization and the Other. Certain instances in these types of lifestyle journalism interrupted constricted representations. Its close connection to the audience, its necessity to follow trends, and its blurring of traditional boundaries between news and entertainment can make lifestyle journalism an arena for active cultural negotiation.

Understanding lifestyle journalism as popular journalism of public value should not lead researchers to assume an automatic democratic and anti-hierarchical potential of all types of lifestyle coverage. The intensive discussions in the 1990s on the potential and shortcomings of popular news equally apply to lifestyle journalism (e.g., Dahlgren and Sparks, 1992). The study of the lived experiences and the attitudes of the audiences will be an important counterbalance to hastily declared celebratory accounts (e.g., Bird, 1998).

What the here presented textual studies demonstrated is that every type of lifestyle journalism follows its specific professional routines and economic conditions. Meaningful analyses will have to stay close to specific examples. The concepts of relevance, productivity and public quality offer strategies for moving beyond evaluating the textual criteria of the content such as narrative openness towards a critical evaluation of lifestyle journalism's democratic role against the background of contemporary social change.

The analysis of lifestyle journalism will always straddle the duality between the naive celebration of its democratic potential as a popular media text and the undifferentiated denunciation as a hyper-commercial format. Yet lifestyle journalism has become such a major part of media output that it would be remiss for scholars not to investigate its public relevance.

REFERENCES

ANDERSON, BENEDICT (1983) *Imagined Communities: reflections on the origin and spread of nationalism*, London: Verso.

BAUMAN, ZYGMUNT (2000) *Liquid Modernity*, Cambridge: Polity Press.

BECK, ULRICH (2008) *World at Risk*, Cambridge: Polity Press.

BENNETT, LANCE W. (1991) "Toward a Theory of Press–State Relations", *Journal of Communication* 40(2), pp. 103–25.

BIRD, ELIZABETH S. (1992) *For Enquiring Minds: a cultural study of supermarket tabloids*, Knoxville: University of Tennessee Press.

BIRD, ELIZABETH S. (1998) "News We Can Use: an audience perspective on the tabloidisation of news in the United States", *Javnost: Journal of the European Institute for Communication and Culture* 3(1), pp. 33–50.

BOURDIEU, PIERRE (1984) *Distinction: a social critique of the judgment of taste*, Cambridge, MA: Harvard University Press.

COSTERA MEIJER, IRENE (2001) "The Public Quality of Popular Journalism: developing a normative framework", *Journalism Studies* 2(2), pp. 189–205.

COSTERA MEIJER, IRENE (2003) "What Is Quality Television News? A plea for extending the professional repertoires of newsmakers", *Journalism Studies* 4(1), pp. 15–29.

COSTERA MEIJER, IRENE (2005) "Impact or Content? Ratings vs quality in public broadcasting", *European Journal of Communication* 20(1), pp. 27–53.

DAHLGREN, PETER and SPARKS, COLIN (1992) *Journalism and Popular Culture*, London: Sage.

DEUZE, MARK (2009) "Journalism, Citizenship, and Digital Culture", in: Zizi Papacharissi (Ed.), *Journalism and Citizenship: new agendas in communication*, New York: Routledge, pp. 18–28.

DU GAY, PAUL, HALL, STUART, JANES, LINDA, MACKEY, HUGH and NEGUS, KEITH (1997) *Doing Cultural Studies: the story of the Sony Walkman*, London: Sage.

EICKELKAMP, ANDREAS (2011) *Der Nutzwertjournalismus. Herkunft, Funktionalität und Praxis eines Journalistentypes* [*Service Journalism: origin, functions and practice of this type of journalism*], Cologne: Halem.

ELIOT, ALEXANDER (1994) "A Cure for Skepticism About Travel Journalism", *Editor & Publisher* 127(46), pp. 56–7.

ENTMAN, ROBERT M. (2004) *Projections of Power: framing news, public opinion and U.S. foreign policy*, Chicago: University of Chicago Press.

FEATHERSTONE, MIKE (2007) *Consumer Culture and Postmodernism*, 2nd edn, London: Sage.

FISKE, JOHN (1989) *Reading the Popular*, Boston: Unwin Hyman.

FISKE, JOHN (1992) "Popularity and the Politics of Information", in: Dahlgren Peter and Sparks Colin (Eds), *Journalism and Popular Culture*, London: Sage, pp. 45–63.

FÜRSICH, ELFRIEDE (2003) "Between Credibility and Commodification: nonfiction entertainment as a global media genre", *International Journal of Cultural Studies* 6(2), pp. 131–53.

FÜRSICH, ELFRIEDE (2002a) "How Can Global Journalists Represent 'The Other'? A critical assessment of the cultural studies concept for journalistic practice", *Journalism* 3(1), pp. 57–84.

FÜRSICH, ELFRIEDE (2002b) "Packaging Culture: the potential and limitations of travel journalism on global television", *Communication Quarterly* 50(2), pp. 203–25.

FÜRSICH, ELFRIEDE and AVANT-MIER, ROBERTO (2009) "Journalism and Social Change: the globalization discourse in world music reviews", paper presented to the Association for Education in Journalism and Mass Communication, Boston, August.

FÜRSICH, ELFRIEDE and KAVOORI, ANANDAM P. (2001) "Mapping a Critical Framework for the Study of Travel Journalism", *International Journal of Cultural Studies* 4(2), pp. 149–71.

GALTUNG, JOHAN and MARI HOLMBOE, RUGE (1965) "The Structure of Foreign News", *Journal of Peace Research* 2(1), pp. 64–91.

GANS, HERBERT J. (1974) *Popular Culture and High Culture: an analysis and evaluation of taste*, New York: Basic Books.

GANS, HERBERT J. (1979) *Deciding What's News: a study of CBS Evening News, NBC Nightly News, Newsweek, and Time*, New York: Pantheon Books.

GILLETTE, FELIX (2011) "How Do You Make Money Answering Questions: Demand Media is trying to find out", *Bloomberg Businessweek*, 31 January, pp. 65–9.

HANUSCH, FOLKER (2012) "Broadening the Focus: the case for lifestyle journalism as a field of scholarly inquiry", *Journalism Practice* 6(1), pp. 2–11.

HARTLEY, JOHN (1996) *Popular Reality: journalism, modernity, popular culture*, London: Arnold.

HARTLEY, JOHN (1999) *Uses of Television*, London: Routledge.

HERMES, JOKE (1998) "Cultural Citizenship and Popular Fiction", in: Kees Brants, Joke Hermes and Lisbeth Van Zoonen (Eds), *The Media in Question: popular cultures and public interests*, London: Sage, pp. 156–67.

HESMONDHALGH, DAVID and BAKER, SARAH (2010) *Creative Labour: media work in three cultural industries*, New York: Routledge.

HÖMBERG, WALTER (2009) "Ratlose Ratgeber? Prämissen, Probleme und Perspektiven journalistischer Lebenshilfe" ["Clueless Counselors? Assumptions, problems and prospects of journalistic self-help"], *Communicatio Socialis* 42(1), pp. 3–20.

HÖMBERG, WALTER and NEUBERGER, CHRISTOPH (1994) "Konturen und Konzepte des Ratgeberjournalismus" ["Contours and Concepts of Advice Journalism"], in: Günter Bentele and Kurtr R. Hesse (Eds), *Publizistik in der Gesellschaft: Festschrift für Manfred Rühl*, Konstanz: UVK, pp. 211–33.

HÖMBERG, WALTER and NEUBERGER, CHRISTOPH (1995) *Experten des Alltags: Ratgeberjournalismus und Recherchenanzeigen* [*Experts on Everyday Life: advice journalism and search ads*], Eichstätt: Eichstätter Materialien zur Journalistik, p. 3.

KLAUS, ELISABETH and LÜNENBORG, MARGRETH (2004) "Cultural Citizenship. Ein kommunikationswissenschaftliches Konzept zur Bestimmung kultureller Teilhabe in der Mediengesellschaft ["Cultural Citizenship: a communication studies approach to assessing cultural participation in the media society"], *Medien & Kommunikationswissenschaft* 52(2), pp. 193–213.

MCGUIGAN, JIM (2010) "Creative Labour, Cultural Work and Individualism", *International Journal of Cultural Policy* 16(3), pp. 323–35.

MOELLER, SUSAN D. (1999) *Compassion Fatigue: How the media sell disease, famine, war and death*, London: Routledge.

NEUBERGER, CHRISTOPH (1996) *Journalismus als Problembearbeitung. Objektivität und Relevanz in der öffentlichen Kommunikation* [*Journalism as Problem Solving: objectivity and relevance in public communication*], Konstanz: UVK-Medien.

SCHUDSON, MICHAEL (2008) *Why Democracies Need an Unlovable Press*, Cambridge: Polity.

SENNETT, RICHARD (2006) *The Culture of the New Capitalism*, New Haven, CT: Yale University Press.

WEBER, BRENDA R. (2009) *Makeover TV: selfhood, citizenship, and celebrity*, Durham, NC: Duke University Press.

LIFESTYLE JOURNALISM
Blurring boundaries

Nete Nørgaard Kristensen and **Unni From**

The article argues that, in contemporary journalism, the boundaries between lifestyle journalism and cultural journalism are blurring. The discussions of the article are based in comprehensive empirical studies, more specifically a content analysis of the coverage of lifestyle, culture and consumption in the Danish printed press during the twentieth century and the first decade of the twenty-first; and secondly, interviews with Danish cultural journalists and editors. The studies reveal that the coverage of lifestyle is expanding and that culture, lifestyle and consumption are today contiguous—sometimes even inseparable—subject matters, which even for journalists are difficult to separate. The findings are interpreted in the light of especially Jansson's approach to mediatization of consumption as an expression of more general socio- and media cultural transformations of society.

Introduction

In this article we argue that, in contemporary journalism, the boundaries between lifestyle journalism (such as journalism on fashion, food and psychology), cultural journalism (such as journalism on movies, music and theatre) and consumer journalism (such as journalism on cars, technology and travels) are blurring. These blurring boundaries make it difficult to categorize at least some subjects or stories as belonging to either one or the other journalistic category: news desks cover music and food, for example, as equivalent matters by articulating them as expressions both of culture, lifestyle and/or consumption. Furthermore, journalistic genres are blending, since product presentations, pre-announcements, reviews, reports and interviews not only include information on cultural expressions and product characteristics but also provide discussions of taste and aesthetics and thus, at different levels, guide the citizen and/or consumer in his or her way of life. Even though all of these subjects and generic approaches are usually categorized as "soft news" in opposition to "hard news", their mutually blurring boundaries indicate that soft news not only challenges existing definitions of journalism, it also challenges existing definitions of cultural journalism in particular as a distinct journalistic subject. Therefore, we analyse lifestyle journalism in comparison with cultural journalism and consumer journalism.

As a point of departure, the article discusses this classical hard news/soft news distinction in journalism, including how cultural journalism, lifestyle journalism and consumer journalism differentiate themselves from the traditional definition of journalism as hard news, as well as how these subjects are both distinct from and similar to one another. These theoretical discussions form the foundation of a discussion of selected findings from both a quantitative and qualitative content analysis of the coverage of lifestyle, culture and consumption in the Danish printed press during the twentieth century and the first decade of the twenty-first century. Since empirical research on lifestyle journalism is very limited, we discuss how the coverage of lifestyle has been expanding in the printed press in some detail, and how it increasingly borrows from and influences coverage of culture and other topics. Secondly, we analyse interviews with journalists and editors which both challenge and confirm the content analysis and the argument about blurring boundaries: culture, lifestyle and consumption are today contiguous—sometimes even inseparable—subject matters, which are difficult to define or demarcate distinctively even for journalists. The specific approaches to these topics adopted by specific newspapers are, however, important trademarks of the news desks and point to lifestyle journalism as important in an increasingly competitive media landscape.

Our empirical findings are discussed in the light of media institutional changes within the Danish media system; e.g. we address how the blurring boundaries of form, content and mode of address reflect structural transformations in the Danish media system. Furthermore, the empirical findings are discussed in the light of Jansson's (2002) discussions of the mediatization of consumption, since he argues that in contemporary society traditional cultural products are launched, communicated and discussed as consumer goods, while functional consumer products are presented as cultural artefacts with priority given to their symbolic value over their mere functional usefulness. This precisely indicates—and accounts for the fact—that lifestyle journalism as topic or journalistic field can function to distinguish and profile the individual newspapers. Specific soft news priorities—literature, food, living, travelling, and so on—serve to brand the individual newspaper in an increasingly competitive news media landscape. This also points at mediatization as a process of "accommodation" (Schulz, 2004) that is characterized by media industries and actors (for example, political actors, actors of sport and entertainment) adapting—or more specifically, how actors "adapt to the rules of the media system trying to increase their publicity and at the same time accepting a loss of autonomy in a close interrelation. On the other hand, the media also benefit from such transactions since they make politics more newsworthy and conveniently formatted" (Schulz, 2004, pp. 89–90). This simultaneous focus on both media systemic transformations and processes of mediatization is a productive approach to explaining the blurring of boundaries of, changing modes of address of and increasing complexity in defining topics such as lifestyle, culture and consumption.

Hard News, Cultural Journalism and Lifestyle Journalism

Defining what constitutes lifestyle journalism is complicated, not least because journalism research within the field is limited and scattered. One way of identifying what constitutes lifestyle journalism is to define what it is not, or, how it differs from journalism as such. Journalism researchers generally distinguish between "hard news" and "soft news" by discussing their differences, similarities and blurring boundaries. Several criticize soft news for increasingly invading hard news—and interpret this invasion as an expression of the tabloidization, commercialization—even corruption—of journalism and the news media as such (e.g. Franklin, 1997; Patterson, 2000; Plasser, 2005). They hereby point to the *subject* of the story as important—that is, whether the content concerns matters of public relevance or lighter matters relating to the private sphere.

Other researchers emphasize the differing production processes which characterize hard news and soft news, respectively (see Boczkowski, 2009 for an overview), pointing to time as an important aspect, including such factors as whether or not a story is breaking news, whether it calls for immediate publication or can be published independently of a specific timeframe. From this perspective the question of time is of greater importance than the question of content or substance.

No matter whether or not one interprets genre, angle and/or temporality as more significant than topic, one might argue that both lifestyle journalism and cultural journalism fall within the "soft news" category, since both usually concern matters relating to the private sphere *and* do not represent breaking news. In the following discussion, we shortly introduce essential characteristics of cultural journalism, lifestyle journalism and at least parts of consumer journalism in order to accentuate the relations between these journalistic fields.

As Hovden and Knapskog (2008), Janssen et al. (2008) and Golin and Cardoso (2008) accentuate in different ways, cultural and industrial transformations have expanded the boundaries of, for example, cultural journalism, which is, consequently, a heterogeneous concept in contemporary journalism, crossing the boundaries of such domains as politics, celebrity culture, lifestyle and consumption. This blurring of boundaries between subjects as well as hard news and soft news can be related to the introduction of service journalism in the second part of the twentieth century—in Scandinavia in the 1980s (Eide, 1992; Hjarvard, 1995). Service journalism provides the reader with guidance on matters of consumption and choices of softer aspects of life in an increasingly complex society and everyday life, and thus addresses the reader as an individual rather than a member of the public—as a consumer rather than as a citizen. Both Eide (1992) and Hjarvard (1995) point to the increasing element of guidance in cultural journalism (both pre-announcements and reviews of cultural products and experiences) as evidence of this tendency. In doing so, they implicitly point to a blurring of the boundaries between cultural journalism and service journalism—or service journalism as a characteristic aspect of cultural journalism. Accordingly, we might understand service journalism as an adaptation or reinterpretation of the classical genre of cultural journalism, the review, as practised in product announcements and tests of a variety of lifestyle products and consumer goods such as children's clothing, wine, and cookbooks. Furthermore, Hjarvard (1995) argues that lifestyle journalism coincides with consumer journalism, since, in terms of content, lifestyle journalism covers a range of consumer-related subjects and objects—living/the home, cars, fashion, food—but also more abstract cultural phenomena such as wellness, subcultures, psychology, human relations, and everyday life. Even within consumer journalism, Sundvor (2008, p. 64) emphasizes the compound nature of this journalistic topic in terms of both content and form: it traverses different topics—politics, economy, business, culture and lifestyle—and genres, from the uncritical product presentation to the critical, investigative story.

This introductory discussion indicates that not least lifestyle journalism is as much a matter of discursive elements and ways of addressing its readers and users, as it is a question of content or time of publication/deadline. It raises at least two central research questions:

RQ1: Since when and how are lifestyle subjects covered by newspapers—and has this coverage changed?

RQ2: How are lifestyle subjects negotiated by journalists and news desks within their daily routines?

Methodology

This article is based on comprehensive empirical studies of lifestyle journalism and cultural journalism in a Danish context (see also From, 2010; Kristensen, 2010; Kristensen and From, 2011). The analysis was conducted using two empirical approaches: a content analysis and a smaller production study. Both studies adopt a broad approach to the same research subject, lifestyle and cultural journalism, and are based on the assumption (introduced theoretically above, and to be explained and developed empirically in the following discussion) that lifestyle journalism and cultural journalism today exist in a continuum between art, popular culture, lifestyle and consumption.

In our analysis, we will draw primarily on selected findings from the content analysis of the coverage of lifestyle, culture and consumption during the twentieth century and the first decade of the twenty-first in four Danish newspapers with different editorial profiles (centre-left broadsheet, *Politiken*; liberal/conservative broadsheet, *Jyllands-Posten*; tabloid newspaper, *Ekstra Bladet*; and in 2008, free newspaper, *metroXpress*). Even though the current media landscape is characterized by a number of media platforms, the content analysis is not cross-medial, but rather focuses on the transformation of the *printed* press in an increasingly cross-mediated and converging media culture. Given that the study covers a long period of time during which everyday life, cultural expressions and media culture have undergone great changes, we have chosen years of analysis, designated as key years relating to different media-institutional and technological changes in the Danish media system, with potential influence on the coverage of lifestyle, consumption and culture in the press. More specifically, we designed a constructed one-week sample from each newspaper for each of the following years: 1890, 1920, 1935, 1960, 1970, 1995, and 2008. Subjects included as lifestyle are: fashion (including beauty, health, shopping); cars (including motorcycles, boats); travels (including tourism); design/living (including gardening and interior decoration), food (including beverages, restaurants) and everyday life (including children, relationships).[1] The findings of this study answer questions of *what* and *how much* has been covered *when*, while qualitative examples from the sample, which consists of 2813 articles in total, will be included to allow us to elaborate on *how* these subjects are covered. This question of "how" is further elucidated and contextualized by findings from the production interviews with journalists and editors (seven respondents who work for the different newspapers included in the content analysis).

More specifically, the empirically-based discussions in the remainder of the article explore whether the assumption that coverage of "soft news" has been increasing, in this case by Danish newspapers, is valid, and moreover which specific subjects are covered within the overall framework of lifestyle journalism. Furthermore, the empirical discussions address the question of lifestyle as converging/overlapping with other subjects and as discursive mode of address.

More Extensive, but Changing Coverage of Lifestyle and Consumption

Based on the content analysis and exemplified by qualitative examples, this first part of the empirical discussion explores *what* lifestyle subjects are covered by the Danish press, and *how* these subjects are covered. On the one hand, the content analysis documents an increasing coverage of topics relating to lifestyle and consumption in Danish newspapers during the twentieth century. On the other hand, the press coverage of lifestyle is not a new phenomenon. However, the mode of address or approach has changed.

One sign of the *increasing* editorial priority given to lifestyle journalism in the printed newspapers relates to Barnhurst and Nerone's (2001) concept of the social mapping of content. Whereas Barnhurst and Nerone (2001, p. 245) identify an increasing segregation between topics relating to the public sphere and civil society (or what could be interpreted as an increasing segregation of hard news and soft news, if one chooses to perceive content or subject as a constitutive aspect of this distinction), this study points to an increasing organization into topics relating to either culture or lifestyle, and thus a segregation of topics *within* the "soft news" category. In the second half of the twentieth century, newspapers, through bars on the top of the pages, such as "House and Garden" or "Family and Consumer" (*Jyllands-Posten*, 1970), divided their stories into increasingly narrow categories, indicating that precedence is given to everyday life and consumption. In 2008 these strategies for mapping content resulted in magazine-like sections such as "Living" (*Jyllands-Posten*, 2008), "Saturday Life" (*Politiken*, 2008) or "Coup" (*Ekstra Bladet*, 2008). These sections present editorially marked and segregated content relating to lifestyle and consumption. This development reflects tendencies within the magazine press, and more recently, in primetime television (Brundson, 2003; Christensen, 2010; Mckay, 2000; Povlsen, 2007), where we have also witnessed an increasing priority given to very specific subjects such as living, garden, food and wellness, targeted at very specific audiences. As in the magazine press, the continual changing and renewal of the special sections of newspapers can be interpreted as a permanent accommodation to changing reader interests and, thus, as part of the branding of the newspapers by means of special sections reflecting the cultural profile of the newspaper (Kristensen, 2010).

On the one hand, this increasing segregation of topics contradicts this article's argument about the blurring of boundaries. On the other hand, it indicates the historical development of lifestyle journalism into a distinct journalistic subject—or a subject of journalistic priority—which can be seen in light of a developing consumer society, an increasing interplay (and interdependence) between the press and advertisers, and changing relations between the public and the private sphere as reflected in the press. Accordingly, not only an increasing number of sections, but also an increasing number of stories concern these subjects (Table 1), even though stories on different aspects of lifestyle and consumption have been covered during most of the twentieth century.

The blurring boundaries are, however, also documented more explicitly by the content analysis, since it shows an increasing hybridization of culture and lifestyle-related matters *within* the same article in the 2008 sample: whereas the distinction between culture and lifestyle/consumption was preserved in the printed press throughout most of the twentieth century, in 2008, more than one in 10 articles touched upon topics relating to both culture and lifestyle/consumption. This mixing of topics seems to have been intensifying, with some fluctuations, especially starting in the second part of the twentieth

TABLE 1

The coverage of overall subjects by year ($N = 2813$)

	1890	1920	1935	1960	1970	1995	2008
Politiken ($N = 1100$)							
Culture	98 (52)	93 (104)	88 (91)	79 (135)	63 (116)	77 (178)	65 (160)
Lifestyle		2 (2)	8 (8)	15 (25)	19 (35)	12 (28)	17 (41)
Culture and lifestyle	2 (1)	5 (6)	4 (4)	6 (10)	18 (34)	11 (25)	18 (45)
Jyllands-Posten ($N = 907$)							
Culture	92 (24)	97 (33)	80 (31)	70 (88)	74 (162)	80 (192)	65 (145)
Lifestyle		3 (1)	21 (8)	21 (26)	17 (38)	16 (39)	28 (63)
Culture and lifestyle	8 (2)			9 (11)	9 (19)	4 (9)	7 (15)
Ekstra Bladet ($N = 673$)							
Culture		80 (37)	89 (88)	66 (76)	77 (65)	92 (109)	68 (141)
Lifestyle		4 (2)	10 (10)	33 (38)	20 (17)	5 (6)	21 (43)
Culture and lifestyle		15 (7)	1 (1)	2 (2)	2 (2)	3 (4)	12 (25)
metroXpress ($N = 133$)							
Culture							64 (85)
Lifestyle							27 (36)
Culture and lifestyle							9 (12)

Values are percentages with numbers in parentheses.

century (Table 1). This hybrid tendency is most noticeable in the broadsheet *Politiken* and least so in the broadsheet *Jyllands-Posten*.

In broader terms, the historical changes in the coverage of lifestyle in Danish newspapers can be summarized in three categories: "stability", "the periodical Golden Age" and "new subjects" (Table 2).

Table 2 confirms an increasing coverage—and increasing variety—of lifestyle-related topics, especially in the second half of the twentieth century. The year 1995, however, stands out, since some topics almost disappear from the agenda (e.g. fashion—a subject that had experienced the periodical Golden Age in the previous decades); the coverage of other topics drops somewhat, even though these topics do not disappear entirely from the agenda (e.g. everyday life), while the coverage of a range of yet other topics increases in 2008 (e.g. food or living). This might explain the fact that 1995 seems to represent a year

TABLE 2

Changes in the coverage of living, fashion, everyday life, food, travelling, and cars

	1890 ($N = 79$)	1920 ($N = 192$)	1935 ($N = 241$)	1960 ($N = 411$)	1970 ($N = 487$)	1995 ($N = 590$)	2008 ($N = 811$)
Living/interior decoration	3 (2)	2 (3)	1 (3)	3 (13)	3 (16)	1 (8)	5 (42)
Fashion		1 (2)	7 (16)	9 (37)	7 (33)	1 (5)	4 (31)
Everyday life	1 (1)		2 (5)	12 (51)	15 (73)	5 (28)	8 (62)
Food				3 (11)	3 (16)	2 (14)	6 (52)
Travelling		1 (1)	2 (5)	2 (7)	2 (9)	3 (15)	4 (34)
Cars		1 (1)		2 (10)	3 (16)	4 (25)	5 (40)
Total	4 (3)	5 (5)	12 (29)	31 (129)	33 (163)	15 (87)	27 (219)

Values are the percentages of the analysed articles each year (numbers in parentheses), which were coded for the given subject ($N = 2813$). In 2008 *metroXpress* was included in the sample.

of transition. In the following discussion, these historical changes will be presented in more detail, with an emphasis on the analysis of qualitative examples of changes in the mode of addressing the topics.

Living—Stable Coverage

One of the topics which has experienced steady coverage during the entire twentieth century quantitatively speaking is "living" (including garden/design/interior decoration), as it is a topic in 1–5 per cent of the sampled stories in each year of analysis. From a more qualitative point of view, the coverage of the subject, and consequently the way in which readers are addressed, has changed considerably. Two articles relating to gardening will serve to exemplify this changing mode of address.

The report "A Thousand and One Varieties of Fruit" (*Politiken*, 3 September 1960, under the page heading "The House in the Garden") reports on the many different and exotic fruit bushes and trees which can be observed in the garden of The Royal Veterinary and Agricultural University (today the Faculty of Life Sciences at the University of Copenhagen). The article emphasizes the mere existence of this impressive collection and its methods of cultivation, addressing the enthusiastic garden-owner who could visit the garden. That is, the article rather narrowly focuses on the garden as aesthetic expression and public good. Decades later the article "Spring in the Windowsill" (*metroXpress*, 4 March 2008, under the page heading "House and Garden") exemplifies how the home and the garden are articulated as lifestyle projects rather than factual information or everyday routine in contemporary journalism (Christensen, 2010). The article presents the very ordinary presence of house plants on the windowsill and the specific choice of their colours as an expression of a strategic action and part of a larger staging of a tasteful and orderly home in a busy daily life: in other words, it points to culture and lifestyle as processes and phenomena rather than products or objects.

More generally, the cases exemplify that even though *living* is a topic which has experienced rather stable coverage and thus attention from the press in quantitative terms throughout the twentieth century, the journalistic approach to—that is the presentation and communication of—the subject has changed considerably, from addressing, informing and educating the readers as (part of a) public to addressing the readers as individuals. It thus exemplifies the theoretical argument of Eide (1992) and Hjarvard (1995) regarding service journalism introduced above, as well as blurring boundaries of living, interior decoration and design in contemporary journalism. We will return to and elaborate on this argument later in the article, since similar transformations can be observed within the coverage of other lifestyle topics.

Fashion—"The Golden Age"

Fashion (including beauty, health and shopping) represents an example of a lifestyle subject which experienced a "periodical Golden Age" measured in terms of the extent of its coverage during the twentieth century. In the analysis, coverage of fashion was most extensive in 1935, 1960 and 1970, whereas it is less important in contemporary journalism (Table 2), just as it has a rather ambiguous status from an editorial perspective, an issue we will return to below. The periodical Golden Age might be explained by the fact that the Danish magazine market was in the early stages of its development in the 1960s and 1970s (Povlsen, 1995). Thus, contrary to the contemporary fashion magazine market, the number of specialized magazines on fashion and beauty in the 1960s and 1970s, which would have been able to compete with newspaper coverage of the subject, was limited. As we will discuss below, newspapers today cannot and will not compete with the many specialized fashion magazines available when it comes to setting the agenda and/or reporting the latest news from the catwalks, new fashion trends, fabrics, or accessories. However, fashion is not absent from the printed press. Instead, coverage is closely linked to the reader profile of the newspaper. The business-oriented newspaper *Jyllands-Posten*, for example, approaches fashion from a commercial angle. This is exemplified by a story in the business section about the movie *Sex and the City* (5 October 2008) on the opening day of the movie. The article gives priority not to the movie as an aesthetic expression but as a vehicle for co-branding commodities such as fashion trends and products (shoes, clothing, etc.) and more importantly, ways of life. The article thus exemplifies the blurring boundaries between lifestyle journalism and cultural journalism, since fashion is approached as a representation of ways of life and a symbolic marker of taste and lifestyle (Jansson, 2002; Kristensen, 2010). Unlike *Jyllands-Posten*, the free daily *metroXpress* covers fashion in a more traditional way by reporting from fashion weeks and presenting fashion and beauty commodities which can be purchased on the way home from school or work. It thus offers coverage similar to that characteristic of the 1960s and 1970s, only supplemented by consumer information such as price and purchase location. Therefore, while fashion is today not a lifestyle topic of top priority in the printed press, it is a topic which journalists feel obligated to cover, even though they also find it very difficult to do so, not least due to competition from the specialized national and international magazine press.

Everyday Life

Like the coverage of fashion, the coverage of everyday life—such as children, family and relationships—was most extensive in the printed press in the 1960s and 1970s, which means it had its "Golden Age" decades ago (Table 2). This is emphasized by page headings such as "The Family" (*Ekstra Bladet*, 1960), "Ekstra Break Recess" (*Ekstra Bladet*, 1970), "For the Entire Family" (*Jyllands-Posten*, 1970), which exemplifies the emerging social mapping of content by the newspapers of that time. Again, specific articles demonstrate how the coverage of the subject has changed qualitatively during the last 40 or 50 years.

The article "Supporting the Child Rather Than Making Demands" (*Politiken*, 1 April, 1970), for example, concerns a new association aimed at helping children with reading difficulties. Accordingly, the article "The School Where Boys Can Be Boys" (*Politiken*, 4 October 1970) tells the story of Bernadotteskolen, a school which seeks to help children, especially boys, through difficult stages of their lives; while the article "Well-being for the Whole Family" (*Politiken*, 4 October 1970) reports on an association that strives to improve the wellbeing of a residential neighbourhood by introducing common areas and shared activities. Even though these stories concern human interest, the angle is on neither the individual nor matters of consumption. Rather, the articles adopt a more general public perspective by informing the readers on social responsibility and community initiatives—or public interests. In other words, they address the question of children and everyday life as a matter of public interest and hereby address their readers as citizens rather than individuals and/or consumers. In 2008, a more consumer-oriented approach could be seen to supplement this public perspective, which is exemplified by an article in the free daily *metroXpress* (2 April 2008, p. 21) that reviews computer games for children with a focus on "a nice weekend". The short article, "Fun for Kids", is written from the child's perspective, inviting four children to describe their experiences with five computer games. It gives priority to the consumer perspective, and thus exemplifies the research discussed above which highlights how a service element and individualization have increasingly come to characterize lifestyle and consumer journalism since the last decades of the twentieth century (e.g. Eide and Knight, 1999).

Whereas fashion and everyday life seem to have experienced declining coverage in the past few decades, the quantitative analysis also discloses that a range of new topics emerged in the newspapers, especially in the second part of the twentieth century. In other words, it reveals an altered focus within lifestyle journalism.

Food—Travelling—Cars

As a new subject, food (including beverages and restaurants) entered the newspapers in the second part of the twentieth century (Table 2), and is covered more extensively in contemporary newspapers.[2] Furthermore, we can observe a changed mode of address and thus discourse in the coverage of food which is similar to the transformations in the coverage of home and garden stories discussed previously. In the 1960s and 1970s, articles focused on everyday life and everyday meals and *instructed* the housewife in how to create inexpensive, nice food. Today the coverage of food includes good advice, recipes, reviews and expressions of taste and lifestyle, and the subject is therefore approached not only as guidance to cultural and/or gastronomic products or experiences (e.g. restaurant reviews) but also, like fashion, as a representation of ways of life and a symbolic marker of taste and lifestyle. Moreover, these articles are often accompanied by large and diverse illustrations, which indicate that reading them is intended to be a pleasurable activity. From a broader perspective, one characteristic of lifestyle journalism and cultural journalism is precisely the visual dimension, which provides not only documentation (if at all), but also (or rather) visual and cultural experiences (Kristensen and From, 2011). For example, on Wednesday 2 April 2008, the broadsheet *Jyllands-Posten* published a two-page spread collage of articles on confirmation party menus and catering, including both price comparisons of catering menus and homemade menus, a handwritten shopping list and budget, illustrated recipes for a three-course party menu and an article on an appropriate wine menu. It thus illustrates a very mixed generic and visual approach to food. Correspondingly, food has been given high priority on television and in the magazine press for the past decade (Brunsdon, 2003; Christensen, 2010) with emphasis on the social, personal, aesthetic and symbolic aspects of food (Povlsen, 2007).

Likewise, printed newspapers began covering consumer goods such as travel/tourism and cars (along with motorcycles and boats) more extensively in the second half of the twentieth century concurrently with the development of consumer society. From a more qualitative perspective, we can, for example in relation to the coverage of cars, observe a consistent interest in technical consumer details, but in contemporary coverage we also observe a considerable interest in the symbolic and social value of these consumer goods as markers of taste and lifestyle, as was the case with the changing approach to the coverage of home and garden, fashion and food. For example, the one-and-a-half page article "We Test: Borgward Isabella" (*Politiken*, 6 April 1960) described and tested the driving capacities and technicalities of a new car in great detail, under subheadings such as "Motor and Gearbox", "Good Roadhandling", "The Rear-end Skids", "The View" and "Equipment". Fifty years later, the interview-based article "Cars and Brotherhood" (*Jyllands-Posten*, 6 June 2008) tells the personal story of a motor journalist and Land Rover enthusiast who is quoted as saying: "A Land Rover has charisma, a curious origin, a fascinating history and suits the ballroom just as well as the stable. It is the key to a national and international spiritual community. And it reflects how simply it can be done, how little it takes to meet the need to get from point A to point B." Even though the article includes traditional technical details on the functionality of the Land Rover as means of transportation or consumer good, the primary approach, as emphasized by the headline of the article and the choice of genre, is the symbolic and social value of the car as symbol of lifestyle and means to social networking and community.

To sum up, the content analysis documents structural changes in the press coverage of subjects such as living, fashion, everyday life, food and cars during the twentieth century (the "what"), while the qualitative examples point to discursive changes in this coverage (the "how"), indicating blurring and closely connected boundaries between lifestyle journalism, consumer journalism and cultural journalism. The blurring boundaries can, on the one hand, be interpreted as a result and reflection of hybridizations of phenomena and subjects in society as such. On the other hand, the journalistic approach to and coverage of these socio-cultural subjects itself potentially influences the cultural circuit, and thus lifestyle journalism itself can also be seen to contribute to the very blurring of the boundaries. This points towards the relevance of analysing journalists' interpretation and approach to different topics in the production phase.

Lifestyle Journalism from a Production Perspective

In the following discussion, we will elaborate on how lifestyle is negotiated as a subject by the seven journalists and editors whom we interviewed about their work. On the one hand, the analysis displays how editorial priority and importance are attributed to lifestyle journalism by contemporary newspapers as part of their branding strategy or specific editorial profile. On the other hand, the analysis confirms the (blurring) boundaries between lifestyle, consumer and cultural journalism from an editorial perspective.

Editorial Importance in a Changing Society and Competitive Media Landscape

Both journalists and editors argue that lifestyle issues are relevant topics which (their) newspapers, at least to some extent, should cover, in a manner that is tailored to the specific target group of the newspaper. They reflect upon how modern (everyday) life has changed and that newspapers nowadays need to show interest in and cover how people live their lives, reflect contemporary existence or living, and provide guidance and information on daily life.

One of the journalists, Poul Tvilum (from the broadsheet *Jyllands-Posten*), articulates the shift in the coverage of lifestyle and consumption from a focus on consumer-related issues as a political topic to a focus on lifestyle-related issues as reflections of everyday life in this way:

> In the old days, consumer journalism was about spoiled meat and consumer complaints about the quality of clothing and so on. We realized very early on that what we needed to gain popular appeal was a focus on lifestyle and weight loss and healthy diets, etc.... We find that modern people's consumer behaviour has changed ... It's no longer just about consuming stuff here and now. There's also a focus on how we live together, how people interact with each other.

This statement confirms that lifestyle journalism is not only a matter of consumer advice, but also—and increasingly so—a matter of guiding the reader on immaterial topics and "the good life" in an increasingly complex society (Hjarvard, 1995).

During our interviews, journalists and editors rarely mentioned specific lifestyle topics as more important than others for their newspapers, but they explained how techniques such as reader surveys are used to pinpoint specific lifestyle issues as important at particular times. In other words, they argue that the coverage of specific lifestyle issues by the newspapers is closely related to trends within society and in the media as such. For example, food is, as mentioned, a topic that has occupied magazines, television programmes—and newspapers. In the words of Ditte Giese (from the broadsheet *Politiken*):

> They do reader surveys all the time, and the second section, Culture, is always rated very highly. This is also how they discovered that their readers are really interested in food, which is why they introduced a food supplement. You can measure it quite clearly.

At the same time, journalists and editors implicitly indicate that lifestyle topics can serve to brand their newspapers. Poul Tvilum (from the broadsheet *Jyllands-Posten*) argues that the establishment of a specific issue as important by the newspaper is closely connected to the interplay between the image/brand of the newspaper, the readers' interest in the subject and the potential to attract advertisers:

> We focus a lot on health in general. We focus a lot on consumer electronics, and motors and diet, for example ... because we think it's important for our brand and because people are interested and because there's money in it. That's the trinity we focus on, you might say.

Thus, editors and journalists argue that lifestyle, as journalistic topic, is a relevant and conventional part of modern newspapers. Accordingly, they contend that the priority given to specific issues by the newspapers reflect trends within society and the media as such. They furthermore indicate, as we have already touched upon above, that lifestyle journalism appears to symbolize and mirror a more general trend within journalism: specific issues, such as food, can be covered as consumer journalism (a political debate on quality), as culture (Asian food culture) and/or as lifestyle (how to choose a wedding menu that reflects your identity or "way of life"). In the following analysis, we will elaborate on these processes of negotiation in the journalistic field, which precisely point to blurring boundaries within journalism.

Blurring Boundaries from a Production Perspective

Both editors and journalists find that most cultural and lifestyle topics are quite distinctive and thus clearly distinguishable. Consequently, they have a clear conception of what, from their point of view, characterizes culture, lifestyle and consumption, respectively, as journalistic topics. They share a common understanding and interpretation of subjects such as theatre, movies and literature as "culture"—or as issues belonging to the cultural section. At the same time, they agree that lifestyle journalism is a more ambiguous topic than cultural journalism. That is, they agree that the boundaries of subjects are, in fact, indefinite, and can thus be interpreted very differently by various journalists and newspapers. And these differing interpretations, as it turns out, are closely linked to the editorial organization of the news desks and, as already indicated, to the editorial profile of the newspaper.

As discussed above, fashion is a recurring example which, according to journalists, can be addressed as an issue relating either to lifestyle, culture and/or consumption, depending on the chosen angle for the specific article, just like food. Fashion is thus an issue under continuous negotiation at news desks, and journalists, even from the same newspaper, disagree on how to approach it and, consequently, where to place it in the newspaper. Nina Ettrup (from the free daily *metroXpress*) describes it as follows:

> In fact, I consider fashion a classic lifestyle topic . . . Of course, it overlaps with consumer journalism. We had this discussion during Copenhagen Fashion Week. Can you put it in the culture section? And I really don't think you can . . . you might as well put it in the money/business section, because it's also about money. Or domestic news. Or foreign news. It's not culture in my view. Unless you turn it into something about what DJs are playing at Fashion Week, or something. But with pure fashion, models, and should it be blue or green, I think that's lifestyle.

The statement demonstrates how the particular focus or approach to the topic in a specific article determines who or which desk writes the story, and where the story is placed in the newspaper. That is, the angle of the story is more important than the subject. It also points to the business section as very important in the discussion of subjects related to lifestyle and culture, because articles on topics such as fashion are often related to economics and market-oriented perspectives, and are accordingly covered in this section and not only in sections on culture, lifestyle and/or consumption. This was precisely exemplified by the already-mentioned article in the broadsheet *Jylland-Posten* on the movie *Sex and the City*—which was published in the business section and covered the opening of the new movie not as a cultural event but as a vehicle for co-branding fashion commodities and, consequently, lifestyles. This confirms one of the opening arguments of this article: that different topics can be addressed differently, as either hard news or soft news. It furthermore points to the theoretical argument indicated above: that the question of blurring boundaries not only relates to culture, lifestyle and consumption, but also to subjects traditionally interpreted as hard news (such as economics and politics).

According to Ditte Giese (from *Politiken*), fashion is an issue for the culture section, even though she simultaneously points to the ambiguity of the subject and its position on a continuum between lifestyle and cultural journalism. More specifically, she explains how her newspaper approaches fashion differently from the weekly and monthly fashion magazines, which, according to her, have a consumer-oriented approach to the topic with priority given to guidance and consumer information.

> Fashion goes in the culture section in *Politiken*, but our angle is not to show "three things in purple" from a consumer angle, but to analyse and contextualize fashion, for example with a long, in-depth article on Fred Perry on the occasion of his 100th birthday . . . We want to have it, but at the same time, we know that people who are interested in fashion

buy the magazines, read fashion blogs and go to fashion weeks . . . And it [fashion] has to be there, because it would seem strange for us as a newspaper not to include it.

These statements thus confirm the ambiguity of fashion as a journalistic topic in newspapers, which was also indicated by the content analysis: fashion is something newspapers cannot ignore, but which they, at the same time, find difficult to cover in a manner that is distinctively different from the competing magazine press.

Jakob Levinsen (from *Jyllands-Posten*) also confirms the empirical conclusion of the content analysis that the categorization of fashion as either lifestyle journalism or consumption depends on the local organization of the newspaper, and that the priority of a specific topic must be seen in the light of the overall brand of the newspaper:

It's more a question of how the newspaper is organized, where it [fashion] arbitrarily ends up. At our place some fashion is lifestyle material with the big fashion shows, and some of it is down at H&M [low-end high street chain] level.

Levinsen's statement points to the influence of subject-external factors (the organizational setting and brand of the newspaper) on the interpretation of, approach to and priority given to a specific issue, in this case fashion. Different newspapers, sections and journalists have their specific fields of interest and specific trademarks. From this perspective the editorial organization and the journalist as agent/subject determine whether a story is characterized as consumer, lifestyle or cultural journalism, not the story as object.

To summarize, from a production perspective, journalists negotiate the definition and placement of lifestyle issues such as food and fashion, and they confirm that some subjects can be defined or interpreted as belonging to the culture, lifestyle and/or consumer desk, depending on the mode of address and the angle of the individual article. These negotiations of boundaries, placement and mode of address are facilitated by the editorial organization of newspapers, which assign priority/importance (or the opposite) to specific issues such as their trademarks, brands or profiles.

Blurring Boundaries and Strategic Trademarks from a Theoretical Perspective

In this article we have approached the issue of blurring boundaries in lifestyle journalism in different ways: through the quantitative analysis and the qualitative examples, we have documented that it is difficult to demarcate lifestyle as a journalistic topic in contemporary journalism: our analysis reveals that boundaries between subjects such as lifestyle, consumption and culture are blurring at the textual level, and consequently so are different modes of address. From the perspective of the producers—journalists—the question of boundaries is constantly being negotiated. These negotiations are themselves manifest in the blurring boundaries between subjects and modes of address.

One framework for interpreting these changes is the development of the Danish media system, including transformations in the relationship between the public and the private, between hard news and soft news. The Danish media system has, in line with global media developments, changed from a party press at the turn of the twentieth century, where Danish newspapers were mouthpieces for political parties and viewpoints, to an omnibus press targeted at a broad audience (that is, a cultural institution providing public service for private money) and most recently to commercial media institutions in a competitive media market, where political and cultural profiles are necessary market strategies. For example, Hjarvard (2010) documents a political parallelism (see Hallin and Mancini, 2004) between Danish broadsheets and niche newspapers and their readers that is particularly evident in the editorial opinions and occasionally apparent in the journalistic content of these newspapers as well. Similarly, Kristensen (2010) and Kristensen and From (2011) document a cultural parallelism between different newspapers and their readers, since readers read the newspapers with which they identify culturally—or the newspapers which confirm their cultural orientation. Accordingly, in relation to lifestyle journalism, this article has documented increasingly demarcated sections within individual newspapers and a changed mode of addressing readers in relation to a range of topics related to lifestyle—from public service to private service, from society to the individual—and that the editorial organisation and the brand of the newspaper/media institution today influence the specific priority given to and negotiation of specific topics, including how specific lifestyle topics are covered and approached. It is thus possible to speak of simultaneous processes or strategies of inclusion and exclusion by newspapers: the many stories and issues which might potentially be interpreted as and subjects for lifestyle journalism force the newspapers to select and prioritize specific topics, combinations of stories and generic approaches, which in the end serve to differentiate, characterize or brand the individual newspaper. The argument of inclusion of topics thus relates to the fact that everything is potentially open to interpretation and representation as lifestyle, while the argument on exclusion relates to the fact that the newspapers brand themselves through very specific topics and journalistic approaches.

Even though our empirical data regarding texts and content is limited to the printed press, the more extensive blurring of boundaries beyond the typical soft news areas might thus be explained in light of the increasingly competitive media landscape of the past decades, which has forced newspapers to develop new or different approaches to a range of topics, since the printed press cannot compete with other media platforms such as television and the Internet when it comes to "breaking" stories. In other words, newspapers cannot compete on timeliness and deadlines. Consequently, other news values have become important.

These media institutional changes reflect the more general socio-cultural transformations which are incorporated in the concept of mediatization of culture and society (Hjarvard, 2008; Jansson, 2002; Schulz, 2004). Jansson (2002) elucidates the close connections between media, economics and cultural and social processes in Western societies and cultures through a discussion of how media products, cultural objects and phenomena, mediatized culture and consumption—including lifestyle—are today linked to an economic, industrial logic which circulates symbolic and semiotic signs rather than fulfilling basic physiological needs. From a theoretical perspective, and departing from the concept of "culturalization", Jansson argues that traditional cultural products are launched and articulated as consumer goods while consumer goods are presented as cultural products. Accordingly, we argue that media, actors and cultural industries in a broad sense "accommodate" (Schulz, 2004) to each other and that the blurring of boundaries between topics in contemporary lifestyle and cultural journalism can be explained as a *result of* but also as *contributing to* precisely these processes. We do not argue that cultural journalism or consumer journalism are being *replaced* by lifestyle journalism, but rather that these journalistic topics are often issues of negotiation, just as they are placed in sections and on news desks where they are (constantly) processed by journalists in ways which *construct* specific (soft) topics as lifestyle journalism, cultural journalism and/or consumer journalism. Accordingly, one might argue that precisely these journalistic negotiations and constructions influence the more general articulation of lifestyle as cultural phenomenon in society.

Even though the empirical perspective of the discussions and arguments presented in this article is Danish, the discussions and results are of broader, international relevance, since they identify more general characteristics of and changes within lifestyle journalism, its production and mode of address. Furthermore, the changing, expanding and blurring boundaries of the form, content and address of lifestyle journalism can be interpreted as a reflection of changes within and blurring of boundaries of journalistic topics and genres as such, documented by and discussed in relation to not least political journalism. This indicates that journalism constantly challenges, reformulates and expands different topics and agendas such as lifestyle, culture or politics.

NOTES

1. Each article could, if relevant, be coded for up to three different subjects—in order to grasp the presumed increasing blurring of boundaries between lifestyle, consumption and culture. Due to a very limited number of articles within some subject categories, e.g. health, these were included in the "other" category in the analysis.
2. One of the newspapers included in the study, *Politiken*, even introduced the Sunday section FOOD in March 2009 (http://www.politikenannoncer.dk/9913/09/04%20MAD:%20Danmarks%20eneste%20dagbl%20, accessed 19 July 2011).

REFERENCES

BARNHURST, KEVIN G. and NERONE, JOHN (2001) *The Form of News*, New York: Guilford.

BOCZKOWSKI, PABLO (2009) "Rethinking Hard and Soft News Production", *Journal of Communication* 59(1), pp. 98–116.

BRUNDSDON, CHARLOTTE (2003) "Lifestyling Britain: the 8–9 slot on British television", *International Journal of Cultural Studies* 6(1), pp. 5–23.

CHRISTENSEN, CHRISTA LYKKE (2010) "Livsstilsprogrammer. Hverdag og underholdning ["Lifestyle Television Programmes. Everyday life and entertainment"]", in: Hanne Bruun and Kirsten Frandsen (Eds), *Underholdende tv* [*Entertaining Television*], Aarhus: Aarhus University Press, pp. 212–45.

EIDE, MARTIN (1992) *Den Fjerde Servicemakt—noter til forståelse av norsk veilednings- og kampanjejournalistikk* [*The Fourth Service Estate*], Bergen: Institut for Massekommunikasjon.

EIDE, MARTIN and KNIGHT, GRAHAM (1999) "Public/Private: service journalism and the problems of everyday life", *European Journal of Communication* 14(4), pp. 525–47.

FRANKLIN, BOB (1997) *Newszak and News Media*, Oxford: Oxford University Press.

FROM, UNNI (2010) "The Reading of Cultural and Lifestyle Journalism", *Northern Lights* 8, pp. 157–75.

GOLIN, CIDA and CARDOSO, EVERTON (2009) "Cultural Journalism in Brazil: academic research, visibility, mediation and news values", *Journalism* 10(1), pp. 69–89.

HALLIN, DANIEL C. and MANCINI, PAOLO (2004) *Comparing Media Systems*, Cambridge: Cambridge University Press.

HJARVARD, STIG (1995) *Nyhedsmediernes rolle i det politiske demokrati* [*The Role of the News Media in Political Democracy*], København: Statsministeriets Medieudvalg.

HJARVARD, STIG (2008) "The Mediatization of Society. A theory of the media as agents of social and cultural change", *Nordicom Review* 29(2), pp. 105–34.

HJARVARD, STIG (2010) "The Views of the News: the role of political newspapers in a changing media landscape", *Northern Lights* 8, pp. 25–48.

HOVDEN, JAN FREDRIK and KNAPSKOG, KARL A. (2008) "Kulturjournalistikken i det norske journalistiske feltet" ["Cultural Journalism in the Norwegian Journalistic Field"]", in: Karl A. Knapskog and Leif O. Larsen (Eds), *Kulturjournalistikk. Pressen og den kulturelle offentligheten* [*Cultural Journalism. The press and the cultural public*], Oslo: Scandinavian Academic Press, pp. 51–70.

JANSSEN, SUSANNE S., KUIPERS, GISELINDE and VERBOORD, MARC (2008) "Cultural Globalization and Arts Journalism: the international orientation of arts and culture coverage in Dutch, French, German, and U.S. newspapers, 1955 to 2005", *American Sociological Review* 73(5), pp. 719–40.

JANSSON, ANDRÉ (2002) "The Mediatization of Consumption: towards an analytical framework of image culture", *Journal of Consumer Culture* 2(5), pp. 5–31.

KRISTENSEN, NETE NØRGAARD (2010) "The Historical Transformation of Cultural Journalism", *Northern Lights* 8, pp. 69–92.

KRISTENSEN, NETE NØRGAARD and FROM, UNNI (2011) *Kulturjournalistik—journalistik om kultur* [*Cultural Journalism—journalism on culture*], Frederiksberg: Samfundslitteratur.

MCKAY, JENNY (2000) *The Magazines Handbook*, London: Routledge.

PATTERSON, THOMAS E. (2000) "Doing Well and Doing Good", KSG Working Paper No. 01-001, John F. Kennedy School of Government, Harvard University, Cambridge, MA.

PLASSER, FRITZ (2005) "From Hard to Soft News Standards? How political journalists in different media systems evaluate the shifting quality of news", *Press/Politics* 10(2), pp. 47–68.

POVLSEN, KAREN K. (1995) *Organisering af hverdagsliv og livsstil: Ugeblade, magasiner og fagblade* [*The Organization of Everyday Life and Lifestyle*], Copenhagen: Medieudvalget Statsministeriet.

POVLSEN, KAREN K. (2007) "Smag, livsstil og madmagasiner [Taste, Lifestyle and food Magazines]", *MediaCulture* 42/43, pp. 46–53.

SCHULZ, WINFRIED (2004) "Reconstructing Mediatization as an Analytical Concept", *European Journal of Communication* 19(1), pp. 87–101.

SUNDVOR, EIGIL (2008) *Forbrukarjournalistikk* [*Consumer Journalism*], Kristiansand: IJ-forlaget.

THE DEVIL MAY CARE
Travel journalism, cosmopolitan concern, politics and the brand

Lyn McGaurr

As journalism scholars' interest in the impact of public relations on hard news has grown in recent years, little attention has been paid to attempts by elite sources to influence soft journalism. In an effort to better understand what can, in fact, be complex interactions between travel journalists and public relations practitioners, this paper tracks one destination's brand over an extended period of cosmopolitan concern. It finds that in times of conflict, government tourism public relations may become politically instrumental, as public relations practitioners seek simultaneously to promote the destination and shield it from media scrutiny. At such times, travel journalists may subvert traditional expectations of their genre by exposing contradictions in the brand. The paper concludes that the power of travel journalism derives not only from its authors' capacity to communicate through their texts but also from their tendency to be enmeshed in the interactivity of the brand.

Introduction

In 2001, Elfriede Fürsich and Anandam Kavoori argued that travel journalism was then an underexplored field of study deserving of greater academic attention in part because of the "special contingencies" of its "tacit allegiance to both advertising and the travel industry" (2001, p. 154). "Freebies" provided by visiting journalist programs (VJPs) are a standard part of government tourism public relations, and the intention of the public relations practitioners (PRs) providing them is to influence travel journalists to write favourably about a destination or product (Dore and Crouch, 2003; Mackellar and Fenton, 2000; Tourism Tasmania, nd b).

According to Lynne Dore and Geoffrey Crouch, hosted visits have become "critically important elements" of the destination promotion strategies of government tourism organisations around the world (2003, p. 140). Nevertheless, recent research suggests that travel journalists have confidence in their professional integrity. Reporting on his survey of Australian travel journalists, Folker Hanusch (2011) found that an overwhelming majority of those interviewed subscribed to "high ethical ideals". In reporting this result, however, Hanusch notes that travel journalists' self-perceptions may not always be reliable and suggests that further qualitative investigation in the form of ethnographic research and in-depth interviews may provide useful insights. This paper responds to concerns over the influence of hosted travel on travel journalists by presenting highly contextualised research into the interconnections between international travel journalists, government PRs and other travel journalism sources in a destination where environmental contestation has been mediatised for decades (Lester, 2007). By following the brand of Australia's island state of Tasmania through an extended period of cosmopolitan concern that has presented both opportunities and challenges for the state's government tourism organisation, the paper exposes some of the complex, often hidden negotiations between brand managers and travel journalists that quantitative analysis is less well suited to investigate.

For the purposes of this article, travel journalism is defined as the print or online texts of staff or freelance newspaper or magazine writers who travel to destinations to write signed (that is, by-lined) accounts primarily for audiences of potential travellers. As noted in an earlier paper (McGaurr, 2010), the term "signed accounts" here specifically links the journalistic imperative of counting as true (Hartley, 1996) to travel writing's attribute of the autobiographical account (Holland and Huggan, 2000), rather than to the journalistic ambition of objectivity (McNair, 2005).

The paper begins by deriving concepts and themes from a consideration of the way in which contemporary branding and cosmopolitanism might intersect with, find expression in and inform travel journalism. It then assembles a biography of the Tasmania brand with reference to these themes using an array of data derived from long semi-structured interviews, government publications, travel journalism and news reports. The paper finds that travel journalism's ability to facilitate or interrupt representations and flows of local concerns in the public sphere can result in government tourism office brand management that seeks to "guide the investments of affect" (Arvidsson, 2006, p. 93) on the part of travel journalists[1] in a manner that is both commercially and politically instrumental. It concludes that travel journalism is one mechanism for restricting or expanding "the margins of indeterminacy" of the brand (Lury, 2004, p. 73) and, as such, its power derives as much from its tendency to be enmeshed in the interactivity of the brand at its margins (Lury, 2004) as from its capacity to speak directly to a tourism destination's consumers and (other) cosmopolitans.

Branding and the Destination

In government tourism offices, VJPs are not only the logistical epicentre of many travel journalists' visits to a destination; they are also a vital hub of brand management. As such they "[put] public communication to work under managed forms by providing a context where it can evolve in a particular direction" (Arvidsson, 2006, p. 67). In today's highly mediatised, intertextual consumer environment, brand management can position ostensibly sovereign consumers—consumers whose reflexivity, sometimes expressed through creative resistance to brands, can nevertheless be commodified (Holt, 2002)— as active participants in the evolution not only of their own identities but also of the brand's (Holt, 2002). In tourism, that evolution finds expression in holidaymakers who are "increasingly seeking lifestyle fulfilment and experience rather than recognizing differentiation in the more tangible elements of the destination product such as accommodation and attractions" (Morgan and Pritchard, 2004, p. 60). In focusing on brands in her attempt to analyse the economic and social implications of contemporary uses of information, image and media, sociologist Celia Lury (2004, pp. 8–9, pp. 131–3) presents a notion of brands as new media objects, in part because they act as an interface that is a site of interactivity facilitating dynamic, two-way but asymmetrical and selective communication between producers and consumers and also separating them from each other. While the brand simultaneously delivers information to and extracts it from customers to be used in marketing, design, production and distribution, it can also severely limit the ability of customers to interact with it (2004, p. 137). In other words, the *interactivity* that brand managers encourage as a source of information about consumers does not necessarily result in consumers having equitable *interaction* with producers (Aronczyk and Powers, 2010; Lury, 2004). As Adam Arvidsson (2006, p. 94) explains, the informational capital of brands depends on consumers producing a "common sociality" that can be appropriated, then filtered and polished before being redeployed.

In the discourse of marketing, a distinction is made between branding destinations and branding places (Anholt, 2004, 2007, 2010; Go and Govers, 2010; Govers and Go, 2009; Kotler and Gertner, 2002). The former relates to tourism marketing whereas the latter in its purest form is synonymous with what place-brand exponent Simon Anholt also refers to as "competitive identity"—a "synthesis of brand management with public diplomacy and with trade, investment, tourism and export promotion" (2007, p. 3). Although Anholt argues against an entirely literal interpretation of the term "branding" when applied to something as multifaceted and dynamic as a country, region or city, he sees tourism as "a refreshingly simple and honest business" (2010, p. 89) and its communications as having a legitimacy that makes the sector the most powerful place-branding "booster rocket": "Publics are generally dismissive of direct communications from national governments or their agencies, and ... are unsure how to react to them. Communications from tourist boards, on the other hand, are seen as a legitimate representation of the country to the global audience" (2007, p. 88). Anholt argues that place branding will only succeed if its communications are honest, ethical and founded on policy-making that incorporates serious consideration of "market feedback" (2007, p. 14) from public diplomacy. Yet, rather than approaching coverage by journalists as market feedback, place-branding literature tends to discuss it in traditional media-management terms (as in Govers and Go, 2009). Positive coverage by independent journalists—who are described as "autonomous" agents—is highly valued by place marketers because it is regarded by potential visitors as more credible than "overt induced image formation" such as advertising (Gartner, 1993). Negative autonomous news coverage is seen to undermine positive messages from induced agents (Schatz and Kolmer, 2010). Travel journalists who have been successfully influenced by place marketers through, for example, hosted visits that are not declared in their published texts are described as "covert induced" agents (Gartner, 1993, pp. 200–1). According to Robert Govers and Frank Go (2009, p. 188) "covert induced agents are becoming increasingly important [in place branding], and the nature of many previously autonomous agents have [*sic*] been changed to become covert induced agents".

While marketing discourse advocates place branding as a means of liberating places—particularly developing countries—from the economic impediment of a poor reputation (Anholt, 2004), Lash and Lury (2007) argue that brands are largely a form of domination, and Lury (2004, p. 163) is ultimately pessimistic about their ability to function as more than "an object of contemporary capitalism". Central to her pessimism is a tension she perceives between the brand's potential to be open and its tendency to be closed, depending on its degree of indeterminacy and the willingness or otherwise of brand managers to act on all of the information they receive (Lury, 2004, p. 162). Yet although VJPs may reasonably be considered public relations tools intended to define the relationship between travel journalists and PRs as one of exchange rather than conflict (see White and Hobsbawm, 2007, for an argument that such arrangements are implicit in the contemporary relationship between many PRs and journalists), they are also, potentially, sites of resistance. By "trying out" destinations on behalf of potential visitors and then mediating their findings, travel journalists, like tourists and other travellers, consume the brand and help (re)produce it: as such they are both consumer– producers and consumer–mediators of destination brands. With this in mind, this paper considers whether travel journalists informed by cosmopolitanism might be willing and able to resist the pressure of defensive public relations strategies that seek to make destination brands more closed in times of political conflict. The following section briefly describes cosmopolitanism and discusses its relevance to travel and travel journalism.

Travel Journalism as a Cosmopolitan Project

As interest in cosmopolitanism has gathered pace over the past 20 years, a plethora of new theories has emerged (Holton, 2009), among which those of anthropologist Ulf Hannerz (2004a, 2004b, 2006) have considerable appeal in relation to the subject of this paper. Hannerz (2004a, 2006) describes cosmopolitanism as having two faces: the happy face of cultural/consumer cosmopolitanism associated with an aesthetic and intellectual appreciation of food, literature, music, etc. from other cultures; and the worried face of political cosmopolitanism that attempts to deal with large-scale concerns such as environmental degradation, species extinction, humanitarian crises, human rights abuses and climate change. Cultural and political cosmopolitanism do not necessarily coexist in individuals or groups: it may be possible for a person to be perfectly satisfied with their level of intercultural connoisseurship without ever feeling the need to participate in, or contribute to, a transnational civic or humanitarian project (Hannerz, 2004a; see also Calhoun, 2002; Urry, 2002). Nevertheless, comparing hard news and features, Hannerz attributes to features an ability to convey a broader variety of sentiments, provide a closer approximation of the complexity of distant others, and make those others, their locations and their situations more "durable" (2004b, p. 33).

Hannerz (2004a, 2004b), and sociologists Ulrich Beck (2006), Bronislaw Szerszynski and John Urry (2006) all acknowledge the possibility of an intertwining of cultural and political cosmopolitanism arising from "banal cosmopolitanism" or "banal globalism"[2]— that is, from the public's everyday encounters with corporeal travel, imaginative travel, cultural diversity, consumer cosmopolitanism and images of connectedness in a world of globalised media and transport. According to Szerszynski and Urry (2006), banal globalism has the capacity to animate both global tourism and the environmental movement, while in Beck's world view journalists have an important role to play in the unveiling and contestation of environmental risks and threats (1995), which he considers to be among humanity's most pressing cosmopolitan concerns (2006). Seen from this perspective, travel journalism that combines praise of a destination's tourism experiences with criticism of government policies that might be considered of cosmopolitan concern, may be indicative of such an intertwining, whereby the happy face of consumer cosmopolitanism lets down its guard occasionally to reveal the more worried face of political cosmopolitanism. In this regard, the interconnectedness of the local, national and global (Beck, 2006; Holton, 2009)—the "polygamy of place" (Beck, 2006, p. 44) so characteristic of many contempor- ary theories of cosmopolitanism—can make travel journalism a forum for the mediation not only of concerns of global significance but also of more localised concerns in instances where distant audiences are grappling with similar issues.

Method

The approach taken in the research for the case study below was to follow a cosmopolitan destination brand through multiple networks over time to "illuminate [its] human and social context" (Appadurai, 1986, p. 5)—in this case with particular reference to travel journalism and public relations. Using a method of data collection similar to that employed by Lash and Lury (2007), I assembled an array of material about the Tasmania brand from various points of view from the mid-1990s to 2010: long, semi-structured interviews with international travel journalists, local tourism operators and PRs, together with published travel journalism, news journalism, government publications, media releases and publicity material. All but one interview for the case study was conducted by phone, Skype or face to face, and all were part of my continuing PhD research into travel journalism. My own experience as a Tourism Tasmania employee from mid-2002 to mid-2008 did not form part of the data analysed but occasionally contributed to the triangulation of data provided by interviewees. Of the 38 interviews, 11 were with travel journalists from Britain or the United States who had visited Tasmania between 2000 and 2010 inclusive and subsequently produced travel features that had appeared in print and sometimes also online. Britain and the United States were chosen because they were Tasmania's biggest international tourism markets. Tasmania was chosen as a case study because it was a destination whose brand both coalesced and atomised around issues of cosmopolitan concern—a destination in which environmental conflict had been media-tised for decades (Lester, 2007). Although the case study does not generally cite secondary sources beyond travel journalism that demonstrate the concern for Tasmania's forests may be considered cosmopolitan, media coverage of related environmental activism in the United States, Europe, Britain and Japan during the period of the case study may be easily discovered (see also Buchman, 2008; Lester, 2007; McGaurr, 2010). Designations of interviewees, where noted, are as at the time of interview.

Case Study

Tasmania's destination brand was born of cosmopolitan concern. In the Australian summer of 1982–83 a protest against plans by a state government authority to dam the Franklin River in the island's newly created Tasmanian Wilderness World Heritage Area resulted in widespread media exposure for the state (Lester, 2007). Immediately following the 1983 Australian High Court decision that protected the river, the state government began looking for ways to capitalise on the publicity the controversy had brought to the island's wilderness (Evers Consulting Services, 1984, Appendix 2, p. 1). The first commercial hut-based tourism operation in the World Heritage Area opened in 1987, and by 1994 the destination was apparently considered well-credentialed enough in ecotourism to host a World Congress on Adventure Travel and Ecotourism. Although there had been a short hiatus in environmental conflict following the Franklin River High Court decision, Tasmania's forests had soon become the next conservation battleground. At the ecotourism world congress, before 450 delegates, 9 per cent of whom were from the media (Busch, 1994), the environment movement attacked the government and its forestry corporation in speeches, protests and petitions (*The Mercury*, 1994a, b). These criticisms were subsequently highlighted in the published proceedings of the congress by then-editor of the US magazine *National Geographic Traveler* Richard Busch (1994) in a move whose penetration would not become apparent for another decade (see below).

Meanwhile, the prospect of hosting the congress had already concentrated the attention of the state government's tourism authority, Tourism Tasmania, on destination branding (Tourism in Natural Areas Project Team, 1993). In the same month as the event was held, Tasmania conducted what was then its "largest ever qualitative consumer research" among interstate Australians. This research found that the island's natural environment and clean, green image were its strongest competitive advantages (Department of Tourism, Sport and Recreation, 1995, p. 8). In 1995, the tourism authority adopted the tagline "TASMANIA Discover your natural state" (Department of Tourism, Sport and Recreation, 1995, p. 8) for the domestic market and "Australia's natural state" for the international market (Department of Premier and Cabinet, 2006), and in 1999 the government established a new joint government and industry place-of-origin branding initiative, Brand Tasmania, which would soon introduce its own VJP targeting foreign correspondents. Brand Tasmania's "umbrella brand" encompassed many "sectoral brands" such as timber, wine, food and tourism, but it was the tourism sectoral brand that the government regarded as the most influential (Department of Premier and Cabinet, 2006). While the government claimed to appreciate that "the Tasmanian brand belongs to us all" (Department of Premier and Cabinet, 2006), the establishment of Brand Tasmania made a previously implicit link between government policy, image management and customer relationships explicit, as the government itself acknowledged some years later in a brand guide that cited some of the early place-branding texts by Anholt (Department of Premier and Cabinet, 2006, p. 3 and outside back cover) and observed that place branding might require "strong alignment of message" across stakeholders "in competition or conflict" (2006, p. 11).

This reconfiguring of the notion of "Tasmania" as more than a tourism brand both supported and guided brand extensions already being energetically pursued by Tourism Tasmania in the food and wine sector. Yet, locally and nationally, the tourism industry was coming under attack for the contradiction between the "natural" image promoted by Tourism Tasmania and the government-sanctioned logging of old-growth forests. From 2002, culture jamming (Arvidsson, 2006; Lury, 2004) attracted news media attention, as brand messages and images were creatively reworked for a Sydney airport billboard, a website URL and a banner on the side of an interstate ferry. In addition, influential international travel journalists would sometimes try out Tasmania, praise its natural environment and other tourism experiences, but then point out the contradictions in the brand. Adventure travel writer Mark Jenkins, whose trip was funded by US magazine *Outside* and who was given interviews by noted anti-logging identities such as novelist Richard Flanagan and the Wilderness Society's Geoff Law, was particularly critical (Jenkins, 2005; interview, 20 March 2009). Similarly, Stephen Metcalf, on a non-VJP-funded assignment for the US edition of *Travel + Leisure*, quoted a restaurateur opposed to a government-sanctioned private pulp mill planned for Tasmania's premier wine-tourism region by a company called Gunns and winemakers with concerns about the same company's acquisition of a major winery in the region (Metcalf, 2008; interview, 26 June 2009). Each writer also quoted a source with opposing views, stressing in their interviews for this case study that balance was important to them as journalists, but their sympathies were clear. For Metcalf, in particular, an environmental dispute in his home community animated his interest in Tasmania's pulp mill dispute (Metcalf, interview, 26 June 2009).

The VJP was an important vehicle for countering challenges to the brand. Throughout the 2000s the success of the VJP in gaining positive coverage in return for hosted travel was listed among the "highlights" in Tourism Tasmania's annual reports, and the authority was comfortable with using public funds for this purpose:

> obviously it's not our place to impinge on journalistic integrity and them pursuing a story. But particularly when we're funding a trip I think that we have to have mutual objectives about what we're trying to do. And I think for most of the journalists that we deal with they completely understand and respect that they're here as the guests of Tasmania and the Tasmanian government and the Tasmanian taxpayer money, then the agreed objectives of the story are what needs to be the focus. (Senior Tourism Tasmania PR Ruth Dowty, interview, 3 June 2009)

International travel journalists who participated in the VJP were far more likely than hosted domestic travel journalists to be guided by a Tourism Tasmania guide throughout their itinerary. During their research in the destination, they were, therefore, generally more constrained than their domestic counterparts—in theory a captive audience for relationship-building on the part of guides. However, international travel journalists were also less likely to return to the state than domestic travel journalists and, thus, less likely to feel a need to please PRs with their published texts purely to secure future "freebies" (Waller, interview, 3 July 2009). From 2000 to 2010 international travel journalists hosted by Tourism Tasmania occasionally included negative comment on the forestry controversy in their features. Among examples were Jeff Greenwald on assignment for the US magazine *Islands* (2008) and, from Britain, *BBC Wildlife Magazine* travel editor James Fair (2000), Paul Miles on assignment for *The Financial Times* (2008a) and *Conde Nast Traveller* (2008b),[3] and travel journalist A. A. Gill (2007) on assignment for *The Times*. Gill's celebrity enabled him to successfully insist that he should be allowed to travel without a guide most of the time, but he was nevertheless shadowed during parts of his trip by a Tourism Tasmania PR (Geoffrey King, interview, 7 June 2009; Gabi Mocatta, interview, 7 September 2009).

On the basis of their personal or professional contacts with environmentalists (Greenwald, interview, 6 March 2009; Miles, interview, 9 March 2009), Miles and Greenwald can be considered mediators of cosmopolitan concern. Miles had worked for Tourism Concern, and Greenwald was the founder and Executive Director of Ethical Traveler, which a few years before his first visit had launched a letter-writing campaign in association with the Wilderness Society in support of protecting Tasmania's forests (Greenwald, interview, 6 March 2009). However, they were also supporters of the travel industry and travel publishing. As consumer–mediators of "Tasmania", Greenwald in particular engaged in a form of brand resistance (Arvidsson, 2006) that expressed itself in the construction of an identity in his first-person narrative (Greenwald, 2008) that combined the passion for place that had traditionally characterised Tasmania's environment movement, and was increasingly part of Tourism Tasmania's branding (Tourism Tasmania, nd a), with the worried face of political cosmopolitanism. This is consistent with an appreciation among travel journalists interviewed for this case study of the significance of branding to tourism public relations and of travel journalism as primarily a celebration of travel (see also Austin,

1999). In the case of articles that unveil threats to that which they simultaneously praise, the genre itself may thus be seen to lend weight and credibility to the criticism.

Although such "talking back", as Lury (2004, p. 137) describes it, has the potential to bring the outside world inside an organisation as a stimulus for policy change, Tourism Tasmania had no direct influence over the state government's forestry policy and its brand management mostly attempted to make the brand more closed (Lury, 2004). In 2005, for example, Tourism Tasmania entered into a partnership with *BBC Wildlife Magazine* whereby the magazine published a marketing supplement on Tasmania with Fair as author (Fair, 2005; interview, 17 March 2009). Such supplements in newspapers and magazines were one of Tourism Tasmania's favoured tactics for maintaining or regaining control of its message, as evidenced by a subsequent supplement in London's *Daily Telegraph* subtitled "Your 16-page guide to one of the most unspoilt islands on Earth", which included articles from a number of travel journalists who had previously participated in the VJP, including Fair (Telegraph Create et al., 2008). Also in 2005, Tasmania began a protracted attempt to move the image it projected of its physical environment away from a heavy focus on abundant nature towards attributes it referred to in its branding literature as "islandness" and "on the edge of the Great Southern Ocean" (Department of Premier and Cabinet, 2006). In international tourism markets, however, the phrase "Australia's natural state" continued to appear in taglines and publication titles (see, for example, Tourism Tasmania North America's 2008 brochure).

Meanwhile, the brand also functioned to regulate staff (see Arvidsson, 2006; Lury, 2004). Overt or perceived pressure not to criticise Tasmania's logging practices—to live the brand by being unfailingly positive about the state (see, for example, Tourism Tasmania nd a)—appears to have caused anxiety among some (though by no means all) Tourism Tasmania PRs and guides—an anxiety that was sometimes evident or reported during interviews for this research. Vice-president of the Foreign Correspondents' Association in Australia Urs Walterlin, who had been hosted on separate occasions by Tourism Tasmania and Brand Tasmania, went so far as to volunteer his assessment that the atmosphere in regard to such matters was one of fear (Walterlin, interview, 26 June 2009).

Yet it is precisely at such moments of tension that "the open-endedness of the brand can contribute to an indeterminate politics or a politics of indeterminacy" (Lury, 2004, p. 141). While some Tourism Tasmania VJP staff with concerns for the environment apparently censored themselves, others talked back (Lury, 2004) by talking to travel journalists. One guide who saw forestry as a concern for the brand and mentioned sometimes giving an opinion on environmental issues she was careful to tell journalists was personal (interview, 24 March 2009), described this as a sign of "authenticity"—an implicit reference to "authenticity" being a noted "core value" of the Tasmania brand (Department of Premier and Cabinet, 2006; Tourism Tasmania, nd a). One former PR who recalled discussing the forestry debate with hosted travel journalists regarded promoting the state for Tourism Tasmania as "conservation work" (Mocatta, interview, 7 September 2009): "I thought that the more people that know about Tasmania, the more visiting journalists that we have, the less trees will be cut down. And that for me was a really fundamental thing." And Tourism Tasmania-sanctioned travel journalism source and (since retired) government wildlife biologist Nick Mooney, who was sometimes brought on board as an expert guide, spoke of helping journalists in his own time:

> People come over to do wildlife stuff and they take 'em off on a wine and cheese tour
> 'cause they just don't want 'em to—they want to avoid the logging issue, you know, this

confrontation. Because it's just so obvious. You go to some of the best wildlife spots and there's fuckin' log trucks everywhere … I used to get many complaints and it was often the last day of the trip when the journalist had half a day free or something and they're desperate to find someone who'd talk about an issue, 'cause they'd been managed and corralled so much, so I'd end up with some frantic bloody run-around for half the day or something, or get them to stay another day and stay at my place and we'd talk about the issue in depth, and that was the origin of these—often the arse end of a trip where they just got really frustrated. That's why I probably get a pretty good run in 'em—because I've been at the end and probably present as someone who's at last someone who will talk about these issues. And because I'm not ambitious career-wise—I'm ambitious in other ways but not career-wise—I don't really care if it pisses someone off, it just doesn't matter. (Mooney, interview, 15 June 2009)

It is a paradox perhaps indicative of the brand's capacity for a degree of autonomy and agency (see Lury, 2004) that the productivity of brand resistance from within was sometimes irresistible to those charged with filtering out incompatible expressions (see Arvidsson, 2006). For example, it was Mooney who guided Fair to the Styx Valley in 2000 in his research for a short travel piece that would feature Mooney and be critical of Tasmania's forestry practices (Fair, interview, 17 March 2009). For many years Mooney had been charged by the government with the task of attempting to verify supposed sightings of the extinct Tasmanian tiger and had gained a marketable cachet from his reputation as a tiger hunter (e.g. Flinn, 2005b). More importantly, he was a Tasmanian devil expert. When the *San Francisco Chronicle*'s travel editor at the time, John Flinn, expressed an interest in tigers and devils prior to his newspaper-funded visit in 2005, Tourism Tasmania enlisted Mooney's assistance again, despite his reputation for speaking his mind:

> He [Mooney] has got an opinion, had an opinion. And he's often got into trouble I think … for being—not overly opinionated, but for having an opinion at all. But he's a character, and I thought that would be the perfect person for John to travel with because he could tell him the science, he knew it all, he was funny, he was interesting, and I felt having talked to John that he would like Nick, and Nick was very happy to drive him up there. He said, "I'll just drive him up there and take him out to Joe's," and that's what he did. (Former senior Tourism Tasmania PR Delia Nicholls, interview, 9 March 2009)

The tourism operator mentioned above—Geoff "Joe" King—operated a night-time wildlife tour that featured devils feeding in the wild and was another government-sanctioned travel journalism source popular with PRs and journalists for his authenticity (Dowty, interview, 3 June 2009; Flinn, interview, 2 March 2009; McGinity, interview, 23 October 2009; Nicholls, interview, 9 March 2009). A fifth-generation Tasmanian cattle-farmer-turned-conservationist schooled in wildlife tourism by Mooney and adopted early by the VJP (King, interview, 7 June 2009; Mooney, interview, 15 June 2009; Nicholls, interview, 9 March 2009), King was vital to what would become Tourism Tasmania's own deployment of cosmopolitan concern. In 2003 the government had admitted that the endemic devil was suffering from a contagious facial tumour; two years later, Tourism Tasmania had invoked cosmopolitan concern for the devil in an effort to manage the potential damage the disease could cause to the brand (Department of Tourism, Parks, Heritage and the Arts, 2005). Within another two years the tourism authority was seeing commercial advantage in supporting the Save the Tasmanian Devil Appeal:

Following the 2007 success of G'day USA, opportunities exist to leverage "cause marketing" (e.g. raising money to fight the Tasmanian "devil disease") activities with philanthropic organisations and develop an education style product targeting affiliate and alumni groups with an interest in nature and wildlife. (Tourism Tasmania, 2007; parenthetical example included in original text)

Any reference in travel journalism to suspicions of disingenuousness could easily have undermined Tourism Tasmania's strategic deployment of cosmopolitan concern for the devil. Positioning themselves as disinterested was important to Mooney's and King's efforts to spread their own conservation messages but it also contributed to the creation of a kind of "ironic, reflexive brand persona" (Holt, 2002, pp. 83–4) that VJP staff knew from experience appealed to travel journalists:

> [King] was smart and funny and eccentric and a passionate person and I just knew he'd make a great story. And he was willing to do it. He learned to put himself out there, because a lot of people don't want to do that. It's hard. (PR Nicholls, interview, 9 March 2009)

> [W]hat I liked about it was that it was so uncommercial. Nick and I just drove over to Geoff's house. We had dinner with his wife and kids, and sat out on the porch and drank a couple of beers. And as it got dark we just got in his truck and just drove over to where his thing was. You wouldn't have anything like that in the States. Everything would have been—the guide would have probably had a little uniform and a badge on and you would have had to sign 18 waivers and it would have been very official. This just felt like it was just very casual. And to me it spoke somewhat to what I said earlier about it being an unaffected place compared to a lot of the rest of the world. (Travel journalist Flinn, interview, 2 March 2009)

In such situations, traditional travel journalism norms and values can and often do operate to stifle noise at the brand's interface. For example, although Flinn and Mooney discussed forestry issues on their lengthy drive to King's remote property (Flinn, interview, 2 March 2009), and although Flinn was travelling at the expense of his paper, he did not refer to Tasmania's forestry dispute in his articles (Flinn, 2005a, 2005b) because he thought it was "a little bit out of bounds" and not "an imminent, huge problem that would have affected an area that a tourist might care about" (Flinn, interview, 2 March 2009). As travel editor of the *San Francisco Chronicle*, Flinn was himself influential but he also had strong affiliations with the elite of popular travel writing and publishing. Despite earlier efforts by Nicholls to entice the *Chronicle* to send a travel journalist to Tasmania (Nicholls, interview, 9 March 2009), Flinn's visit had ultimately been prompted by the personal recommendations of guidebook company Lonely Planet's co-founder Maureen Wheeler, then a board member of Tourism Tasmania (Flinn, interview, 2 March 2009). Having decided to visit the island, Flinn's overriding concern was to serve his readers' interests as expertly as possible (Flinn, interview, 2 March 2009). San Francisco has a large and affluent gay population, and Flinn was aware these readers might have heard that Tasmania had once had Draconian anti-homosexuality laws. As well as writing about the Tasmanian devil—familiar to United States audiences because of its alter ego, the Warner Bros. cartoon character Taz—he wanted to use his article to alert his gay readers to the fact that Tasmania's anti-gay laws had now changed. This change had come about following 10 years of campaigning that had mobilised and deployed cosmopolitan concern locally, nationally and internationally.

At the time of Flinn's visit, the leader of that campaign, Rodney Croome (2005), was working closely with Tourism Tasmania to attract gay and lesbian visitors to the state, and the VJP had arranged for him to guide Flinn around Hobart (Flinn, interview, 2 March 2009; Nicholls, interview, 9 March 2009; Croome, interview, 2 April 2009). While expressing strong personal support for the forestry campaign and stressing the similarities between it and his earlier campaign, in his promotion of the state since his own victory Croome focused on presenting a positive story:

> [I]n my public role, I only talk about gay and lesbian issues . . . in that regard I've got a positive story to tell. And there are plenty of people in Tasmania that are far better qualified than me to talk about the forests, and I leave that to them. That's not my public role. Just as I wouldn't expect them to turn around and say, "Our forests are being trashed, but it's great for gay people". It just wouldn't make any sense. (Croome, interview, 2 April 2009)

Here then, we see cultural and political cosmopolitanism diverging rather than converging in source struggles for publicity via travel journalism. In such circumstances, the happy face of cultural cosmopolitanism can gain ground even when there is extensive coverage of environmental conflict in the local news media, the travel journalists concerned have a news journalism background (e.g. Flinn, interview, 2 March 2009; Sharon Otterman, interview, 20 June 2009) and the journalists are travelling without financial assistance from the VJP. Writing for the *New York Times* two years later and casting Hobart as a stylish "boutique" destination, Sharon Otterman (2007; interview, 20 June 2009) received no freebies, had no contact with the VJP and included no criticism of forestry practices even though she was aware of the debate. Her syndicated article (Otterman, 2007) came to prominence in North America partly because she quoted Brian Ritchie, formerly of the US band the Violent Femmes, who now lives in Hobart. As a travel journalism source, Ritchie offers the kind of celebrity endorsement that brand managers seek to cultivate:

> I won't take any kind of a position, because I think it would somewhat deflate my ability to be an effective cultural force . . . I think if I'm working on art and music and then people are associating me with a cause or against a cause or whatever, I think that doesn't help me in my job. I do realise that the artists and citizens of Tasmania frequently choose to position themselves in some part of this spectrum regarding environmental issues. But knowing people from all the different sides of the spectrum there, I've noticed a common thread is that they all really believe in Tasmania and they all think their position is good for Tasmania. (Ritchie, interview, 20 March 2009)

In the 2000s Tasmania's brand managers projected an increasingly diverse and culturally sophisticated image of the island by promoting heritage, wine and food experiences and providing government support to high-profile cultural events, including one curated by Ritchie. Yet even after more than a decade of concerted brand extensions, in 2010 the most important component of Tasmania's brand was still overwhelmingly its natural environment ("wilderness" plus "coastal nature", in Tourism Tasmania, 2011)—a situation that would have come as no surprise to *National Geographic Traveler*. In 2004 the magazine published a "Destination Scorecard" that ranked Tasmania in the top five of 115 destinations, praised its environment but criticised its record on forestry (*National Geographic Traveler*, 2004; Tourtellot, 2004). At the time the state's government and tourism industry capitalised on the scorecard ranking by successfully directing the attention of the Tasmanian media towards its praise and away from its criticism (Lovibond, 2004). A year later, however, the Director of the National Geographic Society's Center for Sustainable Destinations, Jonathan Tourtellot, reprised the Scorecard criticism in an interview with a Tasmanian newspaper during his attendance as a guest of another ecotourism conference on the island. This time the criticism was reported, as was his observation that Tasmania's arguments about logging were similar to those taking place in North America (Van den Berg, 2005). Nor did the talking back end there: during this same visit Tourtellot was guided on a brief tour by a Tourism Tasmania PR (Tourtello, interview, 24 October 2009) and on his return to the United States he published a travel journalism article in *National Geographic Traveler* that represented Tasmanians as preferring plantations to old-growth logging and concluded with: "Visit Tasmania, and help a logger find a job in tourism" (Tourtellot, 2006).

Finally, in February 2010, even Tourism Tasmania's deployment of cosmopolitan concern for the Tasmanian devil briefly came undone. Shortly before a Tasmanian state election, an article about Tasmania appeared on US newsstands in a recently launched travel magazine called *Afar*—a magazine that markets itself in language consistent with the happy face of cosmopolitanism (Afar Media, 2011). The article, however, was anything but happy. Entitled "Bedeviled Island" (Greenwald, 2010), it was a follow-up to the 2008 article by Greenwald entitled "Sympathy for the Devil" in which he had written about King's devil feeding and expressed overt cosmopolitan concern for Tasmania, describing it as a "global treasure". A year later however, when travelling for *Afar*, the only assistance Greenwald had received from Tourism Tasmania was a hire car (Greenwald, interview, 6 March 2009). At the time, Forestry Tasmania had been planning to seal a section of road to create what it controversially described as a tourist road, and there was concern about the potential of such a road to threaten one of Tasmania's last healthy populations of devils. Now unfettered by a VJP itinerary, Greenwald had focused most of his attention on researching the relationship between King and his brother, whose views on conservation differed. The tagline to the published text summed up his thesis: "Depending on how you view it, Australia's Tasmania island is a paradise of unusual critters and ancient forests or a victim of logging and mining. One family's story illustrates the divide" (Greenwald, 2010, p. 64). Two issues later *Afar*'s letters page contained a paragraph from the King brothers strongly critical of the way their relationship had been portrayed in Greenwald's piece (King and King, 2010, p. 8). Nevertheless, there is little doubt that Greenwald's article accurately reflected views expressed by others closer to home and reported in the national media that Tasmania's brand was being undermined by its forestry practices (see, for example, Denholm, 2009). As one former Tourism Tasmania and Brand Tasmania PR put it, "There's a huge issue and we all pretend that there's no issue, and there is an issue. And the problem is that the argy-bargy's become the issue. This sort of fighting all the time is now becoming our brand" (McGinity, interview, 23 October 2009). By the end of the decade Brand Tasmania was acknowledging the forestry conflict on its own website.

In December 2009, an apolitical Tasmanian community group formed to promote the need to end the conflict. Among a series of television ads it produced, one referred to Tasmania as a "global jewel" and another highlighted the importance of the state's forests to its tourism industry (Our Common Ground, nd). Following the March 2010 state election, after which the Labor Party lost power in its own right for the first time since 1998 and the Greens gained Cabinet positions for the first time in Australian history, environmentalists and representatives from the logging industry came together in a government-sanctioned attempt to resolve their decades-long dispute. In November of the same year, *Afar* won the top award in the magazine category in one of the United States's most prestigious travel-writing competitions, the Lowell Thomas Travel Journalism Awards, run by the Society of American Travel Writers. "Bedeviled Island" won the top award in the category of environmental tourism article.

Conclusion

The case study presented here offers support for Lash and Lury's (2007) argument that branding is largely a form of domination. More interestingly, however, it finds that destination brands can also be sites of meaningful resistance. By following a single destination's brand through time, this paper has shown how international travel journalism's position at the intersection of multiple professional, personal and political networks makes it a mechanism for restricting or expanding "the margins of indeterminacy" (Lury, 2004, p. 73) of the brand. Moreover, in the case of the latter it has shown that cosmopolitan travel journalism can function to undermine attempts by government brand management to use the brand "as a wall or shield, insulating the production process from its environment" (Lury, 2004, p. 159).

The findings of this case study suggest that travel journalists' endorsement of destinations' brands is sufficiently valuable to be sought by governments at the cost of expensive hosted travel, not only because it may increase visitor numbers but also because it can interrupt the flow of local concerns in the public sphere. Moreover, the case study has shown that travel journalists' uncritical support of a destination's brand cannot be assumed, whether or not travel journalists are hosted. Furthermore, pervasive institutional sensitivity to the views of international travel journalists is consistent with the word-of-mouth circulation of travel journalist, PR, guide and source views and experiences through the public sector, the tourism industry and the broader community. In small, tightly-knit communities, such rumours may provide "an effective form of counter publicity in relation to the brand" (Lury, 2004, p. 141) at home, even in the absence of widespread local access to travel journalism texts published internationally or mediatised political action by overseas readers of those texts. As destination brands move through networks in time, travel journalists with cosmopolitan concerns who are prepared to talk back may bring the outside in (Lury, 2004) and a more nuanced interpretation of the inside out. In so doing they can help produce a common sociality that is less filtered, or differently filtered, than governments might wish, thereby contributing to the ability of citizens to participate more fully in their local, national and global communities.

NOTES

1. Arvidsson writes of the investment of affect of consumers, for whom I have here substituted travel journalists.
2. Hannerz (2006) regards these terms as interchangeable.
3. Miles' criticism in the published *Financial Times* (2008a) might best be described as culture jamming (he included the anti-forestry tourism URL mentioned earlier in an

otherwise positive article), while elsewhere (McGaurr, 2010) I have described his article for *Conde Nast Traveller* (2008b) as a travel magazine news article.

REFERENCES

AFAR MEDIA (2011) "Afar Magazine", http://corp.afar.com/products-platforms/afar-magazine, accessed 9 March 2011.

ANHOLT, SIMON (2004) "Editors Foreword to the First Issue", *Place Branding* 1(1), pp. 4–11.

ANHOLT, SIMON (2007) *Competitive Identity: the new brand management for nations, cities and regions*, Basingstoke: Palgrave Macmillan.

ANHOLT, SIMON (2010) *Places: identity, image and reputation*, Basingstoke: Palgrave Macmillan.

APPADURAI, ARJUN (Ed.) (1986) *The Social Life of Things: commodities in social perspective*, Cambridge: Cambridge University Press.

ARONCZYK, MELISSA and POWERS, DEVON (2010) "Blowing Up the Brand: 'new branded world' redux", in: Melissa Aronczyk and Devon Powers (Eds), *Blowing Up the Brand: critical perspectives on promotional culture*, London: Peter Lang, pp. 1–26.

ARVIDSSON, ADAM (2006) *Brands: meaning and value in media culture*, Abingdon: Routledge.

AUSTIN, ELIZABETH (1999) "All Expenses Paid: exploring the ethical swamp of travel writing", *The Washington Monthly*, July, http://findarticles.com/p/articles/mi_m1316/is_1999_July/ai_55215056/, accessed 26 January 2011.

BECK, ULRICH (1995) *Ecological Politics in an Age of Risk*, A. Weisz (Trans.), Cambridge: Polity.

BECK, ULRICH (2006) *The Cosmopolitan Vision*, Ciaran Cronin (Trans.), Cambridge: Polity.

BUCHMAN, GREG (2008) *Tasmania's Wilderness Battles*, Crows Nest: Allen & Unwin.

BUSCH, RICHARD (1994) "Introduction to Collected Speeches, Presentations, and Reports that Came Before the 1994 World Congress on Adventure Travel and Ecotourism Held in Hobart, Tasmania, November 7–10", in: *Proceedings of the 1994 World Congress on Adventure Travel and Ecotourism*, Englewood: The Adventure Travel Society, pp. 1–2.

CALHOUN, CRAIG (2002) "The Class Consciousness of Frequent Travelers: toward a critique of actually existing cosmopolitanism", *The South Atlantic Quarterly* 101, pp. 869–97.

CROOME, RODNEY (2005) *Tasmania: gay and lesbian visitor's guide*, Blackheath: Gay Travel Guides and Tourism Tasmania.

DENHOLM, MATTHEW (2009) "Island's 'Brand' Image in Danger", *The Weekend Australian*, 5 September, p. 6.

DEPARTMENT OF PREMIER AND CABINET (2006) *Tasmanian Brand Guide*, Hobart: Department of Premier and Cabinet.

DEPARTMENT OF TOURISM, PARKS, HERITAGE AND THE ARTS (2005) *Tasmanian Wildlife Tourism Strategy*, Hobart: Department of Tourism, Parks, Heritage and the Arts.

DEPARTMENT OF TOURISM, SPORT AND RECREATION (1995) *Strategies for Growth*, Hobart: Tasmanian State Government.

DORE, LYNNE and CROUCH, GEOFFREY I. (2003) "Promoting Destinations: an exploratory study of publicity programmes used by national tourism organisations", *Journal of Vacation Marketing* 9(2), pp. 137–51.

EVERS CONSULTING SERVICES (1984) *South West Tasmania Tourism Study: main report*, Hobart: Evers Consulting Services.

FAIR, JAMES (2000) "Explorer's Guide", *BBC Wildlife Magazine*, July, pp. 84–5.

FAIR, JAMES (2005) "Tasmania: a BBC Wildlife Magazine explorer's guide", supplement in *BBC Wildlife Magazine*, October.

FLINN, JOHN (2005a) "A Devil of a Time in Tasmania", *The San Francisco Chronicle*, 23 January, http://articles.sfgate.com/2005-01-23/travel/17357830_1_nick-mooney-tasmanian-wallabies, accessed 5 April 2010.

FLINN, JOHN (2005b) "Desperately Hoping to Catch a Tasmanian Tiger by the Tail", *The San Francisco Chronicle*, 23 January, http://articles.sfgate.com/2005-01-23/travel/17357926_1_tasmanian-tiger-creature-abominable-snowman, accessed 5 March 2011.

FÜRSICH, ELFRIEDE and KAVOORI, ANANDAM P. (2001) "Mapping a Critical Framework for the Study of Travel Journalism", *International Journal of Cultural Studies* 4(2), pp. 149–71.

GARTNER, WILLIAM C. (1993) "Image Formation Process", in: Muzzafer Uysal and Daniel R. Fesenmaier (Eds), *Communication and Channel Systems in Tourism Marketing*, Binghamton: Haworth, pp. 191–215.

GILL, A. A. (2007) "Tasmania: the end of the world", *The Sunday Times*, 8 April, http://www.timesonline.co.uk/tol/travel/destinations/australia/article1595903.ece, accessed 5 March 2011.

GO, FRANK and GOVERS, ROBERT (2010) *International Place Branding Yearbook 2010: place branding in the new age of innovation*, Basingstoke: Palgrave Macmillan.

GOVERS, ROBERT and GO, FRANK (2009) *Place Branding: glocal, virtual and physical identities, constructed, imagined and experienced*, Basingstoke: Palgrave Macmillan.

GREENWALD, JEFF (2008) "Sympathy for the Devil", *Islands Magazine*, 22 April, http://www.islands.com/article/Sympathy-for-the-Devil, accessed 5 March 2011.

GREENWALD, JEFF (2010) "Bedeviled Island", *Afar*, March/April, pp. 64–73.

HANNERZ, ULF (2004a) "Cosmopolitanism", in: David Nugent and Joan Vincent (Eds), *A Companion to the Anthropology of Politics*, Oxford: Blackwell, pp. 69–85.

HANNERZ, ULF (2004b) *Foreign News: exploring the world of foreign correspondents*, Chicago: University of Chicago Press.

HANNERZ, ULF (2006) *Two Faces of Cosmopolitanism: culture and politics*, Barcelona: Fundació CIDOB.

HANUSCH, FOLKER (2011) "A Profile of Australian Travel Journalists' Professional Views and Ethical Standards", *Journalism: Theory, Practice and Criticism*, DOI: 10.1177/1464884911398338.

HARTLEY, JOHN (1996) *Popular Reality: journalism, modernity, popular culture*, London: Arnold.

HOLLAND, PATRICK and HUGGAN, GRAHAM (2000) *Tourists with Typewriters: critical reflections on contemporary travel writing*, Ann Arbor: University of Michigan Press.

HOLT, DOUGLAS (2002) "Why Do Brands Cause Trouble? A dialectical theory of consumer culture and branding", *Journal of Consumer Research* 29(1), pp. 70–90.

HOLTON, ROBERT J. (2009) *Cosmopolitanisms: new thinking and new directions*, Basingstoke: Palgrave Macmillan.

JENKINS, MARK (2005) "Bush Bashing", *Outside Magazine*, June, http://outside.away.com/outside/destinations/200506/tasmania-1.html#bio, accessed 5 March 2011.

KING, GEOFFREY and KING, PERRY (2010) "Brothers in Arms", *Afar*, July/August, p. 8.

KOTLER, PHILIP and GERTNER, DAVID (2002) "Country as Brand, Product and Beyond: a place marketing and brand management perspective", *Brand Management* 9(4), pp. 249–61.

LASH, SCOTT and LURY, CELIA (2007) *Global Culture Industry: the mediation of things*, Cambridge: Polity.

LESTER, LIBBY (2007) *Giving Ground: media and environmental conflict in Tasmania*, Hobart: Quintus.

LOVIBOND, JANE (2004) "Tassie in Top Five in World", *The Mercury*, 20 April, p. 3.

LURY, CELIA (2004) *Brands: the logos of the global economy*, Abingdon: Routledge.

MACKELLAR, JO and FENTON, JANE (2000) "Hosting the International Travel Media: a review of the Australian Tourist Commission's visiting journalist programme", *Journal of Vacation Marketing* 6(3), pp. 255–64.

MCGAURR, LYN (2010) "Travel Journalism and Environmental Conflict: a cosmopolitan perspective", *Journalism Studies* 11(1), pp. 50–67.

MCNAIR, BRIAN (2005) "What Is Journalism?", in: Hugo De Burgh (Ed.), *Making Journalists: diverse models, global issues*, London: Routledge, pp. 25–43.

METCALF, STEPHEN (2008) "Tasmania's Gourmet Paradise", *Travel + Leisure*, February, http://www.travelandleisure.com/articles/tasmanias-gourmet-paradise/4, accessed 5 March 2011.

MILES, PAUL (2008a) "Remote Possibilities", *The Financial Times*, 19 April, http://www.ft.com/cms/s/2/a5b82bf0-0cd6-11dd-86df-0000779fd2ac.html, accessed 5 March 2011.

MILES, PAUL (2008b) "Tasmania's Forest Under Threat", *Conde Nast Traveller*, March, p. 34.

MORGAN, NIGEL and PRITCHARD, ANNETTE (2004) "Meeting the Destination Branding Challenge", in: Nigel Morgan, Annette Pritchard and Roger Pride (Eds), *Destination Branding: creating the unique destination proposition*, 2nd ed, Oxford: Elsevier Butterworth-Heinemann, pp. 59–74.

NATIONAL GEOGRAPHIC TRAVELER (2004) "2004 Destinations Rated: destination scorecard—115 places rated: Oceania", http://traveler.nationalgeographic.com/2004/03/destinations-rated/oceania-text/1, accessed 31 July 2011.

OTTERMAN, SHARON (2007) "Tasmanian Goes Boutique, Nice and Slow", *The New York Times*, 29 July, http://travel.nytimes.com/2007/07/29/travel/29next.html, accessed 9 January 2011.

OUR COMMON GROUND (nd) "What We Stand For", http://ourcommonground.drupalgardens.com/what, accessed 24 July 2011.

SCHATZ, ROLAND and KOLMER, CHRISTIAN (2010) "News Coverage of Foreign Place Brands: implications for communication strategies", in: Frank Go and Robert Govers (Eds), *International Place Branding Yearbook 2010: place branding in the new age of innovation*, Basingstoke: Palgrave Macmillan, pp. 134–46.

SZERSZYNSKI, BRONISLAW and URRY, JOHN (2006) "Visuality, Mobility and the Cosmopolitan: inhabiting the world from afar", *The British Journal of Sociology* 57(1), pp. 113–31.

TELEGRAPH CREATE, TOURISM TASMANIA, TAILOR MADE TRAVEL and QANTAS, (2008) "Tasmania: your 16-page guide to one of the most unspoilt islands on Earth", supplement in *Daily Telegraph*, 12 April.

THE MERCURY (1994a) "Ecotourism Summit Ends with Anti-logging Petition", 12 November, p. 7.

THE MERCURY (1994b) "Warning of Fight Ahead to Protect Environment", 11 November, p. 7.

TOURISM IN NATURAL AREAS PROJECT TEAM (1993) *"Ecotourism and Adventure Travel Marketing in Tasmania: 'images & media formats'"*, Hobart: Tourism Tasmania.

TOURISM TASMANIA (2007) "Lighthouse Report Two", http://www.tourism.tas.gov.au/__data/assets/pdf_file/0019/34831/lighthousereport2.pdf, accessed 9 January 2011.

TOURISM TASMANIA (2011) *Motivations Research*, Hobart: Tourism Tasmania.

TOURISM TASMANIA (nd a) *Tasmania Tourism Brand: our brand*, Hobart: Tourism Tasmania.

TOURISM TASMANIA (nd b) "Visit Us: visiting journalist program", http://travelmedia.tourismtasmania.com.au/visit/vjp.html, accessed 9 January 2011.

TOURISM TASMANIA NORTH AMERICA (2008) *Discover Tasmania: Australia's natural state*, December, http://www.discovertasmania.com/__data/assets/pdf_file/0008/57590/MotvBrochure_NAM_web.pdf, accessed 5 March 2011.

TOURTELLOT, JONATHAN B. (2004) "Destination Scorecard: 115 destinations rated", *National Geographic Traveler*, March, pp. 60–7.

TOURTELLOT, JONATHAN B. (2006) "Greenish Tasmania", *National Geographic Traveler*, March, p. 38.

URRY, JOHN (2002) *The Tourist Gaze*, 2nd edn, London: Sage.

VAN DEN BERG, LUCIE (2005) "Logging Concern for Travel Writer", *Examiner*, 29 November, http://www.examiner.com.au/news/local/news/general/logging-concern-for-travel-writer/958332.aspx, accessed 5 March 2011.

WHITE, JON and HOBSBAWN, JULIA (2007) "Public Relations and Journalism: the unquiet relationship—a view from the United Kingdom", *Journalism Practice* 1(2), pp. 283–92.

BREAD AND CIRCUSES
Food meets politics in the Singapore media

Andrew Duffy and **Yang Yuhong Ashley**

While there has been consistent academic interest in the link between the media and politics, this attention has mostly bypassed lifestyle journalism. Yet this can reflect the political and social realities of a country if less clearly than more overtly political coverage. This paper seeks to demonstrate how the Singapore government has used food to help construct a national identity and how the local print media have been a partner in this. It analyses how food has been represented in the Singapore press in relation to attitudes that contribute to nation-building. The findings suggest that the food-related articles studied usually reflected a culture of self-improvement, an ethnic-cultural element and cosmopolitan attitudes, all of which were identified as touchstones of Singapore's government-approved national identity. In addition, there is also marginally more press coverage of cosmopolitan and foreign food compared to local food, in concurrence with government initiatives to place the country as a globalised hub.

Introduction

In the second century, the Roman poet Juvenal used the term *"panem et circenses"* (Juvenal, 1998), or bread and circuses, somewhat critically to describe the two things that people desire—and hence the two factors a state needed to supply to dissuade the populace from revolting. Fast forward 2000 years and it appears that few countries have adopted this as successfully as the South-East Asian city-state of Singapore. In its bid to become an entertainment and cultural hub for the region, it has built a multi-million-dollar concert hall-cum-theatre, the Esplanade; it launched the world's first night-time Formula 1 race; it has built two massive integrated resorts with entertainment, hotels and casinos; and it is revamping its sleepy pleasure island, Sentosa, to make it a world-class destination. Circuses abound, but by far the greatest circus is food. Food is a popular topic of discussion and it fills thousands of column inches each year. It has become axiomatic of the Singaporean identity that they are a nation of foodies, likely to queue for half an hour to eat at the better of two nasi lemak stalls even if they are side by side. Food fads are regular, with recent flurries of excitement over French macarons, Taiwanese bubble tea and US-style doughnuts.

This paper looks at the coverage of food in Singapore's national newspaper, *The Straits Times*, to explore its political impact (Woolley, 2000). It analyses the content of news stories and lifestyle features related to food to establish a taxonomy of food articles and to examine whether the representation of food in the media links with other forms of social control. This study does not suggest that the media are controlled and that therefore the representation of food in newspapers is a form of government intervention. It is more subtle than that. Rather, it seeks to demonstrate how the authorities in the country have used food to help build a national identity following Counihan and Van Esterik's idea that food is "a central pawn in political strategies of states" (1997, p. 1); and how the media has been a partner in this.

Recipe for a Rojak Nation

There are several sobriquets for Singapore, which sits barely one degree above the equator at the heart of South-East Asia. Among them are "little red dot", for its small size and its position as a red (mainly Buddhist) island surrounded by green (Muslim) countries; another is "rojak nation", named for a brightly coloured Malay salad. Internationally, it is variously known as the country where the sale of chewing gum is banned; where drug offenders are routinely hanged; and as the safest, wealthiest place in South-East Asia. These aspects are all connected by the unusual level of control exerted over the nation by its government and from birth to death citizens find their lives, identities and horizons circumscribed by government activity.

One defining characteristic is that it is a multi-cultural society. It became a nation in 1965 and its early years were marked by race riots. These became the starting point for Singapore to label itself a multi-racial country (Chua, 2003). Chua goes on to put it more explicitly that the government adopted multi-racialism as self-definition and used it as a tool for governance based on a strict observance of races. Racial or ethnic festival cultures and food cultures are supported directly by the state and through the multiracial practices of official and unofficial public institutions; race is highly visible in its public sphere (Chua, 2003). Until 2010, every Singaporean was classified at birth as Chinese, Malay, Indian or Other (CMIO) on their identity card, based on the ethnicity of their father (Chua, 2003). But in private, Chinese do not always marry Chinese, nor do Malays stay only with their own, and the country has seen an increased blurring of racial identities, which has led to a recent relaxing in the rules of what goes on a citizen's identity card.

Stauth (1997, p. 51) calls Singapore "a project of a multi-ethnic and multi-cultural polity and a post-modern global city that combines civility, nostalgia and economic functionality". The authorities have chosen whichever aspects of race help them in their aim of building stability and cohesion, taking aspects of Western consumerism and Confucian Asian values to suit. This produces paradoxes: at the same time as decrying the debilitating effects of Westernisation and promoting a culture based on Asian values, the country has developed a consumerist culture, falling in love with the "romance of market expansion" (Evers and Gerke, 1997, p. 2). The government encourages this and Chua (1994) says that there is an added benefit to the government as the good material life reduces criticisms of the regime, especially for the middle class whose existence is a result of highly successful economic policies. Newman and De Zoysa make the point that this is no top-down authoritarianism; it is reliant on voluntary compliance, because "high economic growth levels—accompanied by a firm social contract, full employment, growing prosperity, plus national pride—compensate for the stringent controls over social behavior" (1997, p. 633). Leong (2001) goes further and looks at the national identity as a commodity marketed to domestic consumers in order to inculcate a sense of nationality so that the nation as imagined community (Anderson, 1983) is also a community of consumption united by partaking these same cultural products. This echoes Johnston and Baumann's (2007) idea that American cuisine is a cultural construction produced through discourse as part of an imagined community of America. Stauth draws a connection between "mass consumer culture and social organization, namely, the question of the new possible role of consumer culture as a bridge between state and individual" (1997, p. 57). In other words, the Singapore government has co-opted not just food and shopping, but consumerism as a force to control the populace. Bread and circuses.

Portion Control in the National Kitchen

This result has been achieved through tight controls by the democratically elected People's Action Party which has been in power since before independence. Chua describes the government thus: "financially uncorrupt, manages the economy well, has improved the population's standard of living and governs through due parliamentary process, all with a dash of self-sacrifice on the part of its leaders and members" (1994, p. 657).

But this success has also created a sometimes uneasy relationship between state and people. Velayutham said the government's approach to nation-building based on economic developmentalism and survivalism has "created an ambivalent and tenuous relationship of mutual obligation between the individual and the nation-state" (2004, p. 1). For example, more than 80 per cent of the population live in public housing tower blocks, all of which must keep to a quota of each race according to the national averages to prevent the formation of ghettos. To adapt a food metaphor, unlike America's melting pot, Singapore has kept all the races distinct—a variety of flavours in the rojak rather than a minestrone soup.

The controls extend to food. Chua and Rajah state that, in Singapore, "food and food ways are characterised by a large variety of cuisines that are iconic of the presence of different ethnic communities which make up the nation, reflecting the official categorisation of the populace as a 'multiracial' nation" (1996, p. 1). Equally, they point out that the CMIO classification of Singaporeans similarly classifies the food sold in the ubiquitous hawker centres where inexpensive cooked meals are sold. Consumers can identify the ethnic origins of the food they are about to eat—it comes from an Indian stall, perhaps, or the hawker works under the signboard of Chinese porridge.

The system encourages Singaporeans to see themselves in racial terms rather than as a homogenised whole, and this in turn has led to a challenge in building the national identity, just as Appadurai noted that in India regional cuisines (variety) create a "polyglot culture" and the one arises from the many (1998, pp. 5 and 21). Effectively, it has led to the paradoxical premise that what makes Singaporeans the same is being different. Singapore calls itself a rojak nation—but there are different kinds of rojak. Chinese rojak is a salad of pineapple, cucumber, turnip, fried bean curd and dough sticks with prawn paste and crushed peanuts and chilli sauce; Indian rojak is battered fried tofu, hard boiled eggs, prawn fritters served with a thick, spicy, sweet-potato sauce. The term "rojak" hence incorporates Indian-ness and Chinese-ness, while at the same time reminding the cognoscenti that while the race is important, it is also somewhat indeterminate. Ironically "rujak" is itself an Indonesian word meaning "mixture", and comes from a Malay language.

The media have played a significant part in the construction of the new nation, and food writing may be considered a part of this. One striking feature of Singapore journalism is that it is considered an aid to government in the process of nation-building (Kenyon and Marjoribanks, 2007). In a defining comment at the 1971 International Press Institute's annual assembly in Helsinki, the then-Prime Minister Lee Kuan Yew explained his ideas on the role the national media: "Freedom of the press, freedom of the news media, must be subordinated to the overriding needs of Singapore, and to the primacy and purpose of an elected government" (cited in Latif, 1998, p. 151). A few years later, *Attacks on the Press in 2004* (Committee to Protect Journalists, 2005, p. 118) called the Singapore government "one of the world's most efficient engines of media control". Hence, if the national newspapers may not be a reflection of how all Singaporeans think, then they certainly mirror what the authorities would like them to be concerned about. That includes food. Food links to status and prestige (Powdermaker, 1997 [1959]) which gives another reason why it should be of interest to a government concerned with nation-building. Not just in Singapore. Across the developed world, food writers are increasingly admired, respected and emulated as keepers of the faith, experts to be heeded. As Brown (2004) noted in the United States, heavyweight writers are moving into food journalism, and even the *New Yorker* devoted a double issue to the subject. In Singapore, to be a food writer holds similar kudos to being a political writer, but with few of the attendant risks (Duffy, 2010). This is part of a broader picture, as there have been calls for academics to consider the force and effect of lifestyle journalism, as well as more commonly studied news practices (Hanusch, 2009).

You Are What You Eat

That food has been used to mark cultural boundaries has been well documented, and without doubt food is a hugely powerful system of values, regulations and beliefs (Probyn, 1999). As Counihan and Van Esterik put it, "life can be studied and understood through food" (1997, pp. 1–2). Barthes urged scholars to overcome the idea that food was a trivial subject for study, and saw instead that it constituted "a system of communication, a body of images, a protocol of usages, situations and behaviour" (1997 [1961], p. 21); while Hanke (1989) looks at food as a reflection of a rising culture of conspicuous consumption in America. Mead (1997 [1961]) distinguishes between food as nourishment and food as a source of pleasure as an indicator of an advanced society. Korsmeyer (2005) sees power play inherent in food and flavours as they transmit messages of pleasure, displeasure, power, coercion or submission. Goode says that food is certainly employed and deployed in such a way as to "define inclusion and encourage discipline, solidarity, and the maintenance of social boundaries" (1992, p. 234), while Shugart (2008) establishes that many scholars explicitly note that food functions as a form of communication, and implicit in their characterisation is the more specifically rhetorical function of food as a means to construct and negotiate cultural identity.

But what does it take for one culture to adopt and accept the food of another culture? (Falk, 1991). It does so by establishing a common denominator—in the case of Singapore that of multi-culturalism. Indeed, it is possible that the act of introducing increasingly globalised, cosmopolitan food to Singapore's smorgasbord has had the effect of strengthening commitment and acceptance of CMI food; that is, a Chinese Singaporean may feel little acceptance or kinship for Indian food, and consider it "other"; until he is confronted with Italian, Mexican or Brazilian food, at which point the Indian food may become more Asian, more "us". In this way, the introduction of foreign cuisines can strengthen the Asian-ness of Singapore.

Rozin (1982) also tackles the question of how one culture adopts the food of another, and puts it into a quasi class setting, suggesting that for food to be accepted, it must act as a positive representation, and must represent something of greater value than something else. This is visible in the cosmopolitan attitudes towards food evidenced in the Singapore media, where the idea that foods from around the globe are part and parcel of everyday life is a clear "positive representation".

Certainly, one of the difficulties facing any investigation into food is the way it spills into every aspect of life (Probyn, 1999). "Insofar as food is intimately linked to religious ideas as well as health, nutrition and aesthetics in a civilizational sense, it is also ultimately imbricated with *political* systems of one kind or another", suggest Chua and Rajah (1996, p. 3). Barthes (1997 [1961]) likewise said that food has a political side as well, and is always bound to the values of power. For example, to reverse the brain drain of talented and well-educated Singaporeans overseas, the government has sent missions overseas to try to tempt them back by reminding them of home cooking (*Straits Times*, 13 April 2007). While Nestle (2002) looks at the influence of the food industry on politics, this research is concerned instead with the influence of politics on the cultural power of food, and aims to describe how food is represented in the media—a tool of nation-building—and the social and cultural messages attached to food.

Food and Food Writing

Most academic studies of food writing have concerned themselves with cookbooks, most notably Appadurai's (1998) study of cookbooks in India and how they helped create a national identity. His preoccupation is sociological rather than political, looking at the rising middle classes finding an identity that transcended regional boundaries, and the use of regional cuisines in forming a concerted image of India. He notes the concern with the search for authenticity as a significant value in food writing, a theme echoed by Johnston and Baumann (2007) and Jones and Taylor (2001). The former are more concerned with the representation of food as a signifier of status, and the role of food writers in that process, saying that "food writers have considerable power to shape perceptions of food as high quality, fashionable, and worthy of attention from high status consumer" (Johnston and Baumann, 2007, p. 165). They identify omnivorousness as a marker of high status, when it is framed as authentic or exotic. The latter, meanwhile, quote Anthony Giddens' idea that a principal mechanism of modernism is the way places are "disembedded" from their original locale and brought into contact with other places (Jones and Taylor, 2001, p. 178). Just so, Singapore proclaims itself as a food hub where all cultures meet and all cuisines are available, but at the same time food is expressed in traditional and authentic terms, setting itself against modernism. Jones and Taylor (2001) note the antinomy of novelty and tradition, the former promising excitement and the latter promising authenticity. The challenge facing both the nascent nation-state and the food writer is to communicate both at the same time.

A government desires the reassurance that comes with unchanging certainty; this desire can lead to the urge towards social control which food writing can support. James (1996, p. 78), however, believes that the way food is imagined in academic and popular writings is something fluid and temporal, and suggests that "consumption practices are seen as precariously flexible, rather than fixed and constant, markers of self and identity". Her larger question is whether food in a globalised world can still act as a marker of cultural identity based on distinctions of "we eat this, they do not" between groups. The irony is that food offers a flexible symbolic value because it invokes inflexible cultural stereotypes; but flexible or unchanging, it is the invocation rather than the food itself that is important. Hence the representation of the food in the written word invokes different cultural values, both nostalgia and innovation, authenticity and creativity, the global and the local. "Globalization of food ... is a complex interplay of meanings and intentions which individuals employ subjectively to make statements about who they are, and where and how their Selves are to be located in the world" (James, 1996, p. 92). The variety that comes with culinary globalisation is interpreted differently to find different meanings and create different selves; it is fluid rather than fixed, and is thus a fine tool for a country to use to create an identity, if less effective in maintaining it.

This idea of fluidity reflects a growing idea that a city is the product of what flows through it as much as what is inside it. Beck (2002, p. 17) defines cosmopolitanisation as internal globalisation from within national societies, and in his terms it is helpful to view Singapore as a hub of information and influences flowing through at the same time as the people and the government try to control those influences. It makes it harder to declare one food national: "Anyone who still wants to raise the national flag, when it comes to food, founders on the ever more hollow myths of national dishes, which at best are no more than islands in the broad stream of the dominant and by now banal culinary cosmopolitanism", writes Beck (2002, p. 28). Indeed, the country finds itself in the odd position of having a national dish of chicken rice, although neither chicken nor rice is produced on the island and the dish itself originated on the Chinese island of Hainan.

The media equally reflect Singapore's avowed status as a cultural, culinary and media crossroads of the region and the world, and the fluidity and uncertainty that comes with that role. The country has embraced globalisation more than many and almost one-third of the population are foreigners. Food is used as a magnet, a reason to visit, and a perk of living in the country. Singapore is not alone in using food as a badge of sophistication, reach and power: Appadurai (1998), p. 4) notes that in pre-industrial India it was common for elites to show "their political power, their commercial reach, and their cosmopolitan tastes by drawing in ingredients, techniques and even cooks from far and wide". However, this naturally creates its own tensions as globalisation is complex and shifting (Bokser Liwerant, 2002). Just as it encourages nations and people to forge broader connections, globalisation also encourages small social groups and ethnic communities to create and recreate their own networks side by side or in opposition to nation-states. This interplay between small group identities and national identity brings confusion as well as certainty. Singapore has sought to create a new identity based on the ideal of multiculturalism, that the variety of different groups is a defining element of identity, and food part of that.

Altogether, the role of food in identity is clear and the role of the press in representing both the national food and the national identity offers an interesting area for study, and led to four research questions:

RQ1: What are the common themes of food reporting in Singapore that could help develop a taxonomy for a clearer understanding of how it contributes to the construction of a national identity?

RQ2: What kind of national identity is constructed through food writing, and does this correspond to the image encouraged by the government?

RQ3: How are nation-building tropes encouraged by the authorities manifested in food writing in the national print media?

RQ4: How are controls on society and personal identity replicated in the representation of food in the media?

Methodology

In order to understand how food-related articles in the national press could be seen as supporting government efforts to construct a national identity, the study involved a content analysis of articles in *The Straits Times*, the country's most widely read English-language newspaper and which also has the closest links with government. The research focused on food in the public sphere rather than in the private sphere of the home as this was a more likely arena for the government to seek to control. It also reflects the ease and cheapness of eating out in a country where all public housing estates incorporate a hawker centre—a collection of stalls selling freshly cooked food—and where people can eat a good meal for under $5. Hence the six search terms used to identify food articles in Factiva were: "food", "dining", "hawker centre", "coffee shop", "eating" and "restaurant". Articles from both the news or lifestyle section of the newspaper were considered in order to gather a broader picture of the place food has in society. The selection included articles that made brief allusions to food in order to consider the subject in a broad cultural and political context, as well as when it was the main focus of the article. Articles concerning food outside Singapore were removed.

The study selected articles from two constructed months (one for 2007 and another for 2008) by taking the first day from January, the second from February and so on; and one real month (February 2009) in the interests of completeness. As this gave a small sample size of 244 articles, it was considered expedient to select 20 food-related articles from other months for the inter-coder reliability process, which resulted in an acceptable inter-coder reliability of over 80 per cent. The articles the search yielded were then analysed by one writer, and can be broadly categorised as follows:

- Restaurant or hawker stall reviews.
- Food reviews and the latest food fads.
- Interviews with chefs, expatriates and foreign celebrities in which they tend to give comments about local food.
- Interviews or articles about overseas Singaporeans, in which they tend to mention that they miss the food back at home.
- Interviews with restaurateurs or food company owners about their entrepreneurial experiences.
- Articles about local chefs competing in international cooking competitions.
- Articles about the government, voluntary welfare organisations or religious organisations giving food hampers and vouchers to the needy.
- Articles about food and health-related issues.
- Articles about special occasions and the food associated with them.
- Articles about the importance of civic-consciousness in dining areas.
- Articles about the Agri-Food and Veterinary Authority of Singapore (AVA) recalling tainted food items.

While Titz et al. (2004) looked at the criteria often used in restaurant reviews, including quality and quantity of food, ambience, service and suchlike, this study was more concerned with the broader representation of food in society, and sought other criteria.

Hence, the texts were analysed looking for indicators that they contained references to any of the 10 national tropes discussed by Chua and Kuo (1991), of which further explanation is given below. Chua and Kuo noted that the Singapore authorities have tended to swing between promoting Asian values and building a more Westernised society, or even taking what suited their plans best from each of the two sides. Westernisation led to a backlash that came in the form of a loss of cultural identity that did not sit well with the population and there was a swing towards greater ethnicity in food, language and moral education. Food is one area in which ethnicity can be celebrated without causing tension. Hence Chua and Kuo draw a distinction between two discourses running concurrently, the one on national identity and culture, and the other on ethnic identity and culture. Balancing these two is at the heart of the identity dilemma confronting the country, and has produced different discourses from which one can extrapolate certain national characteristics, or touchstones of a national identity, while acknowledging that this process is both fluid and ever-changing. To these we have added our own operational definitions, arrived at during the inter-coder reliability process.

1. Ethnic-cultural element (defined as any reference to the "Chinese, Malay, Indian, Others" categories).
2. National pride (defined as any mention of the country doing well or when foreigners and expatriates make positive comments about the nation or its people).
3. Strong achievement motivation (defined as the drive to succeed personally or for society).
4. Materialism (defined as an interest in trappings of material and economic success).
5. Generalised social discipline (defined as the social control of individuals, for the benefit of the society as a whole).
6. Culture of self-improvement (defined as a desire to do things better or improve the status quo).
7. Meritocracy (defined as the idea that hard work leads to success for any individual, regardless of their socio-economic position, age, ethnicity or gender).
8. Concern with national interest (defined as the concern with the betterment of society economically and/or socially).
9. Cosmopolitan attitudes (defined as being influenced by the best practices used overseas).
10. Excellence as a national goal (defined as striving for national excellence so that the nation looks good).

The main analysis for this study considered whether the articles reflected any of these 10 touchstones of Singapore's national identity. Reading the articles also suggested a taxonomy of five categories: "Where and What to Eat" (food reviews or the latest food fad), "Experts and Expats" (food interviews with chefs, expatriates or celebrities), "Poverty and Politics" (when the government is giving food vouchers to the poor), "Health" (healthy food) and "Others". This concept of expat food, incidentally, differs from James's (1996), where it represents holiday food eaten by a native of the writer's culture while travelling overseas. Lastly, the research considered whether the cuisine featured was local or foreign; and whether the cost of the dish was low-end ($2–10), mid-range ($11–25) or high-end ($26 and above). The intention was to study whether there was greater coverage of local, inexpensive food, or cosmopolitan, high-end food.

Results and Discussion

A simple statistical analysis showed that many of the articles reflect three main attitudes (Figure 1): a culture of self-improvement (39.3 per cent frequency), a cosmopolitan attitude (31.1 per cent) and ethnic-cultural element (31.1 per cent).

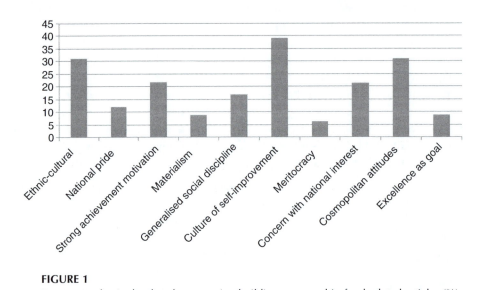

FIGURE 1
Frequency of attitudes that denote nation-building expressed in food-related articles (%)

The findings also show that articles categorised as "Where and What to Eat" most often reflected a cosmopolitan attitude (38.3 per cent) and an ethnic-cultural element (30 per cent frequency). Articles categorised as "Experts and Expats" often reflected self-improvement (45.2 per cent), cosmopolitan attitudes (32.3 per cent) and an ethnic-cultural element (32.3 per cent) as it is commonplace for an expatriate or visiting expert to be asked to demonstrate his or her Singaporean credibility by commenting on the local food. Articles categorised as "Poverty and Politics" tended to reflect a culture of self-improvement (41.2 per cent) and concern with national interest (23.5 per cent). Only one of the articles categorised as "Poverty and Politics" reflected the government's meritocracy policy, which suggests that government-encouraged meritocracy was delinked from poverty. Articles categorised as "Health" mostly reflected a culture of self-improvement and a strong achievement motivation (Figure 2).

Articles featuring local cuisines (29.9 per cent frequency) often reflected an ethnic-cultural element (64.4 per cent), while those featuring foreign cuisines (34.8 per cent) mainly reflected cosmopolitan attitudes (61.2 per cent). In terms of price, mid-range food was most common (21.7 per cent frequency) followed by low-priced (16.4 per cent) and high-priced (12.7 per cent) food (Figure 3).

One common trope was that locals are preoccupied with food. Some equated "Singaporean-ness" with "being food-crazy", such as this article in which a 12-year-old violinist studying in Britain said:

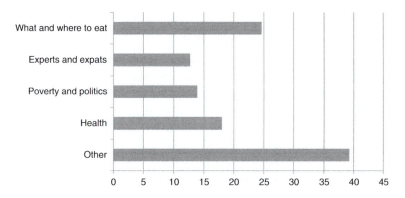

FIGURE 2
Frequency of food-related articles by theme (%)

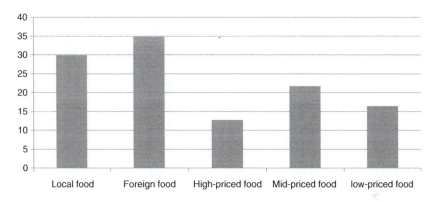

FIGURE 3
Frequency of other attributes of food expressed in articles (%)

The family is also looking forward to the trip back home next month, when they can eat all the food they have been craving. They usually stop at the food centre in East Coast Park on the way home from the airport to fuel up on nasi lemak, satay and chicken rice. "We are Singaporean," Mr Ng said with a laugh. (*The Straits Times*, 18 June 2007)

Others also reiterate this preoccupation with food: "No place is too far for Singaporeans who will drive to Johor Baru and beyond for good food and more" (*The Straits Times*, 17 May 2008). Several articles in *The Straits Times* can also be seen as contributing in other, non-food-related ways to government efforts to construct a national identity, as if the press is one avenue through which locals learn what it is to be "Singaporean".

[Finance Minister Tharman Shanmugaratnam] also said, in his speech, the Singapore spirit of "unity, tenacity and perseverance" will take the nation through these difficult times... (*The Straits Times*, 8 August 2008)

Some who have experienced unemployment and then found jobs, like Mr Loong, adhere to the value of what the Chinese call *zili gengsheng* (regeneration through one's own efforts). "Only if you can't help yourself then look for help. This is the Singapore spirit, it's how we have been brought up", he says. (*The Straits Times*, 7 February 2009)

Hence, although the idea of what the national identity encapsulates may be hazy to some citizens, these articles impart this message: to be Singaporean is to have the desire to persevere and constantly improve. This corresponds with the finding that a culture of self-improvement (39.3 per cent frequency) and a strong achievement motivation (21.7 per cent) are commonly reflected in the food articles.

Foreign foods, as expected, tended to be more expensive (30.6 per cent at the higher end, 42.4 per cent mid-range and 14.1 per cent were low-priced) and associated with cosmopolitan attitudes (61.2 per cent); while local foods tended to be at the cheaper end of the scale (42.5 per cent for lower price, 28.8 per cent for mid-range and 13.7 per cent for high-priced food) and were very often described in ethnic-cultural terms (64.4 per cent). Furthermore, articles may also illustrate the "essence" of the national identity in the dishes they feature:

> The best way to classify her [chef and restaurant owner Devagi Sanmugam] cooking is to call it Singaporean rather than Indian, Chinese or Malay. For example, the stir-fried sliced cabbage ($5.50) is bright yellow with turmeric but tossed with dried shrimps—a Chinese touch. And the *belachan* chicken wings ($8)—a take on the Chinese shrimp paste chicken—are as local as you can get. (*The Straits Times*, 8 February 2009)

This is intriguing because the way the journalist defines the dishes as "Singaporean" seems to hint that such a dish is one that cannot be pigeon-holed into a CMIO categorisation. Rather, it is a dish that has influences from different ethnic groups. The journalist also seems to recognise that the "essentialised notions of ethnicity and ethnic foods" identified by Chua and Rajah (1996, p. 2) cannot be applied to a dish like "*belachan* chicken wings". Hence, because there is culinary hybridisation in this dish, it is termed "Singaporean". This is in line with Benjamin's observation that the term Singapore culture is usually used to refer to an agglomeration of separate ethic cultures rather than any newly synthesised culture they may create (Benjamin, 1976).

Where and What to Eat

The articles classified as "Where and What to Eat" often reflected cosmopolitan attitudes (38.3 per cent frequency) and an ethnic-cultural element (30 per cent), and usually featured food in the mid-price range (33.3 per cent) while cheap food (20 per cent) was twice as well represented as expensive food (10 per cent). These articles were fairly evenly split between foreign cuisines (41.7 per cent) and local cuisines (38.3 per cent). This indicates a focus on the country becoming more cosmopolitan rather than on the individual ethnicities themselves. Many articles featuring foreign cuisines attempt to convey the message that being able to appreciate foreign food is desirable:

> There is absolutely nothing wrong with Heinz or Del Monte or any supermarket ketchup … Sometimes, the palate craves something different though. Enter the artisanal ketchup. (*The Straits Times*, 27 February 2009)

Articles also feature foreign food and regularly associate the taste for foreign food with cosmopolitan attitudes (61.2 per cent).

Chef Steven Ong, 39, of Centre Ps, who sells about 4,000 macarons a month, attributes their popularity to "well-travelled and well-read Singaporeans who are increasingly aware of the famous French cookie". (*The Straits Times*, 11 November 2007)

On the other hand, articles categorised as "Where and What to Eat" that feature local cuisines (38.3 per cent) generally reflect an ethnic-cultural element. The growing discourse on Peranakan (Straits Chinese) culture in the press is one example in which the *Straits Times* journalist not only features Peranakan food, but also delves into what should be considered authentic Peranakan cuisine:

Traditional Peranakan cuisine is riddled with pork. True Blue [a Peranakan restaurant] does not serve pork. Mr Seck acknowledges that some Peranakan customers are fussy about its absence . . . But with so many versions out there, Peranakan purists wonder: Are people getting the real deal? How does one tell what is authentic and what is not? (*The Straits Times*, 2 February 2009)

Experts and Expats

The statistical analysis also showed that articles categorised as "Experts and Expats" often showed a belief in self-improvement (45.2 per cent), and concern for both ethnic and cosmopolitan attitude (32.3 per cent for each) that reflected the cosmopolitan attitudes held by citizens. For example, an interview with Brazilian restaurateur Fabiane Braga shed some light on the growing appreciation of foreign cuisines:

She says: "Singapore is a great place for me and my bistro. Singaporeans like to try new things and that is a good thing for me and my menu of authentic Brazilian dishes." (*The Straits Times*, 23 November 2008)

At the same time, the common references to ethnic food reflect the way that expatriates or foreign chefs gave positive comments about local food, the country's multiracial composition and national excellence. For example:

Singapore has a fantastic blend of cultures and cuisines. I particularly enjoyed Ritz Carlton's Sunday Brunch for its wide variety. I also love Hokkien noodles, *bak kut teh* [pork rib soup] and satay [grilled meat skewers]. (Pascal Tingaud, visiting French chef, *The Straits Times*, 15 February 2008)

Equally, expatriates can be locals overseas, reminiscing about food at home:

"Perhaps being tossed about in a globalised world does that: It teaches you to appreciate little things which are uniquely yours. Like the joy of sweating it out over a simple plate of chicken rice and a cup of kopi-O in a hawker centre. Where else are you able to choose from 20 food stalls in a single space in the warmth of the eternal tropical sun?" (*The Straits Times*, 26 February 2007)

Poverty and Politics

The articles categorised as "Poverty and Politics" most often reflected a culture of self-improvement (41.2 per cent frequency) which suggests that although the government is concerned with the welfare of poor people, giving them food and other assistance, these citizens should improve themselves and not depend on government handouts.

The driving principles behind public assistance, like other forms of financial help, were that it would not be overly generous, should not erode the work ethic and should give room for other helping hands in the community. (*The Straits Times*, 2 February 2008)

However, this culture of self-improvement is also reflected when an article demonstrates government efforts to improve the quality of life for the poor, which reflects positively on the government, that poverty is not seen as a systemic flaw to be criticised but an area for improvement to be praised: "Efforts are also being stepped up to provide more health checks, food packages, free haircuts and home nursing services for the poor and elderly, says Mr Yeo" (*The Straits Times*, 5 May 2008).

Health

Articles categorised as "Health" often reflected a culture of self-improvement (34.1 per cent frequency) and a strong achievement motivation (20.5 per cent). One editorial calls for direct intervention to teach children and their parents to eat well, pointing out that schools have introduced healthy food, but kids can go to a hawker centre or home to eat unhealthily. What is interesting is the assumption of a level of control that people should be taught what to eat in all areas and at all times.

Indeed, guidance that the programme provides might also benefit parents. If their children are not eating right and exercising, very likely neither are they. So, prevention being preferable to and less expensive than treating disease, some adults as well as children need early tailored interventions. (*The Straits Times*, 24 December 2007)

In the same way, other articles urge readers to be more disciplined in eating and exercising, as in an interview with a television presenter who shed 20 kg after committing to a strict dietary and exercise regimen: "You must want to make a change. It's a change of lifestyle and there is no turning back. Trust me. I told myself, this is a personal challenge that I must ensure success in" (*The Straits Times*, 8 August 2007).

Conclusion

This is a single study of one aspect of the interplay between politics and lifestyle journalism, which could be extended to look at other consumerist-driven journalism staples such as fashion, beauty, health and travel. Future studies of food could be augmented with more qualitative research into the opinions of the food writers themselves and of regular media consumers to find out how food influences their own identities and their perception of their nation. But it is hoped that this study could lead to greater interest in lifestyle journalism, particularly in countries with partially controlled press systems (which tend to be thriving at a time when the liberal Western advertising- and subscription-based model is floundering), as a means of social engineering.

To revisit the research questions, it seems that the identity constructed through food writing in *The Straits Times* is one where the ideal of self-improvement is the most common feature across the articles, appearing in 39.3 per cent of them. This correlates to government policies that encourage self-reliance among the population, including the lack of a welfare state and enforced savings programmes. This was followed by cosmopolitan attitudes (in 31.1 per cent of the articles), which correlates to government attempts to place Singapore as a global hub, a finding backed up by the frequency of international food appearing in the articles (34.8 per cent).

From this, it appears that food writing correlates first with government national identity-building, rather than personal identity-building. This latter was more noticeable in the third-most common feature of the articles, that of food having an ethnic-cultural element (31.1 per cent). Evidently, many articles in the local press both reflect and create a preoccupation with food among citizens. Such articles are supplemented by other forms of media such as television food programmes and local food guides such as *Makansutra*. These all feed the idea that Singaporeans love food which then gets embedded into the national psyche. As *Makansutra*'s executive editor K. F. Seetoh says in the guide's 2009 edition, "food is the purest democracy we have", a remark interesting not only for its political undertones, but also for how food is emphasised as a key facet of Singaporean life.

REFERENCES

ANDERSON, BENEDICT (1983) *Imagined Communities*, London and New York: Verso.

APPADURAI, ARJUN (1998) "How to Make a National Cuisine: cookbooks in contemporary India", *Comparative Studies in Society and History* 30(1), pp. 3–24.

BARTHES, ROLAND (1997 [1961]) "Towards a Psychosociology of Contemporary Food Consumption", in: Carole Counihan and Penny Van Esterik (Eds), *Food and Culture: a reader*, New York and London: Routledge, pp. 20–7.

BECK, ULRICH (2002) "The Cosmopolitan Society and Its Enemies", *Theory, Culture & Society* 19(1), pp. 17–44.

BENJAMIN, GEOFFREY (1976) "The Cultural Logic of Singapore's 'Multiracialism'", in: Riaz Hassan (Ed.), *Singapore: society in transition*, Kuala Lumpur: Oxford University Press, pp. 115–33.

BOKSER, LIWERANT JUDIT (2002) "Globalization and Collective Identities", *Social Compass* 49(2), pp. 253–71.

BROWN, DOUG (2004) "Haute Cuisine", *American Journalism Review*, February/March, http://www.ajr.org/Article.asp?id = 3545, accessed 2 December 2010.

CHUA, BENG-HUAT (1994) "Arrested Development: democratisation in Singapore", *Third World Quarterly* 15(4), pp. 655–68.

CHUA, BENG-HUAT (2003) "Multiculturalism in Singapore: an instrument of social control", *Race & Class* 44(3), pp. 58–77.

CHUA, BENG HUAT and KUO, EDDIE (1991) "The Making of a New Nation: cultural construction and national identity in Singapore", paper presented to the Cultural Policy and National Identity Workshop at East-West Center, Honolulu, HI, June.

CHUA, BENG-HUAT and RAJAH, ANANDA (1996) "Hybridity, Ethnicity and Food in Singapore", paper presented to the International Conference on Changing Diet and Foodways in Chinese Culture, Shatin, Hong Kong, June.

COMMITTEE TO PROTECT JOURNALISTS (2005) *Attacks on the Press in 2004*, New York: Committee to Protect Journalists.

COUNIHAN, CAROLE and VAN ESTERIK, PENNY (1997) "Introduction", in: Carole Counihan and Penny Van Esterik (Eds), *Food and Culture: a reader*, New York and London: Routledge, pp. 1–8.

DUFFY, ANDREW (2010) "Shooting Rubber Bands at the Stars: preparing to work within the Singapore system", in: Beate Josephi (Ed.), *Journalism Education in Countries with Limited Media Freedom*, New York: Peter Lang, pp. 31–51.

EVERS, HANS-DIETER and GERKE, SOLVAY (1997) "Global Market Cultures and the Construction of Modernity in Southeast Asia", *Thesis Eleven* 50, pp. 1–14.

FALK, PASI (1991) "Homo Culinarius: towards an historical anthropology of taste", *Social Science Information* 30(4), pp. 757–90.

GOODE, JUDITH G. (1992) "Food", in: Richard Baumann (Ed.), *Folklore, Cultural Performances, and Popular Entertainments: a communications-centered handbook*, New York: Oxford University Press, pp. 233–45.

HANKE, ROBERT (1989) "Mass Media and Lifestyle Differentiation: an analysis of the public discourse about food", *Journal of Communication* 11(3), pp. 221–39.

HANUSCH, FOLKER (2009) "The Public Interest in Researching Travel Journalism Practices: why lifestyle journalism is an increasingly important field of inquiry", paper presented to the International Conference: Journalism Research in the Public Interest, Winterthur, Switzerland, November.

JAMES, ALISON (1996) "Cooking the Books: global or local identities in contemporary British food cultures?", in: David Howes (Ed.), Cross-cultural Consumption: global markets, local realities, London and New York: Routledge, pp. 77–92.

JOHNSTON, JOSEE and BAUMANN, SHYON (2007) "Democracy Versus Distinction: a study of omnivorousness in gourmet food writing", *American Journal of Sociology* 113(1), pp. 165–204.

JONES, STEVE and TAYLOR, BEN (2001) "Food Writing and Food Cultures: the case of Elizabeth David and Jane Grigson", *European Journal of Cultural Studies* 4(2), pp. 171–88.

JUVENAL, DECIMUS IUNIUS (1998) *The Sixteen Satires*, London: Penguin Classics.

KENYON, ANDREW T. and MARJORIBANKS, TIM (2007) "Transforming Media Markets: the cases of Malaysia and Singapore", *Australian Journal of Emerging Technologies and Society* 5(2), pp. 103–18.

KORSMEYER, CAROLYN (Ed.) (2005) *The Taste Culture Reader—experiencing food and drink*, Oxford and New York: Berg.

LATIF, ASAD (Ed.) (1998) *Walking the Tightrope: press freedom and professional standards in Asia*, Singapore: AMIC.

LEONG, WAI-TENG (2001) "Consuming the Nation: National Day parades in Singapore", *New Zealand Journal of Asian Studies* 3(2), pp. 5–16.

MEAD, MARGARET (1997 [1961]) "The Changing Significance of Food", in: Carole Counihan and Penny Van Esterik (Eds), *Food and Culture: a reader*, New York and London: Routledge, pp. 11–9.

NESTLE, MARION (2002) *Food Politics*, Berkeley: University of California Press.

NEWMAN, OTTO and DE ZOYSA, RICHARD (1997) "Communitarianism: the new panacea?", *Sociological Perspectives* 40(4), pp. 623–38.

POWDERMAKER, HORTENSE (1997 [1959]) "An Anthropological Approach to the Problem of Obesity", in: Carole Counihan and Penny Van Esterik (Eds), *Food and Culture: a reader*, New York and London: Routledge, pp. 203–10.

PROBYN, ELSPETH (1999) "Beyond Food/Sex: eating and an ethics of existence", *Theory Culture & Society* 16(2), pp. 215–28.

ROZIN, PAUL (1982) "Human Food Selection: the interaction of biology, culture and individual experience", in: Lewis M. Barker (Ed.), *The Psychobiology of Human Food Selection*, Chichester: Ellis Horwood, pp. 225–54.

SHUGART, HELEN A. (2008) "Sumptuous Texts: consuming 'otherness' in the food film genre", *Critical Studies in Media Communication* 25(1), pp. 68–90.

STAUTH, GEORG (1997) "Elias in Singapore: civilising processes in a tropical city", *Thesis Eleven* 50, pp. 51–70.

TITZ, KARL, LANZA-ABBOT, JE'ANNA, CRUZ, GLENN and CORDUA, Y. (2004) "The Anatomy of Restaurant Reviews: an exploratory study", *International Journal of Hospitality & Tourism Administration* 5(1), pp. 49–65.

VELAYUTHAM, SELVARAJ (2004) "Affect, Materiality and the Gift of Social Life in Singapore", *Sojourn* 19(1), pp. 1–27.

WOOLLEY, JOHN T. (2000) "Using Media-based Data in Studies of Politics", *American Journal of Political Science* 44(1), pp. 156–73.

HEALTH AND LIFESTYLE TO SERVE THE PUBLIC

A case study of a cross-media programme series from the Norwegian Broadcasting Corporation

Roel Puijk

This study traces the changes of a prime-time health and lifestyle television programme (Puls) on the main channel of the Norwegian Broadcasting Corporation (NRK) across the last decade. The overall pattern of change is that as a public-service broadcaster, the NRK continues to broadcast factual programmes in prime time, which incorporate different entertainment and interactive elements to guarantee their popularity and relevance to the viewers. The integration of television and online activity has lessened over the years. The television content has become more lifestyle-oriented, while the Internet content has more stress on factual information and news. The use of reality elements has led to a strong emphasis on motivating the viewer to adopt an active lifestyle, while the viewers' possibilities to participate actively in the programme have diminished.

Introduction

Even though the number of commercial television channels has increased dramatically over the last decade, traditional public-service broadcasters are still significant players on the television market in Europe. In many countries they are performing better than was expected a few years ago (Bardoel and d'Haenens, 2008; Coppens and Sayes, 2006; Syvertsen, 2008). On losing their monopolies during the 1980s, public-service broadcasters introduced traits that were formerly connected to (American) commercial television: more popular programming, infotainment, self-promotion, a more conscious composition of the daily flow, and so on. Accusations abound both in public debate and in research of "commercialization" and "tabloidization" and a tendency to programme "heavier" informational programmes outside prime time or on smaller channels. But, as the former general director of Denmark's public-service broadcaster Nissen (2006, p. 28) argues, public-service broadcasters have to strike a balance between popularity and a distinct profile. They need to reach enough viewers to legitimize their privileges (e.g., a licence fee), but they cannot be just like commercial broadcasters. Because factual programming is an important element in maintaining distinctiveness, factual programmes conspicuously programmed in prime time on the main channel are particularly interesting to analyse.

According to journalists working in the health and lifestyle programme, *Puls [Pulse]*, health-related information is the second-most popular theme on the Internet (after pornography). The programme is scheduled on a highly visible slot on the Norwegian public-service broadcasting corporation's (NRK) main channel NRK 1 immediately after the main newscast on Mondays. *Puls*, along with other science, consumer, and nature programme series broadcast in the same slot on other weekdays, is a part of a "light factual programming timeslot". This timeslot is used to maintain and legitimize the position of the public-service broadcaster that is both informative and popular.

Puls has been on the NRK's schedule since 1999. The present study looks at how this programme and related Internet activity have developed and how *Puls* has incorporated and negotiated the demands for popular public-service programming. The analysis of *Puls* shows that this programme deals with many of the general issues that the NRK faces: the introduction of new technology, cross-media production, competition with commercial broadcasts and reality programmes, as well as the representational issues (gender, homosexuals, and ethnic minorities). The production team strives to be popular, but is at the same time serious in its reporting, which also challenges the viewers.

Changing Factual Programming

Factual Programming

The distinction between "serious" and "tabloid" press has existed for a long time. In television the difference between "serious" and "tabloid" journalism has often been associated with differences between public-service and commercial channels, as well as within the commercial sector. After the abolishment of public-service monopolies in the 1980s, the tendency to choose certain themes and angles to increase the popularity of traditional factual programmes like the news and documentaries has been noticed. The concentration on sensation, emotions, celebrities, the use of personification, allusions to sex, hyperbolical titles and the like have often been denounced by the term "tabloidization", and are considered to be tactics that threaten serious public information based on the accurate, impartial reporting of public affairs.

But other factual programmes, like health, science, and cooking programmes, began incorporating elements that were previously used in fiction and entertainment. One example of what is often called "infotainment" is the breakfast show that became popular in Europe during the 1980s and 1990s, which combines elements from talk shows with news bulletins and informational sequences (Wieten, 2000). According to Hartley (2001b, p. 119), the "infotainment debate" was more prominent in Europe than in the United States, where the mix of rational, personal, and emotional elements in factual programming was more common. Today, the inclusion of more viewer-friendly elements in other factual programmes is widespread—especially on narrowcast television channels like Discovery or National Geographic, where documentaries stress the personal and emotional through a first-person narrative, or where popular programmes like *MythBusters* portray experiments as exciting stories, told in easily understandable vocabulary, intermixed with humour and other entertaining elements.

Health

Several studies have pointed out that health-related issues are dealt with in a broad spectre of television genres, varying from news and informational programmes to advertisements and dramatic series (cf. Wright et al., 2008). Over the past decade, the number of medical shows (such as *Grey's Anatomy*, *ER*, *Scrubs* or *House*) has increased. A study of the top-rated American prime-time television shows has found that the focus was largely on symptoms, diagnoses, and treatment, while preventive messages were less frequent (Murphy et al., 2008, p. 13).

Health is also an important part of news and viewers often draw their knowledge of threatening health issues like HIV/AIDS and SARS from watching the news. Many studies of health programmes on television have looked at how health issues are framed and have assessed the effects of health communication and campaigns (Fannis, 1999; Leask et al., 2010). Conversely, other studies have demonstrated that some health problems are underreported (Wright et al., 2008).

Eide and Knight argue that factual health programmes are part of a more general development towards service journalism, which is "closely related to the popularisation of journalistic idioms, focus and modes of address" (1999, p. 527). They argue that service journalism addresses the viewers as citizen, consumer, and client. They also point out that the term "service journalism" did not appear in Norway until the 1980s and that other terms like "consumer" or "lifestyle" journalism are used alternatively, which indicates that the boundary between health and lifestyle journalism is fluid.

Lifestyle

Lifestyle programmes have from the start taken a viewer-friendly approach. The genre's origins lie in American daytime television during the 1950s, which was directed at women (Hartley 2001a). According to Hartley, the daytime lifestyle programmes addressed women as domestic "workers" and also as consumers with purchasing power. The notion of lifestyle television has changed over the years, and today it refers more generally to programmes that deal with ordinary people's domestic lives and daily preoccupations. Still, the domestic context persists, as does the genre's association with women. According to its Web pages, the BBC's Lifestyle Channel, for example, describes itself as "Serving up six programming strands covering food, fashion and beauty, home and design, parenting, personal development and health" (BBC Lifestyle, 2010).

According to Brunsdon, lifestyle programmes that accommodated mostly women's leisure activities and hobbies, such as cooking, gardening, travelling, and home decoration, held a prominent position in the 8 pm slot on British television during the 1990s (Brunsdon, 2004). She argues that social changes were important reasons why these programmes were aired in prime time: the increase in home ownership, expansion of females in the workforce, and the tendency for women to postpone their first child (Brunsdon, 2004, pp. 77–8). But she also observes that lifestyle programmes vary widely— from realist styles similar to those used in old-fashioned instructional and leisure programming to those with a melodramatic focus on human drama (Brunsdon, 2004, p. 89). An analysis must, therefore, take the characteristics of each programme into consideration.

This article analyses *Puls*, which is foremost a health programme that also covers physical, psychological, and relational issues related to modern lifestyle. Accordingly, it has a more serious and journalistic approach than most lifestyle programmes. But it also has feature elements and during the course of its existence it has changed and adopted reality and participatory elements that have renewed traditional reporting.

Reality and Participation

Hill (2007) argues that factual television has recently been restyled in a number of ways, not least by the proliferation of different reality concepts. Although she describes factual television as "a container for a variety of genres, sub-genres and hybrid genres", factual programming still "tends to be used by audiences to signify non-fiction programmes that make truth claims and are based on facts" (Hill, 2007, p. 3). Hill's research indicates that different forms of reality television are disputed in general, and public-service broadcasters in particular are cautious not to stretch the reality line too far. This does not prevent public-service broadcasters from engaging in the production of reality concepts, but they are on the whole more selective, avoiding especially programmes where participants run the risk of being humiliated.

One refreshing aspect of reality television is the participants. Many reality programmes cast "ordinary people", people who differ markedly from those who were normally portrayed in the past. Further, audience participation is often encouraged with voting, taking part in online meetings, leaving comments, and more. Jenkins (2006) argues that we are witnessing a whole new "convergence culture", where fans contribute actively and interact with producers. But participation and interactivity also involves problems. When the mass media make participation possible, the individual contributions may easily conflict with journalistic norms (Enli, 2007, p. 181).

Cross-media Production

Today, almost every broadcaster engages in online production. This varies from simple re-usage of content on different media to more differentiated productions where the content for each medium is carefully designed to complement each other.

> The term "cross-mediacy" refers to situations when media texts or communication are shown or used in more than one medium: the communication is split up and arranged in several media in order to make sure that users or fans are kept interested, loyal, activated, updated, informed and amused. (Philipsen, 2010, p. 119)

Cross-media production thus aims at integrating the different media into a synergetic whole. But in practice this is often difficult to achieve. Several studies have revealed a struggle between representatives of the different media and a hierarchy with television on top, followed by radio, and the Internet at the bottom (Erdal, 2008).

The introduction of the Internet has also led to changes for public-service broadcasters. Public-service broadcasters have used the Internet not only to give additional information about their programmes, but also to provide archival services, to get commentary and input from viewers, and more. Extending their activities beyond broadcasting, public-service broadcasters are now becoming multimedia production houses. The term "public-service media" implies a more general public service covering a range of platforms (Lowe and Bardoel, 2007). Murdock (2006, p. 227) even envisages public broadcasting "as the central node in a new network of public and civil institutions that together make up the digital commons". While this opens up new activities for public broadcasting, European Union (EU) regulations somewhat limit their possibilities. With the "Television Without Frontiers Directive" (EU 1989) and the "Audiovisual Media Service Directive" (EU 2007), the EU plays an important role in promoting the free circulation of programmes in the television sector and in increasing the pressure on public-service broadcasters to compete on equal terms with commercial competitors. The Treaty of Amsterdam (1997) requires that the core areas and aims of the public-service broadcasting remit are clearly described, while the public-value test of new services demands that value added to the market is compared with potentially competition-limiting effects.

The NRK operates within these developments and is constantly adapting its organization and programmes. In the following, I shall analyse the changes that occurred on the level of a single programme series, and consider whether their programmes have become more popular in relation to content and viewer participation. In addition, I shall analyse how the relations between television and the Internet have developed.

Method

The present study is based on a combination of methods. I started in 2003 with two months' participant observation of the editorial board. At that time the programme *Puls* was re-launched as a multimedia programme using the latest developments in digital technology and the Internet. During this period I observed daily production, talked to the editors and journalists, attended editorial meetings, and collected written material. I also interviewed each member of the editorial board as well as a number of people from other departments at the NRK. As I was mainly interested in the use of new technology, I did not follow reporters to on-location recordings. Of course, I also watched the programmes and analysed the Web pages they produced. I continued to follow the editorial board by watching its production over the years and came back to interview the editor, the online editor, and the project leader of the *Bedre Puls* series in 2007. In 2009, I re-interviewed the editor, and in autumn 2010 I carried out a final series of interviews with the editor, the online editor, and the editor of the "genre desk". These interviews were semi-structured. In the first phase I asked the staff members about their professional backgrounds, their experiences of producing the television programme and with the Internet, their opinions on internal co-operation, about the editorial policy, and so on. I noted their answers during the interview and transcribed them in the evening. In the next phase, I prepared questions on the developments I had observed from the broadcasts or Web pages, questions I had while analysing my previously collected material and questions that arose from the public discussions on the NRK. I then recorded the interviews and wrote down the most interesting parts verbatim. I also coded each programme and Internet page they produced during the fall season of 2003 and 2010.[1]

The collection of a wide range of material over almost a decade made visible the internal developments and changes in the programme and its online activity. The study is a case study and not representative for the development of the NRK and its programmes as a whole, as there are many other programme areas, changes, and adaptations that are different from the developments noted with *Puls*. Nevertheless, the study provides insight into developments in the area of factual programming. In addition, this approach can contribute to our understanding of not only the internal logic of the editorial board, but also of how contextual and institutional changes are reflected in the microcosm of concrete programme production. Before embarking on a description of the programme, I shall first describe some of these contextual and institutional changes.

NRK—Adapting to Competition

The NRK has been quite successful, and still has the largest television market share in Norway.[2] Over the past decade the organization has implemented changes at all levels in order to adjust to the present situation of increased competition, with emphases on viewers' preferences, tighter regulation, digitization, and convergence. Factual programming in the NRK covers a large range of programmes and themes—from news and debate to documentaries, magazines on culture and the arts, consumer and science programmes, and more. Many of these programmes are broadcast in prime time. From 2000 to 2008 factual programmes (excluding news) went slightly down from 28.8 to 27.6 per cent of the total offer on NRK 1, while most documentaries were shown on NRK 2.[3]

Reorganization

Around the turn of the century public-management systems were introduced successively—the NRK became a state-owned, limited company in 1996 (as did all major publicly-owned cultural institutions in Norway); strategic planning was introduced in 2001; a separate broadcast division was established the same year (Ytreberg, 2001). In addition, a reorganization of the radio and television departments took place, integrating parallel departments in multimedia departments producing for television, radio, the Internet, and mobile platforms.

By introducing managerial systems that originate in the commercial sector, the management has tightened its grip on what often are considered unruly programme creators at the ground level of production. This new system of management has manifested itself in the introduction of strategic planning and a broadcasting department, in the composition of the schedules, and in the commissioning of programmes from production departments or external producers (cf. Born, 2004; Puijk, 2007).

The introduction of the Internet also contributed to a redefinition of the NRK. The first Web pages were published in 1995, and when Internet activity increased to a level where it had to be taken into account in the formulation of the remit, a separation between core and auxiliary activities was introduced in 2004 (Moe, 2007). The main radio and television channels were defined as core public-service activities to be financed through licence income, while Internet activity was to be financed by other sources of income (mainly advertisements on the Web). In response to the EU directives and the Court of Europe's decisions, the remit was revised in 2008 and Internet activity was included as part of the public-service obligations financed by the licence fee.

Health Programmes

Programmes about physical and psychological health have been a part of NRK television's menu since the 1970s. The first programmes, *Helsenytt* [*Health News*] and *Fra medisinsk forskning og praksis* [*From Medical Research and Practice*], had a rather top-down approach to health, mostly featuring interviews with medical professors and practitioners about advances in the medical field. A much more socially engaged and critical programme *Sosialkanalen* [*Social Channel*], which had a bottom-up perspective, was aired during the 1980s. During the first part of the programme, one or two individual cases were shown with on-location reports. The second part consisted of a studio debate where governmental representatives were challenged (Puijk, 1990).

As part of a major reorganization of the NRK in the early 1990s, a weekly health and consumer programme series was started—each week alternating between health programme *Helsereflleks* [*Health Reflex*] and consumer programme *Forbrukerreflleks* [*Consumer Reflex*]. *Helsereflleks* was a magazine programme consisting of three or four unrelated items, covered by on-location reports where ordinary people told their stories while experts (often medical) gave their professional opinion about the case. Sometimes short dramatizations were included to enliven the broadcast. In addition, the host interviewed experts and representatives in small studio-based sequences. In 1999, *Helsereflleks* was renamed *Puls* and was from then on broadcast on a weekly basis, during prime time on Mondays, right after the main newscast. During an internal struggle for a light factual timeslot, the concept of *Puls* was rejuvenated, and under the internal name *Nye Puls* [*New Pulse*], a fully digitalized, multimedia editorial board emerged in 2003.

Establishment of *Nye Puls*

The introduction of a broadcaster division in 2001 had direct consequences for factual programming on NRK 1. One of the proposals of this new division in 2001 was the establishment of a daily news hour (newscast and debate programme) from 7 to 8 pm. This proposal entailed either the termination or moving of existing informational programmes in this timeslot. This proposal was met with considerable resistance; the editorial board of the science programme, *Schrödingers Katt* (produced in Trondheim), initiated a campaign among scientists to support the programme. In Oslo, the factual department wrote a report urging for a "light factual timeslot" from 7.30 to 8 pm or from 8.30 to 9 pm on weekdays, asserting that removing programmes like *Puls* and the consumer programme *FBI* from NRK 1 would "take away power from the viewers to influence their daily lives" (NRK, 2002, p. 2). In addition, the report argued that these themes are important for strengthening the NRK's profile and brand; not to follow these recommendations would be to leave an important field open for their main competitor, TV2, to exploit. The income potential of these themes on the Internet was also underlined.

This focus on new media was rather new. As online activity was not defined as part of the NRK's core activity, one of the options was to provide commercial online services. In 2002, both *Puls* and *FBI* had been included in a project where NRK and the commercial telecom operator, Telenor Plus, tested the commercial potential of Internet services (NRK, 2003). The pre-emptive approach was successful and a light factual timeslot was established right after the main newscast at 7.35 pm. One reason why *Puls* was allowed to continue was its plans to utilize new technology as the basis for a new concept. Together with *FBI* it shared a fully digital production chain that enabled it to produce in 16:9 format, furnished its open office space with spotlights so it could be used as a studio, and integrated technical staff (photographer/editor) among the editorial staff.

Puls on Television—Form and Content

Puls is marketed under the slogan "the programme that gives you a better life". This includes not only giving viewers information on health- and lifestyle-related issues, but also encouraging them to take control over their own lives—whether it be training, eating more healthily, or registering complaints with authorities. There are also fewer consumer-related issues and more socially orientated ones, like bullying, caring for others, and loneliness, and a concentration on issues connected to modern lifestyle, the use of social media, and the "see-me generation".

The new multimedia concept did not change the structure of the television programmes very much, but it added different forms of audience participation via the Web. The programme in 2003 still consisted of a mix of on-location reports and studio items where the host introduced new items and interviewed experts and authorities. The basic combination comprised four items: a "news item" based on critical journalist reporting, a "consumer item" based on input from viewers, a more feature-like "lifestyle item", and an item where the host interviewed one of a contracted group of experts (in medicine as well as training, nutrition, sexuality, alternative medicine, and psychiatry). When asked what kind of journalism they used, the editor stated in 2009:

> We have a rather fixed template. The first item should be a news story. And preferably one that can be broadcast on the radio news as well. But we also want to give a sense of experience—even in the news item. So our news stories are quite feature-like, but we still want something newsworthy. (Editor *Puls*, 19 May 2009)

Through the years, *Puls* has experimented with different forms. In one period the host left the studio and interviewed the expert on location or took part in exercises outdoors. In another the studio segments were broadcast live, but after a while they returned to "live on tape" recordings during the normal working hours on Monday. In addition, several series were integrated in the programmes.

From 2009 to 2010 the form gradually changed towards more theme-oriented programmes that treated only one theme each broadcast. In autumn 2010 these programmes included studio segments where "ordinary" or well-known people (well-known from areas other than the one discussed) as well as experts on the theme were interviewed, interspersed with on-location reports with ordinary people on the same theme. The contracts with *Puls'* experts were terminated. When I asked the editor about the choice of themes, she answered:

> The themes should be broad. It can be narrow, but then it has to have a broad appeal. And then we also think about the age group 30–40 years old and what interests them. Things like hospital reforms are simply too boring. The themes now are more about mastering life—mastering stress, mastering daily life, mastering parental responsibilities, mastering cancer. It should be useful for people but also innovative. (Editor *Puls*, 4 November 2010)

When asked whether they consciously thought about their public-service obligations and NRK's remit, she replied:

> We think we should be a public-service programme. We should make people a bit wiser—but we should also inspire and not teach. This is also the reason we don't have these experts anymore—those who sit and teach. People should instead find out for themselves—think a little and be inspired to do that. If we could do that, that would be very nice. We work intensively to do that. (Editor *Puls*, 4 November 2010)

According to the editor the dramaturgy changed, from a series of unrelated items, starting with the most important (news) item, to an integrated dramaturgy with a peak in the middle of the programme. But the making of a theme-based programme requires new routines:

> We don't think theme-based broadcasts are easy to make. It is harder to make a coherent theme-based broadcast than to make a broadcast with three or four unrelated elements. The whole bunch has to think team-wise and that is a bit difficult. (Editor *Puls*, 4 November 2010)

For the sake of variation the programme switches from on-location reports to interviews and conversations between the host and her guests in the studio. One of the elements used to soften the programme is a humour sequence. While the reporters in most on-location reports assume an invisible style (i.e., their questions are edited from the report), a more entertaining section appears in the middle of the broadcast, where a visible reporter engages with people "on the street" with small experiments, intriguing questions, and the like.

Over time, *Puls* has provided both "heavy" and traditional items, as well as "light" lifestyle items (Brinch and Iversen, 2010). Table 1 gives an overview over the themes of the television programmes during the autumn seasons. As the programmes in 2003 were composed of several separate sequences, the total number of items for 2003 is higher than for 2010, even though there were fewer broadcasts.

We can note that specific health- and treatment-related issues are declining, while more lifestyle-related issues are increasing. Social issues, like "bitching", "friendship", and "caring for each other", were the subjects for a programme each in 2010, in addition to more physical-health issues, like "ME virus", "tooth bleaching", and "obesity among children".

One change since 2003 has been the diminishing focus on criticism of authorities (e.g., not giving the people the best treatment, lack of resources, failing actors in the market). This was often a main element in the "news issues" (and the corresponding Web pages), but in 2010 there was much emphasis on our stressful daily lives, social pressures, and media use.

Reality Series

In 2006, a form of "reality" programming was introduced in *Puls'* spring seasons. Under the segment "New Year's Resolution", *Puls* recruited two "ordinary" people to realize their goals for the New Year. They got advice from *Puls'* experts on training and

TABLE 1
Themes of *Puls'* television broadcasts (%)

	Autumn 2003	Autumn 2010
Illness, medicine, treatment	55	30
Psychological health	9	18
Social relations	20	30
Exercise, nutrition	12	11
Combination/other	4	11
Total	100	100
Number of broadcasts	14	17
Number of themes	58	17

nutrition to get into better shape. As they progressed, short reports on their activities were shown during the television broadcasts. This was the start of the regular series *Bedre Puls* [*Better Pulse*], which showed ordinary people how to improve their living situation, and it has been aired during the spring season since 2007. These series can be characterized as a variation of a makeover reality programme. Still, the focus is on rather ordinary people realizing a better life for themselves through training and improved nutrition, instead of on grossly overweight persons (as in *The Biggest Loser*) or on physical beauty (as in numerous other commercial makeover programmes).

While the project leader expressed that she would have liked to have had non-white participants, there were none among the volunteers. Still, the participants in 2010 were not average—a gay couple were instructed in wrestling and a biker was challenged to train for bobsleighing. The only female participant was motivated to do a more traditional Norwegian sport, cross-country skiing. In addition to the television reports, this project included various supplements on the Web pages: training videos, a competition based on step counting, a calculator for one's "physical age". Further, one could log on to a personal page, keep a training diary or create a training group. These personal pages were much inspired by the growth of social media at that time.

The Internet activity during the first broadcast of *Bedre Puls* in 2007 boomed: while the average number of clicks on *Puls'* Web pages the month before had been under 2000 per day, on the day *Bedre Puls* was launched, it reached 125,000, averaging 45,000 the following week. But the interest in creating personal pages and *Puls* groups was low, and these were abandoned as part of a major reorganization of NRK's site in December 2009.

Multimedia Production

In 2003 *Puls* was re-launched as a playground for new digital technology. Not only was the production chain fully digitized and in 16:9 format, it also emphasized different online functions, cross-media production, and audience participation.

Cross-media Publishing

Nye Puls was to be a multimedia production team from the start. Like many other television programmes, *Puls* publishes Internet articles for each of the items dealt with on television. This activity is supposed to add value to the programme, and not simply to recycle the same material. One aspect is that efforts used for research could be used more efficiently to provide the users with more background information online. Another aspect is that the different outlets were intended to support each other, although in practice it meant primarily that the other media would support the main product: television. The timing of the different outlets is essential (Puijk, 2007). Normally, the main (news) item is converted into a radio news item that is broadcast on the morning news. When I asked the editor of *Puls* whether they also were interested in getting these items as part of the main television newscast, she responded:

> We are not that keen on getting these news issues on the television newscast because they are right before us. And we don't have the capacity to edit a variation of our issues for them. It is more like: when we have something newsworthy in our broadcast—when one of our guests makes a surprising statement or something like that—we tip the late

news [at 11 o'clock]. But the radio news [broadcast in the morning] is important for us. Then the news spreads and it is good advertisement for our programme. The newspapers and the Norwegian news agency catch it and then there is a spin-off effect. (Editor *Puls*, 4 November 2010)

The news items are thus deliberately timed in relation to the television broadcast: they are published on Monday morning, supposedly to generate interest for the main product, television. For the same reasons the programme's Internet pages are published early Monday morning. Other forms of cross-media production have also been introduced through the years. In co-operation with the commercial publisher Allers, a paper magazine was published from 2005 to 2007, as were several books written by *Puls* journalists. Moreover, the *Bedre Puls* project, with the different offers it provides on the Internet, is an attempt to provide more useful information, to motivate and engage users, and to help them to improve their physical condition.

Independent Web Publishing

Puls' online desk consisted of two journalists in 2003. Their main task was to provide content and to maintain *Puls'* Web pages. They processed texts from the reporters, added pictures, and moderated user-generated content. Every item produced for television— which at that time had a magazine form—was also represented as a Web page. As these tasks took most of their time, the aim of producing additional Web-only content was restricted to a few articles. Over the years the tight connection between television and Web articles loosened. In an interview in 2007, the online editor told me that most of the news items still had their related on-line texts, but more feature-based items were no longer re-published on the Web. Instead, an effort was made to increase the amount of on-line stories, mostly generated by surfing the Web and taking their own angle to the story, or by using viewers' tips.

In 2009, a more dramatic change was introduced as part of a total rejuvenation of NRK's Internet site. The Internet pages of *Puls* and *FBI* were joined in a "Health, Consumer, and Lifestyle" site. Instead of maintaining a programme-related site, and sometimes pitching a story for the front page, the main task now is to produce stories that can be presented on NRK's front page (www.nrk.no). This implied more independence for the on-line editorial board.

[B]eing an editorial board that works for *Puls* and *FBI* is something we want to get away from, because, with the new front page and the launch last year, the NRK web is becoming more independent and has moved away from television. Our task as online journalists is to produce stories for the front page of nrk.no, and not to produce stories for the television board. (Online editor *Health, Consumer and Lifestyle*, 4 November 2010)

This model is also followed in other areas. "Clusters" are also formed for "Culture & Entertainment" and "Science & Technology". The main aims, according to the editor of the co-ordinating Web desk, are to increase the journalistic level of the sites and to get more traffic on NRK's site. But the offer is also reduced: many of the older articles and interactive offers connected to the programmes have disappeared in the process.

Table 2 illustrates the radical change in the routines and content of the Web pages. The attempt to disconnect the online production from the television programmes shows in the number of pages that have an explicit connection to the television programme.

TABLE 2

Selected characteristics of *Puls*/*Health and Lifestyle* Internet pages (%)

	Autumn 2003	Autumn 2010
Norwegian experts cited	49	71
Based on published research or figures from authorities/non-governmental organizations	8	53
Critical journalism	14	7
Advice to reader	44	58
Journalistic reporting not connected to television	10	76
Connection to television of which:	68	24
Articles connected to television reports	44	22
Articles based on advice from viewers	7	–
Articles encouraging viewers to participate	17	2
Total page number	167	120

While 68 per cent of the Internet pages were connected to the television broadcast in 2003, only 24 per cent were in 2010. The routine in 2003 involved three to four Web pages for each television report (about the individual case shown on television, background information and an interview with an expert, etc.). In addition, there was at least one Web page each week urging viewers to participate in Net meetings, to pose questions to experts, and to provide advice for the "interactive" television segment.

The Web pages in 2010 looked quite different. Although each television programme normally also had one or two related Web pages, most online production was not directly related to the television broadcasts. Most of the Web pages reported scientific studies on health and lifestyle themes. Many of these originated from other websites (e.g., BBC, Denmark Radio and Forskning.no). In addition to referring to these studies, the Web page featured interviews with a Norwegian expert who explained some of the implications of the findings. The Web pages also regularly included a fact frame about the theme and links to relevant official sites and non-governmental organizations.

In 2003 and even more in 2010 much attention was directed towards implications and concrete advice for the readers: what to do and what not to do, what to eat and which products to avoid. The increased professionalization has led to more careful references to sources and more news that can be used on NRK's front page. Yet, critical journalism, generated mostly by television's news-item reporters, has declined. One reason might be that the Internet journalists have less time to dig up these kinds of stories.

User Participation

When *Nye Puls* started in 2003, the Internet was seen as a way of increasing the opportunities not only to engage the viewers, but also to let them contribute actively in the production process. Many productions tried out new, participatory programme elements by using new platforms (the Internet or mobile phones) as forms for instant viewer input—voting in reality programmes like *Big Brother* and *Idol*, crawls on discussion programmes or chats in SMS-tv (Enli, 2007). Net meetings where users could communicate with experts or programme creators were also introduced. *Puls* also tried out different interactive forms.

In 2003, a Web-streaming extension of the television programme was introduced. The television programmes ended with a studio sequence where the host interviewed one of the affiliated experts, who answered questions that viewers had posed on the Internet site. When the television broadcast ended, this studio interview continued as a live Web stream for about 30 minutes. Viewers could pose their questions on *Puls'* Web pages, from which some were selected and relayed to the host's monitor. She would read the questions and the expert answered them. As few people watched the streamed version, it was abolished in 2004, but turned up as a television broadcast on NRK 2 in 2007.

That year the broadcaster had commissioned *Puls* to produce some broadcasts for the smaller channel NRK 2. According to the editor they did not have enough capacity to fill this slot with on-location reports, so they decided to use this broadcast on NRK 2 to extend the programmes on NRK 1. Thus, following the main broadcast on NRK 1 at 7.55 pm, the experts and guests from this programme would stay in the studio and participate in a Net meeting where viewers could pose questions and discuss the topic of the day. From 9.30 to 10 pm questions from this meeting were discussed in the studio and broadcast live on NKR 2.

Other forms of user participation were also facilitated. Apart from the traditional Web pages where *Puls'* experts answered people's questions, an effort was made to enable users to influence the television programme itself. The "consumer" item of the main television broadcast in 2003 was based on viewers' comments: during the programme the viewers were asked to contribute their own knowledge on a health-related issue (e.g., treating a cold, relieving a sore back). The viewers could write their solutions on *Puls'* Web pages on Tuesday, and, from this information, the next week's consumer item was produced.

This form of "collective intelligence" television was abolished after some years for two reasons. During my interviews the journalists responsible for this item said they thought it was neither a very challenging nor inspiring task (see Puijk, 2007). Further, according to the editor, the items were not very popular and journalists' time was needed for other tasks.

As part of the NRK's debate forums, *Puls* had its own. With the exception of a few themes (especially a debate on "bullying" in 2002), these pages did not generate much response. Still, they had to be moderated,[4] and when the opportunity arose to terminate them as part of the restructuring of the NRK's Web pages, they took it.

Even though most of the possibilities for giving commentary and providing input to the programme through the Web pages have been abandoned, the use of a Facebook group (constructed in January 2010) gives viewers a chance to respond. It serves as a channel to promote the television programmes and to collect tips and reactions. In December 2010 approximately 2000 persons were fans of *Puls'* Facebook page. Still, the medium is not used very systematically.

> Facebook came as an initiative of some staff members . . . but we don't use it very much. We are quite new to this, so maybe in the future, but it is traditional journalism that drives the programme for the moment. (Editor *Puls*, 4 November 2010)

Conclusions

Public-service broadcasting has to be distinctive in order to justify its privileges, but it has to be popular enough not to become irrelevant. Factual programming used to be the prerogative of public-service broadcasting. But as factual television has developed into more entertaining variants, including different forms of reality television, commercial channels have taken an interest in factual programming. In their attempt to rejuvenate their factual programming while also maintaining their aim to offer more than mere entertainment, public-service broadcasters have employed different means, some of which are also used in commercial broadcasting. On the basis of this case study, I want to point to three areas: changes in content, participation/interaction, and online production.

Content

Presenting information in an entertaining way has become a widespread and acceptable form of information dissemination, including for public-service broadcasters (Brinch and Iversen, 2010). NRK has aired entertaining health-related series like *Embarrassing Bodies* (Channel 4, produced by Maverick Television Production) and *Make My Body Younger* (BBC Three) on their youth channel NRK 3. In 2010, it produced an entertaining sexual-information series for youth (*Trekant*). In its health and lifestyle production for prime time on the main channel, it has continued a style that was developed during the 1990s—a combination of light and heavy themes, based on personal on-location filmed stories, combined with interviews of experts either in the studio or on film. It has also, to a rather limited extent, introduced more "popular" elements (e.g., humour, celebrity) to increase interest in its programmes, not unlike those already used in the 1980s (Puijk, 1990). As we have seen, the attempt to reach the 30–40-year-old population has involved less emphasis on physical illnesses and treatments and more on lifestyle items and how our way of living influences our physical, psychological and social well-being.

The most radical change in the programme has been the *Bedre Puls* series, which can be considered a weak "makeover" reality concept. It fits in with the tendency to serialize television production, which has both organizational and narrative advantages. The organizational advantages include more regular and streamlined planning, production, and distribution. The narrative advantages are that *Bedre Puls* has a continuity of persons and a narrative development throughout the season. While normal *Puls* items are based on individual stories that get exposure for five to seven minutes, the characters taking part in *Bedre Puls* were exposed over a range of 10–12 programmes. This enables the viewer to get to know these characters and to follow their development. Introducing a target to be reached in the end, these sequences also build up to a climax, along with a dramatic development of the characters, just as other reality series do.

User Participation and Interactivity

Some variants of reality programmes make use of the Internet to provide earlier episodes, additional material, and a channel for viewers' comments so they can discuss both the programme and its participants. In some cases viewers can influence the development of the programme itself. These developments, which can also be seen in gaming and motion films, contribute to what Jenkins (2006) calls convergence culture, where fans and active consumers take part of the process of cross-media production.

This emphasis on the users fits well with the changes in public-service broadcasting, where audiences' priorities are more in focus today. Still, programmes like *Puls* are more anxious to promote socially active viewers and to empower and give a voice to minority groups and individuals. There was also an attempt to utilize collective intelligence, but most interactive elements have been eliminated, owing either to low popularity or to difficulties. This reduction of interactive and participatory elements has also been observed in other fields of journalism. As Domingo summarizes his findings from studies on online news producers:

> Findings suggest that the professional culture of traditional journalism has a strong inertia in the online newsrooms that prevents them from developing most of the ideals of interactivity, as they do not fit in the standardized news production routines. (2008, p. 680)

Online Journalism

Less interactivity correlates with the separation of television and the Internet. In the beginning, Internet production was seen as an extension of television, either to expand the offer on television (background information, programme archive, etc.) or to provide input for television. Today, Internet production is much more independent, generating content not presented on television. This represents a professionalization of Internet journalism and a greater focus on producing interesting texts for the front page. We also registered both a sharp increase in the use of scientific research as the basis for this journalism and a decrease of the critical dimension.

The overall pattern of the changes is that as a public-service broadcaster, NRK continues to broadcast factual programmes in prime time, which incorporate different entertaining and interactive elements to guarantee their popularity and relevance to the viewers. The television content has become more lifestyle-oriented, while the Internet content has more stress on factual information and news. The use of reality elements has led to a strong emphasis on motivating the viewer to adopt an active lifestyle, while the viewers' possibilities to participate actively in the programme have diminished. The development of the Internet as an independent medium seems to establish it as a place for the head, while television is more a place for both heart and head. It is not possible to generalize these findings to other stations or countries, as each has their own history and development. More research would be needed to separate the general from the unique factors that determine the patterns.

ACKNOWLEDGEMENTS

I would like to thank the staff of *Puls* and other interviewees at the NRK for their co-operation in this study.

NOTES

1. I coded the television programmes according to the themes they covered, and the Internet pages were coded in two periods (12 August 2003 until 8 December 2003 and 8 September 2010 until 26 November 2010), according to: their relation to television, presence of Norwegian experts, references to research, user advice, and critical approach.
2. Market share NRK 1: 31.9 per cent, TV 2: 22.1 per cent, NRK total 39 per cent, TV 2 Group total 25.3 per cent (2009, source: TNS Gallup).

3. The numbers include programme categories: Information, Art/Culture/Media, Nature, Education and Science., The total broadcasting time rose by more than 50 per cent to 8315 hours in 2008.
4. The moderating was necessary not only for liability, but also because some users link to their commercial enterprises, which the NRK as a neutral and advertisement-free organization disapproves of.

REFERENCES

BARDOEL, JOHANNES and D'HAENENS, LEEN (2008) "Reinventing Public Service Broadcasting in Europe: prospects, promises and problems", *Media, Culture & Society* 30(3), pp. 337–55.

BBC LIFESTYLE (2010) "About BBC Lifestyle", http://scandinavia.bbclifestyle.com/aboutbbcl.html, accessed 3 January 2011.

BORN, GEORGINA (2004) *Uncertain Vision: Birt, Dyke and the reinvention of the BBC*, London: Secker & Warburg.

BRINCH, SARA and IVERSEN, GUNNAR (2010) *Populær vitenskap: fjernsynet i kunnskapssamfunnet [Popular Science: television in the knowledge society]*, Kristiansand: Høyskoleforlaget.

BRUNSDON, CHARLOTTE (2004) "Lifestyling Britain: the 8–9 slot on British Television", in: Lynn Spigel and Jan Olsson (Eds), *Television After TV*, Durham, NC: Duke University Press, pp. 75–92.

COPPENS, TOMAS and SAYES, FRIEDA (2006) "Enforcing Performance: new approaches to govern public service broadcasting", *Media, Culture & Society* 28(2), pp. 261–84.

DOMINGO, DAVID (2008) "Interactivity in the Daily Routines of Online Newsrooms: dealing with an uncomfortable myth", *Journal of Computer-mediated Communication* 13(3), pp. 680–704.

EIDE, MARTIN and KNIGHT, GRAHAM (1999) "Public/private Service: service journalism and the problems of everyday life", *European Journal of Communication* 14(4), pp. 525–47.

ENLI, GUNN SARA (2007) *The Participatory Turn in Broadcast Television*, Oslo: Acta Humaniora.

ERDAL, IVAR JOHN (2008) *Cross-media News Journalism*, Oslo: Acta Humaniora.

EUROPEAN UNION (EU) (1989) "Television Without Frontiers Directive", http://eur-lex.europa.eu/LexUriServ/LexUriServ.do?uri=CELEX:31989L0552:EN:HTML, accessed 3 January 2011.

EUROPEAN UNION (EU) (2007) "Audiovisual Media Service Directive", http://ec.europa.eu/avpolicy/reg/avms/index_en.htm, accessed 3 January 2011.

FANNIS, BOB M. (1999) *Health on Television: studies on the content and effects of mass messages*, Amsterdam: Thela Thesis.

HARTLEY, JOHN (2001a) "Daytime TV", in: Glen Creeber (Ed.), *The Television Genre Book*, London: BFI, pp. 92–3.

HARTLEY, JOHN (2001b) "The Infotainment Debate", in: Glen Creeber (Ed.), *The Television Genre Book*, London: BFI, pp. 118–22.

HILL, ANNETTE (2007) *Restyling Factual TV*, London: Routledge.

JENKINS, HENRY (2006) *Convergence Culture: where old and new media collide*, New York: New York University Press.

LEASK, JULIE, HOOKER, CLAIRE and CATHERINE, KING (2010) "Media Coverage of Health Issues and How to Work More Effectively with Journalist: a qualitative study", *BMC Public Health* 10: 535, doi:10.1186/1471-2458-10-535

LOWE, GREGORY F. and BARDOEL, JOHANNES (Eds) (2007) *From Public Service Broadcasting to Public Service Media*, Gothenburg: Nordicom.

MOE, HALLVARD (2007) "Commercial Services, Enclosure and Legitimacy", in: Gregory F. Lowe and Johannes Bardoel (Eds), *From Public Service Broadcasting to Public Service Media*, Gothenburg: Nordicom, pp. 51–69.

MURDOCK, GRAHAM (2006) "Building the Digital Commons", in: Gregory F. Lowe and Per Jauert (Eds), *Cultural Dilemmas in Public Service Broadcasting*, Gothenburg: Nordicom, pp. 213–30.

MURPHY, SHEILA T., HETHER, HEATHER J. and RIDEOUT, VICTORIA (2008) "How Healthy Is Prime Time? An analysis of health content in popular prime time television programs", www.kaisernetwork.org, accessed 3 January 2011.

NISSEN, CHRISTIAN S. (2006) *Public Service Media in the Information Society. Report prepared for the Council of Europe's Group of Specialists on Public Service Broadcasting in the Information Society* (MC-S-PSB), http://www.coe.int/t/dghl/standardsetting/media/doc/H-Inf%282006%29003_en.pdf, accessed 3 January 2011.

NRK (2002) "Slik vi ser det" ["As We See It"], internal document, Oslo: NRK.

NRK (2003) "Sluttdokument. Bredbåndspilot for PULS, Barmeny, FBI og STYRK live" ["Final Document. Broadband pilot for PULS, Barmeny, FBI and STYRK live"], internal document, Oslo: NRK.

PHILIPSEN, HEIDI (2010) "Creative Cross-media Communications and Concepts", in: Heidi Philipsen, Lise Agerbæk and Bo Kampmann Walther (Eds), *Designing New Media. Learning, communication and innovation*, Aarhus: Academica, pp. 111–36.

PUIJK, ROEL (1990) *Virkeligheter i NRK: programproduksjon i fjernsynets opplysningsavdeling* [*Realities at the NRK: programme production in the television enlightment department*], PhD thesis, University of Oslo.

PUIJK, ROEL (2007) "Time and Timing in Cross-media Production: a case study from Norwegian television", in: Lekalos George, Chorianopoulos Konstantinos and Doukidis Georgios (Eds), *Interactive Digital Television: technologies and applications*, Hershey, PA: IGI Publishing, pp. 262–80.

SYVERTSEN, TRINE (2008) "Allmennkringkasting i krise—not!" [Public Service Broadcasting in Crisis—not!]", *Norsk Medietidsskrift* 3, pp. 211–29.

WIETEN, JAN (2000) "Breakfast Television: infotainers at Daybreak", in: Jan Wieten, Graham Murdock and Peter Dahlgren (Eds), *Television Across Europe*, London: Sage, pp. 175–97.

WRIGHT, KEVIN B., SPARKS, LISA and O'HAIR, H. DAN (2008) *Health Communication in the 21st Century*, Oxford: Blackwell Publishing.

YTREBERG, ESPEN (2001) *Programskjemaarbeid i NRK fjernsynet, beslutningsprosesser i et maktsentrum* [*Programme Timetable Work at NRK Television: decision-making processes in a centre of power*], Oslo: IMK, Oslo University.

HYPERTEXTUALITY AND REMEDIATION IN THE FASHION MEDIA
The case of fashion blogs

Agnès Rocamora

Since their appearance in the early noughties, fashion blogs have established themselves as a central platform for the circulation of fashion-related news and information. Often the creation of fashion outsiders, they have entered the mainstream fashion media, bringing to light the shifting nature of fashion journalism. The paper discusses the rise of the fashion blogosphere and the impact of new technologies on the mediation of fashion. Drawing on the notions of hypertextuality and remediation, it contributes to a recurring question in academic studies of digital culture: how new are new media? The paper looks at the ways fashion blogs define themselves in relation to traditional fashion journalism and the traditional fashion press. Their relation of co-dependence and mutual influence is unpacked to shed light on the contemporary field of the fashion media, and the role of new technologies in the production, circulation and consumption of fashion-related news.

Introduction

The 1990s saw the birth of blogs—a contraction of the terms web and log shortened into its present form by blogger Peter Merholz in 1999 (Rettberg, 2008, p. 26)—with their number soaring from 50 in 1999 (Kaye, 2007, p. 128) to 184 million in 2008 (Technorati, 2008). When in 2003 the genre—a regular, often daily, online posting of one's musings on a variety of topics—was appropriated by a young American woman to document her style, the first blog devoted to fashion—*nogoodforme*—was created. The fashion blogosphere, now constituted by both independent and corporate sites, has since rapidly expanded with Blogger.com evaluating in July 2010 at 2 million the number of blogs "with an industry of fashion" (Blogger, 2010).

Blogs are generally included in the category "new media", a term which, although in use since the 1960s, acquired high currency in the mid-1990s (Hui Kyong Chun, 2006, p. 1). This categorisation according to novelty has been debated by some, a question being: how new are new media? (see, for instance, Lister et al., 2009). As Fuery notes:

> the new is a complex intersection of issues requiring recognition at a moment in time. It is not always—perhaps very rarely—something that appears for the first time. The new is not always new at all. One of the ways in which the new gains its status is the transformation of vision that allows us to see the new, and the social consequences that allow us to evaluate this status of the new. (2009, p. 20)

In this paper, I revisit this issue of the newness of new media in the light of fashion blogs, to ask, then, how new are fashion blogs? Asking the question forces us to reflect on the particularities of blogs as opposed to the printed press, which also means gaining a better understanding of fashion discourse as articulated in the media. I first look at a key dimension of fashion blogs that constitutes a novel way of conveying fashion news, and a departure from the printed press: hypertextuality. I discuss "the transformation of vision" of fashion it has supported insisting on some of the changes fashion blogs have brought to the production, circulation and consumption of fashion discourse. Drawing on the work of Bolter and Grusin (2000 [1999]), I then discuss some of the ways blogs have refashioned old media, incorporating some of their defining traits in their own digital pages, to then look at how the print media have in turn refashioned themselves by capitalising on the success of blogs.

Before I do so, however, I present a brief overview of existing studies of the fashion media—all studies of print media, for no work has been produced yet on their digital counterparts (see, however, Rocamora and Bartlett, 2009)—as a way of situating the present study in the slowly growing body of work on the field of the fashion media.

Studying the Fashion Media

Studies of the fashion media constitute a corpus of work different from studies of women's and men's magazines (see, for instance, Crewe, 2003; Edwards, 1997; Hermes, 1997; Gough-Yates, 2003) in that it takes as its main subject of enquiry fashion images and/or fashion writing, in contrast with studies of women's and men's magazines, where fashion tends to be addressed only briefly.

Studies of the fashion media have privileged textual analysis. Amongst them is Barthes's (1990 [1967]) *The Fashion System*, where he appropriates Saussurian linguistics to analyse what he terms "written fashion", that is, fashion as put into words. Borrelli (1997) also looks at fashion writing. Deploring the little attention that has been given to written fashion, she focuses on an analysis of American *Vogue*'s "Point of View" section from 1968 to 1993. Moeran (2004, p. 35) also is concerned with written fashion, observing that "it is, indeed, the use of language that transforms clothing into *fashion*". Parting with Barthes and his endeavour to systematize the relation between the signifiers of written fashion, he sets out to look at the signifieds of fashion writing as occurring in the pages of Japanese fashion magazines. Where Barthes, Borrelli, and Moeran focus on fashion as written in magazines, Rocamora (2002) looks at newspapers in a comparative analysis of the British *The Guardian* and the French *Le Monde* to discuss the values attached to fashion in both.

Not only has written fashion been interrogated, but so have fashion images. Thus, Rabine (1994, p. 66) addresses the female body as represented in contemporary fashion magazines to argue that it is caught between "two bodies": a "confident, free, sexually powerful" body, and a subordinate and objectified one. Jobling (1999, p. 66) also concentrates on the discursive construction of the body of fashion photography, here *Vogue*, *The Face* and *Arena*, also insisting on the "complementarity" between words and images in the creation of meaning, a complementarity Rocamora (2009) considers to analyse the discursive construction of "Paris" and the reproduction of the Paris myth in the contemporary French fashion media.

Other authors have privileged neither words nor images, preferring instead to explore fashion journalism as a genre, often focusing on a particular title. Thus, Benhamou (1997) looks at the first publication to have reported on fashion, *Le Mercure* (1672–1791), discussing the changes in discourses on fashion and women triggered by a change of editors, whilst in her analysis of *La Presse*'s "Courrier de Paris" column (1836–39), Hahn (2005) discusses the rise, in the nineteenth century, of the fashion press as a commercial press. She argues that by the mid-1840s commerce and advertising had become a dominant feature of fashion magazines, with fashion constructed as a pleasurable experience addressed to "an emerging female consumer's subjectivity" (Hahn, 2005, p. 224). A specific title—*Vogue*—is also the object of study of a special issue of the journal *Fashion Theory* (Conekin and de la Haye, 2006), in which authors attend to different aspects of a range of national editions of the magazine, also privileging textual analysis over studies of production and consumption. Indeed, such studies are rare. Amongst them, however, is Moeran's analysis of four fashion magazines, where he addresses the issues of production and reception. He reminds the reader that fashion magazines "are both cultural products and commodities" (2006, p. 727) and that understanding them means interrogating not only their content but also their production and consumption. Attention to the latter also informs Lewis's study of "the lesbian gaze", where she discusses the "different forms of pleasure and identification activated" (1997, p. 92) in the reading of the fashion pages of a range of lifestyle magazines, including gay title *Diva*.

Finally, although McRobbie's (1998) *British Fashion Design* does not focus on the fashion media, her study is worth mentioning in that it includes a rare investigation of fashion journalists. Drawing on a Bourdieuian framework, she discusses the "fluid field of fashion journalism" (1998, p. 151) to insist on its lack of "serious discussion" of fashion. Bourdieuian theory also informs Entwistle and Rocamora's (2006) study of fashion journalism and fashion buying during London Fashion Week, an event, they argue, that materialises the field of fashion, its logic, structure and rules.

The fashion media, then, have proven to be a rich platform for the investigation of a broad range of issues. With the rise of fashion blogs this platform has widened, offering new opportunities for enquiry. In the remainder of this paper, I present some avenues for reflection on their role and specificity in the production and circulation of fashion discourse, starting—as a way also of engaging with the idea of the newness of new media mentioned earlier—with the idea of hypertextuality.

Hypertextual Fashion

The blogosphere is a hypertextual space. Hypertextuality has come to commonly refer to the electronic linking of a wide range of written texts and images, brought together in a constantly shifting configuration of networks—the sense used in this paper. A link—also called hyperlink—is one which allows Internet users to move through this configuration, jumping from one site to the other by clicking on the related signifier, usually a word displayed in a different colour, font, or style. As Lister et al. (2009, p. 26) remind us: "The prefix 'hyper' is derived from the Greek 'above, beyond, or outside'. Hence, hypertext has come to describe a text which provides a network of links to other texts that are 'outside, above and beyond' itself".

The term and essential principles of hypertextuality are not in themselves new. The concept, coined in 1965 by Theodor Nelson to refer to "a body of written or pictorial material interconnected in such a complex way that it could not conveniently be presented or represented on paper" (Nelson, cited in Rettberg, 2008, p. 45), was actually pioneered in the 1940s by Vannevar Bush and his idea for a machine, the memex, that would store and link texts together in a manner akin to the way, Bush argued, the human mind works: through associations and connections (Bush, 1945, cited in Landow, 1997).

This idea at the core of hypertextuality, that texts are inscribed in a complex formation of texts, a network, that they connect to other texts and exceed their limits, is also present, Landow (1997) reminds us, in the work of Foucault, Derrida, Barthes and Bakhtin. Indeed, the latter's thinking behind the notion of intertextuality (see Bakhtin, 1981)—a term coined later by Kristeva (1969)—finds a materialisation in the hypertext. Academic writing itself, with its annotations, footnotes, and endnotes is premised on the practice of a degree of hypertexuality (Landow, 1997, p. 4).

With the World Wide Web, however, and the blogosphere in particular, hypertextuality has proliferated. It is the very structure blogs rest on. When the reader clicks on a link, images (both still and moving), words and sounds can come at once on the screen, quickly succeeding and completing each other, making of fashion blogs, in contrast with magazines, texts in perpetual movement, always new, never-ending. Indeed, although a magazine is always caught in a wider discursive formation, this formation is kept outside of the material boundaries of the magazine. The reader's experience of the text, here the magazine, is contained by its materiality, the limits of its pages. The network of texts the magazine is inscribed in can be invoked but it can never be made fully present. With fashion blogs, however, a broad range of texts a post relates to can be made accessible by the "here and now" of the Web.

When accessing Tavi's *thestylerookie*'s 12 November 2010 post, for instance, I may decide to read the text from beginning to end without any interruption, or I may decide to click on the first link included in the post—the word "how"—which immediately takes me to an earlier post Tavi refers to in her entry. A further link at the bottom of the page can take me to the comments section where I will encounter other readers' reactions to the post, and possibly enter their own blogs to then move towards yet more diverse possibilities, across various historical times, textual genres and authorial voices, for blogs also always link to other websites.

Thus, the many sites, images and posts a blogger is referring to can appear on the screen at any time, taking over the text I had begun with, or rather turning it into a multi-layered text whose many threads lead me towards a potentially unending flow of images, words, and sounds. As Landow notes, hypertext "creates an open, open-bordered text, a text that cannot shut out other texts" (1997, p. 80); it "blurs the distinction between what is 'inside' and what is 'outside' a text", making "all the texts connected to a block of text collaborate with that text" (1997, p. 83).

The reading experience described above in the case of Tavi's blog parts with traditional, linear, modes of engagement with the printed text, for a hypertext is nonlinear, that is, "an object of verbal communication that is not simply one fixed sequence of letters, words, and sentences but one in which the words or sequence of words may differ from reading to reading because of the shape, conventions, or mechanisms of the text" (Aarseth, 1994, p. 51). Multiple entries and trajectories are possible, dependent on the reader's whims, making of the blogosphere a nonlinear space of interrelated textual nodes that can be read in any order, a feature that Manovich (2001, p. 77) also argues is characteristic of new media.

Although a magazine can be opened at any page it is still premised on the idea of a linear organisation of its content from page one to page x with a sequence of sections generally shared by all magazines: contents, editorial, features and other articles, fashion stories, beauty pages. With blogs, there is no beginning and no end, only a moment in one's encounter with a text. As Bolter observes: "Where printed genres are linear or hierarchical, hypertext is multiple and associative. Where a printed text is static, a hypertext responds to the reader's touch" (2001, p. 42). The centre can always be decentred; "it never tyrannizes other aspects of the network in the way a printed text does" (Landow, 1997, p. 85).

Thus, linking is one of the key traits distinguishing hypertexts from print technology (Landow, 1994, p. 6). Where fashion magazines never refer to any other magazines—clearly implying their independence from the rest of print publications and a status as the one authoritative fashion source—linking "produces a network organization" (Landow, 1994, p. 24) whereby fashion blogs constantly relate to other blogs, be it through directly linking to them in a post or by including them in their blogroll, the list of blogs and the related links bloggers favour.

Rhizomatic Fashion

Hypertextuality brings to mind the Deleuzian notion of rhizome, a concept helpful for reflecting on the structure of the Web (see also Landow, 1997, pp. 38–42), and of the fashion blogosphere in particular. A rhizome, following Deleuze and Guattari (1980)—whose own *A Thousand Plateaus* constitutes a "print proto-hypertext" (Landow, 1997, p. 38)—is an a-centred system that is always changing and made up of units—so-called "plateaus"—that are linked together in a non-linear way, in a network formation (Deleuze and Guattari, 1980, p. 32). "Plateaus can be read in any order and linked to any other plateaus", to which they are joined by what Deleuze and Guattari call "lines" (1980, p. 33). In the blogosphere they are the links that allow Internet users the constant movement from one page to the next, from one site to the next. Indeed, the blogosphere, like the rhizomes Deleuze and Guattari discuss, is a space in a permanent state of becoming, never fixed. Its plateaus are the many pages blogs and the blogosphere are made up of, and which, in a perpetual movement of displacement and replacement, open on to a limitless number of sites and signs that allow the reader to be always on the move within a continuously changing textual space.

A rhizome by virtue of being never fixed is "a short memory, or an anti-memory" (Deleuze and Guattari, 1980, p. 32), a state that aptly defines fashion with its constant quest for, and production of, the new. In that respect the rhizomatic structure of the blogosphere aptly lends itself to fashion. The latter's logic of renewal of clothes and styles is mirrored in the rapid renewal of posts and the endless replacing of one site by another that links enable. This is a logic of replacement that, as Bolter and Grusin (2000 [1999], pp. 43–4) observe, is also that of the Web: each new page takes over another *ad infinitum*.

The short memory of blogs draws attention to the idea of temporality and the role of time in the definition of the blogosphere, and the fashion blogosphere in particular. Time, Bauman argues,

> is no longer cyclical (time), but not linear either because events and actions succeed each other randomly rather than in a straight line, and seem to change direction on their way . . . Nowadays we are held together by short-term projects, moving constantly from one project to another—what model of time can be derived from such experience? I suggest a "pointillist" time. Much like canvasses of Sisley, Seurat or Signac, which consist

of points only, no broad brushstrokes and no continuities. That is, though, as far as the analogy goes, because in pointillist paintings you have pre-designed and in-built meaningful configurations. However, in liquid modern life configurations are not given beforehand. They are just randomly scattered points: episodes, fragments—but of what whole? Living through the moment, one point in time, you cannot be sure to what configuration you will eventually belong when scrutinized retrospectively. (Bauman, cited in Deuze, 2007a, p. 673)

Blogs clearly articulate and feed into this conception of time, a time made of fragments, of a succession of brief moments: the moments made of one's encounter with a succession of interlinked Web pages and sites; of written texts, still images, sounds and videos; and of the snapshots of life bloggers narrate in their posts.

Time as articulated in the blogosphere, a new time of interconnected *points*, time as "a fluid, networked entity" (Fuery, 2009, p. 31), echoes time as articulated in the field of fashion. Indeed, where once fashion time was neatly paced by the twice-yearly collections and the monthly publications of glossies, now fashion time has accelerated, fragmented into a series of moments that have shattered its orderly pace. Pre-collection, pre-fall, cruise, resort, high summer, and Christmas collections are all new moments in this restructured fashion time, a time now ruled by the imperative of immediacy, which Tomlinson (2007) has identified as constitutive of today's "culture of speed". Indeed, where in the field of fashion newness was once restricted to a twice-yearly event, it is now a permanent present, a situation the Internet has fed off and sustained. As Lovink puts it: "Technology such as the Internet lives on the principle of permanent change . . . The 'tyranny of the new' rule" (2008, p. xi). Thus "the goal of 'immediacy'", he argues, has become "a professional media value" (p. 90). Witness the live streaming of fashion shows, events once the preserve of an elite given the privilege to see the collections months ahead of their appearance in print media and in shops. Witness also the "what's new", "just in", and "new arrivals" sections of online fashion shops, in which collections are constantly updated. Bolter and Grusin (2000 [1999], p. 43) argue that "replacement is the essence of hypertext" and the Web "an exercise in replacement", a comment also true of the very content of websites in online fashion.

In their constant, often daily, updating of sites with new posts, fashion blogs feed into this tyranny of the new, constructing, more than any other media, fashion as transient, passing, already gone. The flow of posts replicates the flow of goods, with the posts and goods of today promised to rapid take-over, out-fashioned by newer arrivals that freeze time, and fashion, online into a perpetual present. As Virilio (1991, p. 14) notes, "Chronological and historical time, time that passes is replaced by a time that exposes itself instantaneously". "It is a pure computer time", which "helps construct a permanent present, an unbounded, timeless intensity" (1991, p. 15).

The transience of blogs contrasts with the lasting quality of glossies with many often kept by their readers like books on bookshelves (see Lynge-Jorlen, 2010). Thus, where Bolter talks about "the qualities of the computer" as being "flexibility, interactivity, speed of distribution", he defines that of print as "stability and authority" (2001, p. 3), a stability then, which contrasts with the un-fixity of hypertexts such as blogs.

Deleuze and Guattari (1980) encapsulate rhizomes' state of short memory and constant change in the notion of nomadism, which translates into the digital wandering and flânerie often constitutive of one's virtual movement through the Web. Within the fashion blogosphere, this flânerie brings to mind another type of flânerie at the heart of fashion: shopping. Where In Real Life (or IRL as off-line life is also called on the Web) consumers move from one shop to the next, wander around and *browse*—a term that aptly captures the link between shopping and digital deambulation—in the fashion blogosphere they move from one site to the next.

> Instead of Parisian streets, shopping windows, and the faces of the passers-by, the virtual flâneur travels through virtual streets, highways, and planes of data; the eroticism of a split-second virtual affair with a passer-by of the opposite sex is replaced with the excitement of locating and opening a particular file or zooming into the virtual object. Like Baudelaire's flâneur, the virtual flâneur is happiest on the move, clicking from one object to another, traversing room after room, level after level, data volume after data volume. (Manovich, 2001, pp. 274–5)

Flicking through a magazine is akin to flânerie too. However, shopping remains imaginary, a distant project. With blogs it becomes real, thanks to the many links that take readers straight to a digital point-of-sale, triggering and responding to the desires of "the society of immediate satisfaction" (Laïdi, 2000, p. 115). Laïdi notes "the logic of never-ending choices to be made on the spot" with which contemporary individuals are confronted (2000, p. 115). They are "submerged with possibilities. But these possibilities are in open access. They are here. They are no longer a horizon" (2000, p. 115). The Web has intensified this collapsing of the there/later into the here/now. Thus, in the fashion blogosphere, fashion news can immediately be conducive to the act of buying, a process which also draws attention to the role of discourse in the circulation of fashionable goods and, more particularly to that of bloggers as intermediaries between readers as consumers and fashion companies.

Digital hypermedia, Bolter and Grusin (2000 [1999], p. 53) write, "seek the real by multiplying mediation so as to create a feeling of fullness, a satiety of experience, which can be taken as reality". In the fashion blogosphere the profusion of pages, words and images also evokes that of the goods encountered whilst shopping In Real Life. The profusion of digital signs echoes the abundance pertaining to fashion, once again fittingly matching its logic and serving its interest.

Decentred Fashion

A hypertext is a space where margins can be brought to the fore. It "reveals differences that turn out to be, no longer, inevitabilities and invisibilities" (Landow, 1997, p. 87). So does the fashion blogosphere. Objects, subjects which, in a print magazine have been left outside its pages, excluded from its discourse, can in the fashion blogosphere become visible. Indeed, far from simply recycling or appropriating stories already covered by the traditional media, bloggers often generate new, alternative content, as Bruns (2005) notes of news blogs. Bloggers are not mere users of the Internet, they are producers too ("produsers" as Bruns, 2005 puts it), active participants in the creation of news, or citizen-journalists, an idea I return to later.

In print media the showcasing of designers is ruled by advertising: editorial pages have to feature the brands that have earned titles some income by advertising in their pages. Although numerous independent blogs have started monetizing their sites by way of banner ads, such ads are few, leaving bloggers more control over the content of their sites. A platform can be given to designers whose lack of economic capital has excluded them from the media, a space crucial to success in the field of fashion. The popular Susie Lau, for instance, whose blog, at the time of writing, does not feature any ads—except for the mention of two independent fashion titles called *Dazed Digital* and *Another*—has made reporting on the margins of the field of fashion a crucial element of her popularity. In a 6 November 2010 post for instance, she discusses the work of the little-known Anna Jazewitsch, whose "first graduate collection . . . entitled 'Oftimica' was a geometric and structured affair". By clicking on the words "Anna Jazewitsch" and "Oftimica" the reader is given direct access to the designer's blog and to some images of her collection, some of which are also featured on Lau's blog. She says: "I do get designers who contact me about their work, to get features on the blog, and I'm happy that they're approaching bloggers as well, because they recognise that it's a different platform and that their clothes aren't always going to be called in for magazines" (Lau, cited in Hanssen and Nitzsche, 2010, p. 15).

On her *punkyb*, the French Géraldine Grisey, another highly popular fashion blogger, often features little-known names such as Heimstone, a company launched in 2007 and embraced by independent bloggers. When in 2008 Grisey "introduced" it to her readers by way of a video, many enthused about the label:

- "Superb discovery show of Heimstone." (steph, 3 July 2008)
- "I didn't know Heimstone and the clothes look really cool." (littlejujube, 3 July 2008)
- "I knew Heimstone a little . . . but seeing the look of the two designers makes me feel like trying the whole look." (clémentine, 3 July 2008)
- "HEIMSTONE, a label that will quickly grow." (Sophia 3 July 2010).[1]

Decentring also informs the fashion blogosphere in its construction of a network of fashion cities. Where the field of fashion is dominated by Paris, London, New York and Milan, the cities the printed press almost exclusively focuses on, in the fashion blogosphere, these cities are only a few in a wider topography of fashion locales. This is particularly evident in the case of street fashion blogs, blogs that report on fashion as seen on the streets of various cities across the world (see, for instance, *thesartorialist*; *dublinstyle*; *sofiastreetstyle*). When accessing such blogs, readers enter a network of cities that covers a wide territory, and where no particular cities dominate others, but each is just a node, a moment, in a larger formation. Centres in hypertexts, we saw earlier, are always transient; "As readers move through a web of network of texts, they continually shift the center— and hence the focus or organizing principle—of their investigation and experience" (Landow, 1997, p. 36). As a new fashion blog replaces another to which it is linked, becoming the new centre of attention of the user, so, too, do the cities linked to change, endlessly reconfiguring the fashion map.

When the reader logs on *stylefromtokyo*, for instance, Tokyo becomes the city at the heart of the fashion blogosphere. The "world friend" section then allows her to move to Amsterdam by clicking on *DamStyle*, which can then take her to Lisbon with *fashionstreet-lisboa* and from there to Moscow or Warsaw, and so on towards more destinations. In contrast with print fashion magazines, the fashion blogosphere allows a wide range of places to become visible, extending the boundaries of the geography of fashion. As Manovich (2001, p. 333) observes, with new media "cultural possibilities that were previously in the background, on the periphery, come into the center".

In the fashion blogosphere, the geography of fashion has been decentred but so has the geography of fashion taste makers. Indeed, where until recently the sole influential fashion media intermediaries were those fashion journalists, stylists and photographers linked to established titles such as *Vogue*, *Harpers* or *Elle* and avant-garde niche magazines such as *Purple* or *Pop*, the rise of the fashion blogosphere has resulted in the coming to prominence and the growing influence of individuals who had no institutional affiliation to the field of fashion when they started their blog. The French Géraldine Dormoy, of *cafe-mode*, writes that her blog "aims at making you share my personal point-of-view on fashion. Not really a fashionista, I consider myself more passionately eager for info" (*blogs.lexpress.fr/cafe-mode*, "L'Auteur"). Lau was working in digital media when she started *stylebubble* and now defines herself as "a freelance writer, full-time blogger and dabbling in all sorts of projects. I'm still a fashion-outsider" (Lau, 2010), whilst one of the most famous fashion bloggers, the aforementioned Tavi, is a 14-year-old girl who still attends school in America.

The popularity of such bloggers has been greeted with intense criticism by fashion insiders. *ES Magazine* cites a fashion director:

> I complimented Tavi on her skirt and she told me it was vintage Prada. I said, "It's not vintage, it's from the collection five seasons ago". She was astonished that I remembered it—but of course I remembered it. This is my world. I remember everything. These bloggers, they don't understand about the history. (27 August 2010, p. 14)

Similarly, according to Robert Johnson (cited in Mesure, 2010), associate editor of men's magazine *GQ*, bloggers "don't have the critical faculties to know what's good and what's not". As Bridget Foley (2010), of print magazine *WWD*, also puts it, implicitly contrasting traditional journalists' informed knowledge (such as those working for her title) with bloggers' lack of it:

> Are we in competition with bloggers? Absolutely. I'd like to think that knowledge of what you are writing is still considered important. I'd like to think that some bed of knowledge about a designer and the history of the house remain important. I think we are starting to feel a little backlash toward the whole immediacy of things.

Such statements must be seen in the light of what some have argued is a crisis of the "expert paradigm" (Walsh, cited in Jenkins, 2006, p. 52). Jenkins puts it thus: "Walsh argues that our traditional assumptions about expertise are breaking down or at least being transformed by the more open-ended processes of communication in cyberspace" (2006, p. 52). Deuze (2007b, p. 112) talks about a "liquefaction of the boundaries between different fields, disciplines, practices, and categories that used to define what media work was". In the field of journalism, including fashion journalism, this is compounded by the absence of official credentials, the lack of an established educational trajectory and that of "professional boundaries" (Carlson, 2007, p. 265). As a result, "the line between journalist and non-journalist is perpetually blurry and dynamic" (Carlson, 2007, p. 265), a blurriness that has paved the way for the concept of citizen-journalism, mentioned earlier, and that has allowed independent fashion bloggers to enter the field of fashion and claim legitimacy.

Hypertext "does not permit a tyrannical, univocal voice" (Landow, 1997, p. 36). In the fashion blogosphere this means a decentring of the voice of traditional fashion experts, print fashion journalists, whose authority has been displaced by the shifting into focus of other voices such as that of bloggers. Thus, "The newness of new media", Fuery (2009, p. 21) writes, "is not necessarily its technical inventions, it is the transformation of vision that affects how we make sense of, and even actually make, the world and its social orders". The newness of fashion blogs partly resides in the shifting approach to fashion they have conveyed, a fashion that is not centred on established designers and key cities only, on the voice of the traditional expert, but that echoes the openness and the decentredness pertaining to blogs' hypertextuality.

Fashion Remediation

However, Bolter and Grusin (2000 [1999]), drawing on the work of McLuhan (1967 [1964]), remind us that new media may well transform established visions, but they never totally supersede old media, for a new medium always appropriates some of the characteristics of an older medium. Where McLuhan (1967 [1964], pp. 15–16) argued that what characterises all media is that "the 'content' of any medium is always another medium", Bolter and Grusin (2000 [1999], p. 15) note that "What is new about new media comes from the particular ways in which they refashion older media and the ways in which older media refashion themselves to answer the challenges of new media". They call this process "remediation", a process whereby both new and old media represent and refashion each other.

Thus, the Web "is the remediation of print" (Bolter, 2001, p. 42), a process clearly at play between fashion blogs and print magazines. Bloggers, for instance, regularly borrow visuals taken from the printed press to illustrate a post, when they're not directly writing about and celebrating the visual in question. As Bolter (2001, p. 23) reminds us, remediation involves "homage". On 13 November 2010, for instance, Marie of kingdomofstyle congratulates Harper's Bazaar "on such a captivating golden Christmas cover!". She adds, having reproduced the cover: "At Christmas . . . I want to feel the magic and the fantasy that only a big glossy cover can convey. When I first saw this cover I actually gasped." Marie's enthusiasm for Harper's Bazaar lends support to Rettberg's argument that "While use of the Internet is clearly increasing, this does not seem to be at the cost of other media usage, which remains stable. It seems likely that some media are used simultaneously" (2008, p. 45). Jaja Hargreaves, of july-stars, for instance, states that she reads

> a disconcertingly enormous amount of fashion blogs and magazines. Anything from French VOGUE, JALOUSE, PURPLE, SELF SERVICES, LULA, RUSSH, ENCENS, FANTASTIC MAN, MONOCLE, POP and NYLON to the more conventional fashion publications like ELLE, UK VOGUE, GRAZIA, and the style supplement of the FINANCIAL TIMES.
> (Hargreaves, cited in Hanssen and Nitzsche, 2010, p. 44)

Similarly, in her blogroll, Anabelle (fashionpirate) links to the magazines she reads, including Pop, Vogue Nippon, and Another Magazine.

Fashion blogs also remediate print magazines by way of some of the poses personal fashion bloggers adopt when putting themselves into the frame of the computer screen, poses that evoke those of models in glossies. A recurring trope of fashion photography, for instance, are images of a model photographed from behind whilst walking away from the camera. Evans and Thornton (1989, p. 104) call it "the disappearing woman" (see also Rocamora, 2009, Chap. 6). The popular Rumi of Fashiontoast and Karla of Karlascloset regularly utilise this type of shot. On 9 June 2010, for instance, Karla is shown crossing a zebra crossing in a New York street, a visual evocative of Williams Klein's famous 1960 photograph of two models in Rome, the black and white lines of the zebra they are crossing a striking echo, as in the case of Karla's picture, of a pattern on their dresses. On 8 September 2010, Rumi is shown standing in the middle of a busy city road, her post reading: "I decided that I like the backs of things more than the fronts of things". In images set in city streets more generally the bloggers are often shown taking long strides, another trope of fashion photography, and one that—like much contemporary fashion imagery— constructs the street as a space of fashionable display (see Rocamora, 2009; Rocamora and O'Neill, 2008).

In many posts bloggers are shown in movement, albeit frozen in time by the camera, but they are also featured at rest, on the street, often standing against a city wall, in a seemingly unelaborated pose reminiscent of the straight-up, a genre of fashion photography that came to prominence in the early 1980s in the British style press (see Rocamora and O'Neill, 2008), and which bloggers—street fashion bloggers in particular— have capitalised on. Indeed, British style magazine *i-D*'s first issue in August 1980 featured a spread entitled "straight-up" showing full-length portraits of ordinary people seen on the street, a city wall as prop. In the 1990s this take on style became the *raison d'être* of print magazines such as *FRUiTS*, *STREET* and *TUNE*, exclusively devoted to fashion as "found" on city streets, whilst also being regularly mobilised in the fashion pages of various other glossies and newspapers. Thus, when fashion blogs such as *thesartorialist* and *facehunter* took up the genre it had already been a regular feature of the printed press.

The blogs, however, have given it a new visibility, to the point that it has become tightly associated with the fashion blogosphere as if no other media before it had represented it. Indeed, independent fashion blogs are often seen as the one space where real fashion, fashion as worn by real people, can be seen. In April 2006, a reader tells Susie Lau: "i'm so sick of fashion magazines which are almost always overpriced boring commercials (except purple. i love purple). i'm so much more engaged by what real people think and wear. so thank you and keep up the good work" (Sarah). French blogger Betty (2008) puts it thus: "people love to be inspired by real people and also they see that there is fashion in real life and not only in the magazines", whilst—according to Eirik Slyngstad and Andreas Schjønhaug of *thestreethearts*—"blogs are often started by ordinary people like you and me, and that makes them more real and effective for a large number of readers than magazines do" (cited in Hanssen and Nitzsche, 2010, p. 73). The inside cover of Scott Schuman's 2009 book *The Sartorialist*, the print version of his eponymous blog, a phenomenon I return to later, reads: "His now-famous and much-loved blog, the sartorialist.com, is his showcase for the wonderful and varied sartorial tastes of real people across the globe".

Such claims to the real are re-enforced by visions and representations of the Web as an unmediated space, which has consolidated the association of street fashion/fashion blogosphere, thereby somewhat occulting the significance of print media in popularising the genre. Indeed, the Web, as Bolter and Grusin (2000 [1999], p. 200) argue, "rivals" all media "by promising greater immediacy". This is "immediacy" in terms of rapidity, as discussed earlier, but also immediacy in terms of authenticity and truth, "in the name of the real", for immediacy also refers to a seemingly non-mediated relation to an image or representation (2000, p. 65). As Tomlinson (2007, p. 99) observes, the goal of immediacy is premised on the idea "that mediated material should be delivered both rapidly and with the rather illusive quality of 'liveness'". Bolter puts it thus:

claims of immediacy are what govern the circulation and consumption of new media products. What producers of new media artefacts are selling are experiences of immediacy. They engage in an ongoing struggle to define or redefine immediacy or authenticity of experience in a way that particularly enhances their own products. Often the immediacy of the product is expressed as transparency: you can see through the product to the ostensible reality behind it. (2001, pp. 70–1)

The idea that street fashion blogs present fashion as it is, unmediated, is reinforced by the absences of words and writing, which distinguishes such blogs from other fashion blogs. Indeed, the "value of immediacy", Tomlinson argues, translates into "the removal of symbolic barriers and conventions (the newsreader's desk) which signal the media as *mediators*, rather than as, say, everyday acquaintances and interlocutors" (2007, p. 100). In most independent fashion blogs this is articulated in writing through the adoption of a casual, often confessional tone, for as Tomlinson also notes, the value of immediacy informs a style of media presentation "which favours informality, direct conversational modes of address, and a certain assumption of intimacy (sometimes even of ironic complicity) with the audience" (2007, p. 100). In street fashion blogs this is expressed through the privileging of images over words, as if the former spoke for themselves, with no need for the mediating work of the blogger's words. In his book, Schuman puts it thus: "I like people to draw their own conclusions, to find their own inspiration, without the influence of a guiding hand. That's why you won't find a lot of text in this book". This is an explanation, one can assume, that is equally applicable to the minimally captioned blog.

This claim to immediacy as unmediated reality is supported by the claim to immediacy as rapidity discussed earlier, for images of street fashion in fashion blogs are images of the t/here and now, they are the present "reality" of city life, even more real, even more alive, than they are "now".

The street fashion images many blogs have championed have in turn become an influence on the printed press. Indeed, as mentioned earlier, remediation is a two-way process: new media borrow from and refashion old media, which in turn refashion new media to absorb some of their characteristics in their pages. Thus, "Newer media do not necessarily supersede older media because the process of reform and refashioning is mutual" (Bolter and Grusin, 2000 [1999], p. 259). The British *Grazia*, for instance, has a section entitled "Style Hunter", which clearly brings to mind the street-style blog *facehunter*. Like many other glossies its website also hosts a range of blogs, now a common tool of corporate fashion.

Print magazines have also remediated fashion blogs by incorporating the latter's visuals and take on fashion in their own pages. This is the case, for instance, of the British *Elle*'s "Show Me Your Wardrobe" section. The section is the print version of Jackie Dixon's eponymous blog, started in 2008. Some of the pictures she takes for it appear in *Elle*, and vice versa, with the British magazine also inviting readers to explore the blog by way of a "for more, see showmeyourwardrobe.com", and with the blog announcing in its digital pages the release of the newest *Elle* issue that features it. This collaboration between blog and print medium draws attention to a defining trait of today's media culture, that of convergence, or "the flow of content across multiple platforms and networks" (Jenkins, 2006, p. 274). As Bolter also notes:

in the late age of print, we see the move to heterogeneity and hybrid forms, including on-demand printing from digital databases, printed books and magazines that refer to

Web sites, Web sites that preview and sell books, and so-called "information appliances" that combine the characteristics of books, notebooks, and calendars ... All such hybrids work against closure, because both in form and function they refer their users to other texts, devices, or media forms. (2001, p. 79)

Amongst the hybrid forms Bolter evokes features the putting into print of a blog such as Dixon's, and so do the book by-products of popular blogs. Indeed, 2009 saw the publication of Schuman's *The Sartorialist*, followed in 2010 by Rodic's *Face Hunter*, both made of images previously published in the blogs. This remediation of fashion blogs into books is part of a wider trend that has seen the release of books based on blogs, with the "blooker prize" aptly capturing the proliferation of this new hybrid form.

Conclusion

The blogosphere is changing rapidly. It is only by paying careful attention to its many texts, producers and consumers that current shifts in practices of media production, representation and consumption will be identified and understood, shedding light on the shifting nature of the contemporary field of fashion media. In this paper, I have started addressing some of these shifts, shifts in the representation of fashion, for instance, shifts in the coming to dominance of new taste makers. Thus, I have paid attention to some of the defining traits of fashion blogs, to their novelty in contrast with print media—also arguing, however, with Bolter and Grusin (2000 [1999]) that new and old media, rather than excluding each other, feed into each other. This process forces us to see their relation as one of co-dependence rather than pure rivalry, as one that can lead towards constructive redefinition of each genre rather than the annihilation of the one by the other, contrary to the many apocalyptic statements on new media.

In the present article I have focused on blogs as texts, privileging a textual analysis of fashion blogs. However, as mentioned in the first section, studies of the fashion media should not limit themselves to such an approach, as understanding media products means understanding not only their textuality but their modes of production and consumption, too. Such a project falls outside the remits of this article but it is hoped that it will be undertaken in future times, through, for instance, ethnographies of fashion blogging and blog audiences. Only then will the full extent of the changes currently taking place in the fashion media be captured, shedding light on the shifting nature of the contemporary field of journalism and the redefinition of practices of production and consumption within.

NOTE

1.   In quoting from blogs, grammar, spelling and stylistic choices such as abbreviations and capitalisation are reproduced unchanged.

REFERENCES

AARSETH, ESPEN J. (1994) "Nonlinearity and Literary Theory", in: George P. Landow (Ed.), *Hyper/Text/Theory*, Baltimore, MA: Johns Hopkins University Press, pp. 51–86.
BAKHTIN, MIKHAIL M. (1981) *The Dialogic Imagination*, Austin: University of Texas Press.
BARTHES, ROLAND (1990 [1967]) *The Fashion System*, Berkeley: University of California Press.

BENHAMOU, REED (1997) "Fashion in the Mercure", *Eighteenth-Century Studies* 31(1), pp. 27–43.

BETTY (2008) "'Press' Section, interview", *Express Australia*, August, http://www.leblogdebetty.com/, accessed 21 December 2009.

BLOGGER (2010) http://www.blogger.com/profile-find.g?t =j&ind =FASHION, accessed 9 July 2010.

BOLTER, JAY DAVID (2001) *Writing Space*, New York: Routledge.

BOLTER, JAY DAVID and GRUSIN, RICHARD (2000 [1999]) *Remediation: understanding new media*, Cambridge: MIT Press.

BORRELLI, LAIRD (1997) "Dressing Up and Talking About It", *Fashion Theory* 1(3), pp. 247–60.

BRUNS, AXEL (2005) *Gatewatching*, New York: Peter Lang.

BUSH, VANNEVAR (1945) "As We May Think", *The Atlantic Monthly* 176(1), pp. 101–8.

CARLSON, MATT (2007) "Blogs and Journalistic Authority", *Journalism Studies* 8(2), pp. 264–79.

CONEKIN, BECKY and DE LA HAYE, AMY (Eds) (2006) "Vogue", *Fashion Theory* 10(1/2).

CREWE, BEN (2003) *Representing Men*, Oxford: Berg.

DELEUZE, GILLES and GUATTARI, FELIX (1980) *Mille Plateaux* [*A Thousand Plateaus*], Paris: Minuit.

DEUZE, MARK (2007a) "Journalism in Liquid Modern Times: an interview with Zygmunt Bauman", *Journalism Studies* 8(4), pp. 671–9.

DEUZE, MARK (2007b) *Media Work*, Cambridge: Polity.

EDWARDS, TIM (1997) *Men in the Mirror*, London: Cassell.

ENTWISTLE, JOANNE and ROCAMORA, AGNES (2006) "The Field of Fashion Materialized", *Sociology* 40(4), pp. 735–51.

EVANS, CAROLINE and THORNTON, MINNA (1989) *Women and Fashion*, London: Quartet Books.

FOLEY, BRIDGET (2010) "100 Years of WWD", *The New York Times*, 1 November, http://runway.blogs.nytimes.com/2010/11/01/100-years-of-wwd/, accessed 9 November 2010.

FUERY, KELLI (2009) *New Media*, New York: Palgrave.

GOUGH-YATES, ANNA (2003) *Understanding Women's Magazines*, London: Routledge.

HAHN, HAZEL (2005) "Fashion Discourses in Fashion Magazines and Madame de Girardin's Lettres parisiennes in July Monarchy France" (1830–1848), *Fashion Theory* 9(2), pp. 205–28.

HANSSEN, KIRSTIN and NITZSCHE, FELICIA (2010) *Fashion Blogs*, Zwolle: d'Jonge Hond.

HERMES, JOKE (1997) *Reading Women's Magazines*, Cambridge: Polity.

HUI KYONG CHUN, WENDY (2006) "Introduction", in: Wendy Hui Kyong Chun and Thomas Keenan (Eds), *New Media, Old Media*, New York: Routledge, pp. 1–10.

JENKINS, JAJA (2006) *Convergence Culture*, New York: New York University Press.

JOBLING, PAUL (1999) *Fashion Spreads*, London: Routledge.

KAYE, BARBARA (2007) "Blog Use Motivations", in: Mark Tremayne (Ed.), *Blogging, Citizenship, and the Future of the Media*, New York: Routledge, pp. 127–48.

KRISTEVA, JULIA (1969) *Séméiôtiké*, Paris: Seuil.

LAIDI, ZAKI (2000) *Le Sacre du Présent*, Paris: Flammarion.

LANDOW, GEORGE P. (1994) "What's a Critic to Do?", in: George P. Landow (Ed.), *Hyper/Text/Theory*, Baltimore, MD: Johns Hopkins University Press, pp. 1–48.

LANDOW, GEORGE P. (1997) *Hypertext 2.0*, Baltimore, MD: Johns Hopkins University Press.

LAU, SUSIE (2010) http://www.stylebubble.co.uk/style_bubble/faq.html, accessed 18 December 2010.

LEWIS, REINA (1997) "Looking Good: the lesbian gaze and fashion imagery", *Feminist Review* 55, pp. 92–109.

LOVINK, GEERT (2008) *Zero Comments*, London: Routledge.

LISTER, MARTIN, DOVEY, JON, GIDDINGS, SETH, GRANT, IAIN and KELLY, KIERAN (2009) *New Media: a critical introduction*, New York: Routledge.

LYNGE-JORLEN, ANE (2010) *"Reading Niche Fashion Magazines"*, PhD thesis, University of the Arts London.

MANOVICH, LEV (2001) *The Language of New Media*, Cambridge, MA: MIT Press.

MCLUHAN, MARSHALL (1967 [1964]) *Understanding Media*, London: Sphere.

MCROBBIE, ANGELA (1998) *British Fashion Design*, London: Routledge.

MESURE, SUSIE (2010) "Fluff Flies as Fashion Writers Pick a Cat Fight with Blogger", http://www.independent.co.uk/life-style/fashion/news/fluff-flies-as-fashion-writers-pick-a-cat-fight-with-bloggers-1884539.html, accessed 6 March 2011.

MOERAN, BRIAN (2004) "A Japanese Discourse of Fashion and Taste", *Fashion Theory* 8(1), pp. 35–62.

MOERAN, BRIAN (2006) "More Than Just a Fashion Magazine", *Current Sociology* 54(5), pp. 725–44.

RABINE, LESLIE (1994) "A Woman's Two Bodies", in: Shari Benstock and Suzanne Ferriss (Eds), *On Fashion*, New Brunswick, NJ: Rutgers University Press, pp. 59–75.

RETTBERG, JILL WALKER (2008) *Blogging*, Cambridge: Polity.

ROCAMORA, AGNES (2002) "Le Monde's Discours de Mode", *French Cultural Studies* 13(1), pp. 83–98.

ROCAMORA, AGNES (2009) *Fashioning the City*, London: I. B. Tauris.

ROCAMORA, AGNES and BARTLETT, DJURDJA (2009) "Blogs de mode", *Sociétés* 104(2), pp. 105–14.

ROCAMORA, AGNES and O'NEILL, ALISTAIR (2008) "Fashioning the Street", in: Shinkle Eugenie (Ed.), *Fashion as Photograph*, London: I. B. Tauris, pp. 185–99.

RODIC, YVAN (2010) *Face Hunter*, London: Thames and Hudson.

SCHUMAN, SCOTT (2009) *The Sartorialist*, London: Penguin.

TECHNORATI (2008) "State of the Blogosphere 2008", http://technorati.com/blogging/feature/state-of-the-blogosphere-2008/, accessed 27 October 2008.

TOMLINSON, JOHN (2007) *The Culture of Speed*, London: Sage.

VIRILIO, PAUL (1991) *Lost Dimension*, New York: Semiotext(e).

SERVICE JOURNALISM AS COMMUNITY EXPERIENCE
Personal technology and personal finance at *The New York Times*

Nikki Usher

This paper looks at service journalism and its evolution as a community platform through blog comments and social media through a case study of two sections of The New York Times' *business section: the personal finance section and the personal technology section. The paper proceeds through a discussion of the importance of networked journalism, and relies on in-depth qualitative interviews with the journalists closest to the decisions being made about how service journalism at the Times becomes a participatory experience for readers. The article argues that a Web 2.0 world facilitates a community experience that changes the one-to-many relationship that journalists have with their readers; instead, journalists make decisions about coverage and engage in conversations with readers in response to this new relationship with readers.*

Introduction

At a time when so-called "serious" business journalism has been faulted by scholars, the public and academics for failing to anticipate the global financial crisis, there is a "softer" side of business journalism that has comfortably been on the rise. This form of business journalism, which is often categorized under the umbrella of "service journalism," serves to help people make sense of consumer affairs. This article looks at two specific forms of service journalism, personal finance journalism and personal technology journalism, through a case study of *The New York Times*.

This article argues that this news has changed in the Web 2.0 era as the service journalists become facilitators of an online community focused around the news that they cover. Furthermore, the community surrounding personal technology and personal finance news helps suggest and direct coverage at *The New York Times*. In short, news you can use has in a much more literal sense become news the user/reader wants to know, now.

First, the article provides a discussion of service journalism and a theoretical breakdown of the ideas surrounding journalism and community through the framework of networked journalism. Then the specific relationship between business news and service journalism is discussed. The article explores how personal finance and personal technology have evolved within business news, and more specifically, their development at *The New York Times*. It then turns to an empirical analysis of service journalism at *The New York Times*, relying on interviews with journalists covering and editing both personal technology and personal finance journalism to show the changing dynamic between journalists and audiences.

Service Journalism and Community Foundations

Service journalism has been a much over-looked area of scholarship in journalism studies. Not to be confused with public service journalism, service journalism can best be thought of as journalism that "represents the development of a hybrid social identity—part citizen, part consumer, part client—that is oriented to resolving the problems of everyday life" (Eide and Knight, 1999, p. 527). Eide and Knight go on to talk about service journalism as having a pattern of problem and resolution. Service journalism focuses on an individual issue or an answer, and should be considered more than just a simple throwaway section of news. Instead, as Eide and Knight argue, service journalism is connected more broadly with issues of the public sphere. Service journalism may help coalesce social movements and arm advocacy groups with information. One example is the role personal finance journalism has played in the wake of the financial collapse with regard to questions about how to deal with mortgages.

Significantly, as Hanitzsch et al. note, service journalism represents a fundamental shift in the "social function of the news" (2005, p. 109) with journalism moving away from being an information distributor to helping select relevant information. Similarly, as Hartley (2000) contends, "softer journalism" or what might be seen as "smiling journalism" can be useful to public knowledge because it runs contrary to the idea of journalism of opposition, or of journalism as negativity. At its core, service journalism is a distinct form of news that is instead based around the idea of community. This role ties into much older ideas of the social function of news in the public sphere, as Dewey (1954 [1927]) helped elucidate.

Service journalism has much in common with what Beckett and Mansell (2008) and Jarvis (2006) call "networked journalism" in the Web 2.0 era. Citizens are involved in the news-making process, but it is a process of citizens and journalists working together to create a professional news product. As Beckett (2008a) explains:

> The journalist still reports, edits, packages the news. But the process is continually shared. The networked journalist changes from being a gatekeeper who delivers to a facilitator who connects.

Networked journalism relies on interactivity such as blogging and social networking "not just as add-ons, but as an essential part of news production and distribution itself" (Beckett, 2008b, p. 5). As Jarvis (2006) notes, "In networked journalism, the public can get involved in a story before it is reported, contributing facts, questions, and suggestions." Service journalism in the Web 2.0 world works in a collaborative fashion at *The New York Times* where readers work with journalists to create news as a collective product—in the vein of "networked journalism."

As Benkler (2006) has explained, the architecture and properties of the Web enable anyone, anywhere (so long as they have a computer) to publish. The outsides of the conversation now have the capacity to contribute to the conversation. While Benkler sees the end of the "institutional information economy" and the hub and spoke model of mainstream media, I see networked journalism as facilitating a way where a networked public can work with mainstream media to have its concerns articulated for a wide, predictable and regular audience. Mainstream media helps informal networks unite around a specific and permanent community—though this is not to say that other independent online communities cannot also offer users similar gratification.

The importance of user content in creating a community around mainstream media content has been studied by researchers, who have looked at the BBC's extensive use of community collaboration (Williams et al., 2011). While community content can result in an unequal balance of power between mainstream media and the user (Usher, 2011), when this community is facilitated appropriately in a way that respects the potential contributions of users, coverage can be crafted in a cooperative manner.

Business News Scholarship and Service Journalism

It is important to locate business news within the existing scholarship in journalism studies. Business news journalism is a form of specialty journalism: it can appear both in the specialty press but it is also often a special section in general news. *The New York Times*, for instance, is a general news outlet with a specific business section. Business journalism that appears in business sections has been critiqued, among other things, for being written for "investors" (Gans, 2010). Even if this critique is correct, service journalism in business news is written instead for consumers. It serves an important role in the ecology of business news: there are plentiful magazines devoted to personal finance, personal technology, and travel (among other topics), and both *The New York Times* and *The Wall Street Journal* dedicate portions of sections or entire sections to this form of news, respectively.

Business journalism itself has not been the subject of much scholarship in recent years—if ever. If anything, it has been all but ignored in academia and in journalism education (Roush, 2006). As Roush points out, most of the major histories of American journalism leave out business news—aside from mentions regarding the Great Depression. If these histories talk about business news, it is most often in concert with a discussion of the rise of advertising, and then these histories move on. Recent business news scholarship has focused on the training of business journalists (Ludwig, 2002). Others focus more on the history of business journalists (Quirt, 1993), or on how business journalism can be used to predict moves in the market (Brooks and Gray, 2004). A new contribution to this scholarship focuses on *The New York Times* itself (Chernomas and Hudson, 2011). This book argues that newspaper's economic coverage has largely been directed by its publisher's interests in making the newspaper profitable; however, my time in the newsroom and other accounts of the newspaper's activities (Mnookin, 2008) seem to reject this hypothesis.

Because of the relatively limited scope of business journalism scholarship, it is a promising area of research. Careful study requires thinking about whether the audience actually does consist primarily of investors, for instance. Alternatively, an analysis could help reveal the particular values and imperatives of business journalists. In this article, networked journalism is a useful theoretical construct to understand service journalism, as the business journalists I observed were actively trying to understand what it meant to engage with their community so as to better understand the everyday consumer experience.

Method

To gain insight into the way that service journalism worked in the business section of *The New York Times*, I analyzed specifically the personal finance section, "Your Money," and the personal technology section. I chose these sections because during my research for a larger five-month in-depth ethnography, I learned that these sections had active online communities. As such, I thought they represented a promising entry into the evolution of journalism.

I employed three different modes of data collection. First, I collected and analyzed five months of *Times* business desk content, including archiving online blogs and the online website after it had been updated for the following day. While I did not conduct a content analysis, I used this exhaustive inquiry into *The New York Times* content as a starting point for questions for research. Second, as part of a larger five-month ethnographic study at the *Times*, I attended meetings where personal finance and personal technology coverage were discussed. These meetings included formal editors' meetings and more informal meetings with reporters and editors. In addition, I observed more informal conversation between the editors and journalists charged with producing this content. These ethnographic methods, though slightly updated to account for the Web, are in keeping with many news ethnographies, such as Gans (1979), Tuchman (1980), Epstein (1973) and Fishman (1980).

Finally, for the bulk of this article's content, I rely on interviews conducted with people most closely associated with the personal finance coverage and personal technology coverage. I spoke to the two columnists, the one main blogger, and the main editor of the personal finance section of business news coverage. I also spoke with two columnists and two editors of the personal technology section, as well as with people who could comment on the histories of these sections, and who could talk about the role of the audience in *Times* content. The majority of interviews were conducted with individuals who are the people primarily responsible for creating and crafting the personal finance and personal technology content, following semi-structured guidelines. The questions that were specific for this analysis were part of a larger set of interview questions that discussed the role of business journalists at the *Times*, their views of coverage, their sense of business news in the financial crisis, their experiences with online and multimedia, and their views of the audience.

Specifically, I added questions about whether journalists saw themselves as doing service journalism, asked them to further explain what they did and how they saw it as fitting into the overall ecology of the business news section. I also asked them to talk about their relationship with the audience, as I had observed that these journalists had an especially active audience following. I conducted a thematic analysis of the data, focusing on what journalists understood as service journalism, what they saw as their role in the newsroom, and how they viewed their audience. From this, I also teased out the theme of the influence of new technology on their work.

This is a case study of just one newspaper. In fact, the scope is even narrower: two small areas of coverage—personal finance and personal technology—within a much larger newspaper. But *The New York Times* is an excellent place for a case study. Though it may not be comparable to other newspapers because of its breadth of resources and its prominence in the United States, the *Times* still retains important similarities with other US newspapers. Like many newspapers, the *Times* is working to adjust to the digital age both with regard to its financial model and with its editorial strategies. Part of this adjustment includes trying to understand how readers fit into the process of newsmaking. But one of the strengths of the uniqueness of this site is that the *Times* may be an exemplary place to look for the best of service journalism; problems with Jayson Blair and Judith Miller notwithstanding, the paper has been a bulwark of top journalism in the United States. Service journalism at *The New York Times* is treated with the same standards as "serious news" and this journalism is an important forum for consumer advocacy.

The History of Personal Finance and Personal Technology Journalism at *The New York Times*

Personal Finance at the Times

The term "personal finance" in *The New York Times* first appears as a term in relation to the personal finances of major political and social figures in 1913. The *Times* routinely began using the word "household budget" and articulating advice (particularly for women) starting around this time. For example, in 1919, we see the term "household budget" used in connection with the idea that "in these days of increased efficiency, each household should run its affairs on a scientific business basis with as careful an accounting for every penny as is the case with business organizations," though this does not appear in any special section on personal finance or business (*The New York Times*, 1919).

Right before the 1929 Wall Street crash, the *Times* noted that housewives were big stock buyers, investing millions in the stock market along with their husbands (*The New York Times*, 1927). During the Great Depression, the majority of stories featuring news about personal finance and budgets were not about advice but instead focus on how schools or the girl scouts are educating children in personal finance. In other periodicals, though, we see what can be the birth of personal finance journalism on a regular basis starting in the mid-1930s, with personal finance columnist Sylvia Porter's weekly column in *The New York Post* (which would eventually become widely syndicated).

Before World War II, the *Times* had "Food News of the Week" (*The New York Times*,1938); news which featured advice to consumers about bargains in the markets; news about how housewives could stretch the household budget for food became a repeating theme. This became the "News of Food" column during and after World War II. Other articles provide information about budgeting in war-time. Household budget news was also followed with information about how to pursue home decorating on a budget, but not with personal investing news. By the 1950s, the "News of Food" column became the "Food" column, and it disappeared by the 1960s.

Personal finance news in the way that we think of it—news about investing decisions, saving, mortgages, college plans, and beyond, was not particularly prevalent until the late 1970s (Saporito, 1999). This is because fewer than 4 per cent of Americans were invested in the stock market in 1950, rising to only 15 per cent by 1970, whereas now, more than half of all households are invested in the stock market in some capacity (Roush, 2006).

Though market coverage has been part of the *Times* since its inception, with stock quotes in the 1850s and market coverage from all over Europe by 1900, market news as it applied to individuals did not appear in earnest until the redesign of the *Times* from a two-section paper into a four-section paper in 1978. One of these four sections would be a stand-alone business section designed to cover the "story" of business, providing more in-depth analysis than just market coverage—news that extended into the drama of corporate life and also addressed the concerns of individuals about personal finance (Quirt, 1993). As the section's first editor, Lee Andrews, noted in an interview with Quirt: "As you go out across the country, you find that people nearly everywhere are interested in what Wall Street is thinking and what is happening in the economy, as well as in personal finance." The first "Your Money" column, a column explicitly devoted to personal finance, appeared on November 11, 1978.

At present, personal finance and personal technology are what the business desk calls "verticals" or specific areas of coverage targeted at niche demographics. Personal finance has its own presence (as "Your Money") on the website. This was reorganized as a specific presence on the website between 2008 and 2009. "Your Money" has an associated blog, Bucks, which is the source of much of the community life that I will discuss and selected portions are reverse published into the paper. "Your Money" has a lead writer, Ron Lieber, and a secondary columnist and reporter, Tara Siegel Bernard. Both of these journalists also cover "straight" business news, as well as write blog posts. There is also a regular blogger, Jennifer Saranow Schultz.

Personal Technology at the Times

The beginning of regular personal technology coverage started with small developments being covered in the 1980s and early 1990s out of *The New York Times'* business and science sections. Personal technology was covered, according to deputy business editor Kevin McKenna, almost as an "oddity." On a historical note, the first appearance of the word "personal computer" in *The New York Times* was in 1977, in a story focusing on the coverage of a computer trade show; in the article, the journalist predicted that microcomputers would soon be like the personal calculators people "now" had (McElheny, 1977). From the inception, personal technology was of interest to the business section because of its connection to industry but also because of its connection to consumers.

The personal technology section in its modern form began in earnest as part of the *Times'* first experiment with the Web. Started as CyberTimes in 1996, the section covered personal technology and technology in general. The coverage included new information about the latest gadgets. There was a column about life in the digital age, as former CyberTimes editor John Haskins put it, "A column on how life was so much easier thanks to the Internet" (personal communication, April 23, 2010). The section also talked about computing in everyday life, the beginnings of e-commerce, legal issues, education issues, and other issues. This experimental Web technology news section was considered a fairly safe bet for the *Times* because it was assumed that early adopters would be interested in technology, according to McKenna, who was at that point editorial director of what was then called The New York Times Electronic Media Company.[1]

The section was so successful online that it was spun-off into a weekly print section in 1998 called Circuits. At that point, the Web version of CyberTimes ceased to exist and was pulled under technology coverage on the *Times'* website. Circuits featured columnist David Pogue's "State of the Art" personal technology column, the very same column he writes today for the business section, and the one he speaks about in this article. Circuits lasted from 1998 to 2005, at which point personal technology coverage moved inside the business section as a once-a-week section, with Pogue's column to run on the front once a week.

When the business section launched its vertical strategy, Pogue got his own blog and the section inaugurated the blog Gadgetwise. This personal technology column was, according to editor Sam Grobart, designed not to be a "gadget porn" blog like other technology blogs. Instead, it was intended to provide thoughtful commentary in addition to providing information about the latest models; it was not supposed to be inclusive of all developments in personal technology, but a curated blog of all the best (Grobart, personal communication, February 9, 2010). This blog, too, also had posts chosen for reverse publishing into the newspaper.

How do Personal Finance Journalists and Personal Technology Journalists Understand Service Journalism?

To understand how journalists think about their relationship with their audience—and to examine the changing role of the reader in shaping community in service journalism—it was first important to understand how journalists understood service journalism. Most journalists did see what they did as service journalism and were quite proud of what service journalism represented to them. Only one journalist did not recognize the term, but he spoke to the ethos of helping people make their lives easier by instructing them in how to make better choices about products and services. All of these journalists shared a common belief that their goal was to help people understand their choices as consumers and saw themselves as serious journalists committed to serving their public.

One of the complicating factors that should be noted is the degree to which companies promote their ware for inclusion in service journalism coverage. Service journalism has an uneasy relationship with advertising; for instance, in the same pages where personal technology columnists talk about new gadgets, the advertising shows off some of the newest personal technology gizmos. The personal finance pages feature far less advertising, however.

Nonetheless, part of the reason the business section divided personal technology and personal finance into separate sections on the Web was to take advantage of new Web advertising opportunities. However, most journalists saw what they do as divorced from the products that happened to be advertised in their section, and in fact, viewed it as their role to act as an advocate for consumers in a world where ads make choosing the best product increasingly difficult. On a larger scale, this suggests that service journalism reflects the ideals of journalism in the public interest.

Personal technology columnist David Pogue, who does not use the term service journalism, said it was his job to guide people to the products that could make their lives better—articulating a premise of service journalism. But his words also demonstrate his intention to depart from commercial interests.

> My real job is to separate the worthy [products] from the unworthy and to save people money. Frequently what I advise is to save and to not have you fall victim to the [technology] rat race...I love simple elegant stuff that is reasonably priced. (personal communication, May 13, 2010)

Though Pogue is a columnist who advises people about how to make purchases, he takes pride in journalism values. His comments suggest that he holds himself to adhering to a method which weighs claims for veracity with the audience in mind, even if Pogue ultimately takes a stand in his writing.

Bob Tedeschi, personal technology columnist for App Smart, a column devoted to applications for smartphones, also described how he saw service journalism as fitting into the basic ideals of journalism itself.

> I personally use service journalism as a way to frame what I do in those columns. When I am approaching one of these stories, I don't think I approach it any differently [from traditional journalism] in terms of the questions I ask. My task is to test out stuff from the perspective of a person with average technology abilities . . .

> I don't think I approach these stories any differently than a story I would report about lifeguards who text while on duty. [What] I am doing in both of those cases [is] I am just trying to focus really hard on what the reader needs to know at that moment about that topic. (personal communication, September 13, 2010)

Nonetheless, Tedeschi does see service journalism as serving a particular purpose:

> Service journalism is more advisory: that's it in a nutshell. It's offering the advice to somebody [from somebody] who has the advantage of instant access with company executives. It's asking [questions] for those average users: What would you say if you had the experience of having the president of a company in same room with you?

What is interesting about service journalism is that it does, in fact, take a stand—and in this respect it differs from traditional objective journalism. At the same time, however, these journalists are still rigorously questioning the merit of the products they evaluate, and in offering guidance, are doing so with the goal of serving the public *consumer* interest. Financial columnist Ron Lieber expressed a similar thought in his understanding of his role in covering personal finance for the *Times*, noting that service journalism does not depart from the standards of traditional journalism, though it has a different aim in its reporting.

> The business section is the most natural place for personal finance . . . Personal finance is about everything that hits you in the wallet . . . service journalism is taken seriously here. They've run a bunch of "Your Money" on page one since I've been here . . . it is elevated across the paper. (personal communication, April 8, 2010).

Between the lines, Lieber articulated that personal finance journalism has a place at the *Times* because it is important to everyone who reads the newspaper. Some of what he has written about has been considered important enough to be on the front page of the paper. So Lieber brings an additional wrinkle to the idea of service journalism—it is not just about solving problems, it is also about doing high-quality journalism that can represent the best that a place like *The New York Times* has to offer.

Personal finance columnist and reporter Siegel Bernard sees her work not only just as specifically meaningful to people's everyday lives but also as being connected to larger ideas about business and finance.

> We're not writing about industry, we're writing about real people. Much of what we do is very service-y. But it still ties into business products and services because what we write about is often created by big business. (personal communication, April 6, 2010)

However, at its core, much of what Siegel Bernard writes is about "strategies, planning, choosing the right products or services, and how best to use them." These topics are stories that are "relevant to the news but a lot of topics are evergreen," or stories that have a staying power because they remain applicable to situations beyond just the news cycle.

Each of these perspectives suggest that service journalism is part of a continuum of journalism that embodies the same high standards maintained elsewhere in the paper but with a slightly different tone that keeps in mind the consumer. Service journalism is about helping people but its public interest work takes on an advocacy and advisory role, and should not simply be dismissed as fluff. It is newsworthy, but its topics may retain a longer shelf-life past their appearance in the daily news. However, this discussion of service journalism seems to put the idea of audience at a distance. But these journalists are actively involved in having a conversation with their audience, one that helps them to craft their coverage, as this next section will indicate.

Connecting Service Journalism and Community

Personal finance and personal technology journalism at the *Times* in the Web 2.0 world espouses a new ethic of community participation. This relationship between journalist and reader builds on the idea of networked journalism, where professional journalists rely on a partnership with community members/citizens to help them craft their coverage. Of course, service journalism has always been a back and forth between community. One can think of basic advice columns—from personal issues (Gudelunas, 2007) to broader issues of home repair. As Gudelunas noted, advice columnist Dan Savage said he writes half his column and the letter-writer writes the other half. Traditionally, this conversation has been one that has relied on a tedious exchange of letters back and forth, or journalists' own sense based on their lives and others in the newsroom about common household issues.

In a departure from previous service journalism, the Web has enabled a community to form around content online and around the journalists, who act as facilitators for this community. Instead of being fans of columns reading alone, they can directly correspond with each other about the content of what journalists are writing about through online forums. This is just one of the facets of networked journalism—the idea that community can be created around co-produced content. Similarly, another aspect that has shifted at the *Times* is an increasingly collaborative relationship between readers and journalists, one that helps direct and influence journalists.

Twitter and Community

Not all of the journalists on the personal finance and the personal technology verticals use Twitter, but for journalist David Pogue, it has been an invaluable way to connect with his readers. He monitors his audience and is able to have an ongoing conversation with readers about their views on his coverage, and even things as simple as the movies he watches. This conversation makes Pogue more than just an anonymous journalist but someone who also has a personality beyond just what he writes on the page. His one-million-plus followers can talk to him, but they can also talk to each other through the Twitter platform, and they are united by their common interest as followers of

Pogue content, mentioning "David Pogue" or "@pogue" in their tweets. Pogue notes the power of Twitter:

> I have big presence on Twitter where there's a lot of give and take . . . It's all wonderful gravy that all this happened. It was never an ambition. It was never a calculated plan . . .
>
> But, it's an obligation to the readership . . . to try to be responsive. A lot of times they will lead me to new products and new column topics.
>
> I use it for crowdsourcing. [You can get answers] in 15 seconds using it that way. Answers help me out with jokes for a column [even]. It's very useful. (personal communication, May 13, 2010)

Pogue has actively created a fan base around his work. He could never pick up the phone to hear what all of these people are saying, and he may not read all these tweets. However, a quick look at his tweeting reveals that he is replying to people in this fan base and encouraging them to answer his questions. In crowdsourcing his reporting, for example, he is doing precisely the kind of journalism espoused by the ideals of networked journalism.

Because of the way that Twitter works, Pogue actually has to actively curate all of these tweets to make them visible to his readers. In Figure 1, he is asking a question, perhaps for a column or a blog post, and he is soliciting answers from the crowd.

Through this conversation and others, his fans are united by the fact that they are engaging in a direct conversation with Pogue in a way never before possible. Though Twitter does not allow for the same kind of back and forth comment that other platforms provide (such as some of the blogs that the personal finance team uses), Pogue's use of

Pogue David Pogue
Many of you are suggesting snap-out components to help with gadget sustainability (new chip, keep the computer). But why would mfrs want to?
16 Dec

harvrock Adam 🔁 by Pogue
@Pogue common power cord charging and syncing (USB/mini-USB)
16 Dec

eclisham Elaine Clisham 🔁 by Pogue
@Pogue People love shiny new gadgets with new features, so if they're going to upgrade every two, make recycling mandatory or charge a fee.
16 Dec

eolsson Eric Olsson 🔁 by Pogue
@Pogue Modularity - gadgets past their prime can be disassembled relatively easily, and many of the parts reused in another gadget
16 Dec

FIGURE 1
David Pogue's tweets. Printed with permission

Twitter is clearly an exemplar of a new relationship between journalist and audience member where he is using the audience as an instant resource.

For example, as part of Pogue's work, he is charged with making a regular multimedia video. However, he often finds that he wants to include his fans as part of his videos—he needs "extras." So he recounted to me how he has been able to go on Twitter and ask for people to volunteer to be in his online videos and suddenly have "30 people volunteering for 4 spaces who are willing to come up to my house in Connecticut."

Siegel Bernard uses Twitter, but how she has used it has changed over time. At first, she noted, "I use it as a news service, as a wire, for headlines about what we're up to. People interested in personal finance will hopefully follow that, and that may bring us more readers" (personal communication, April 6, 2010).

Then when I spoke with her a few months later, she said:

> It's kind of funny, but my outlook on Twitter has evolved since then [April 2010]. At first, it was something else to think about. But I've warmed up to the idea over time . . . I've also started to use it to reach out and communicate with people interested in the subject, as well as my peers. I've also created a personalized newswire for myself, which helps me keep track of what others are doing on a variety of topics.

So Siegel Bernard is using Twitter to help facilitate community and to help build her audience. Others, however, are not as invested in using Twitter to facilitate a conversation with their readers and do not use it in the way that Pogue does. As Lieber says, he goes "off and on with Twitter" and says he tries it for a month, and then will go silent. "I'm not sure what it gets me." Even if Twitter is not the ultimate way to engage the audience for everyone, community for service journalism is still being facilitated online in other ways.

Service Journalism and Community Through Commenting and Blogs

Networked journalism through service journalism at the *Times* is best illustrated through the way that the personal finance team relates to its audience through story comments and blog comments. The personal finance blog, Bucks, features daily posts about personal finance. These posts often reflect issues that are going on in the news. For example, during the Toyota recalls of 2010, Bucks writers wrote stories about how to buy a car and whether this was actually a good time to buy a new car. During tax season, Bucks brings on guest bloggers who speak to a variety of tax issues. Similarly, the blog, according to Siegel Bernard, "provides space to the issues we don't have space for in the paper."One of the aspects that Siegel Bernard has noticed as being particularly valuable about the blog is the form of community that has generated around the blog.

> I've started to notice screen names that I recognize, so it's clear that many of the same commenters are coming back. Some readers will ask additional questions in the comment section, and we jump in with the answers. The readers also help each other out by answering questions. We've started to create a mini-community here at Bucks.

In addition, Siegel Bernard notes that the commenters can provide ideas about what to cover and give her a better sense of the audience.

I do feel like I have a relationship with readers given the combination of both the blog and what we are writing about being so personal. There's often an emotional component to money.

Furthermore, Siegel Bernard notes that the commenters help her decide what to cover. "Sometimes they tell me some things that weren't clear or some things I could do that are of more interest to them." Bucks blogger Jennifer Saranow Schultz put it this way:

I feel that it's a community sharing tips and tricks. The ones that are really clever, we can blow up into a post. With the Ask an Expert Q&A, you can send your questions in and get them answered. In the print format, it would be a lot harder to get [that] and it might take up a lot of space. (personal communication, May 7, 2010).

The feedback between commenting and the creation of content is one of the key aspects of networked journalism. Personal finance columnist Ron Lieber's role in reaching out to readers through commenting back to them has been widely held up as an exemplar at the *Times*. As assistant community news manager Vanessa Schneider noted:

It just means the world to readers when Ron Lieber writes back to them or comments back to them on a story. For something like the "Your Money" vertical, it is so important to readers. For Ron Lieber they know him [commenting]. They want to interact with Ron. He finds leads [through commenting], for instance with credit cards and how people got screwed over. (personal communication, April 19, 2010)

Lieber also spoke to the nature of the blog and the relationship with the audience. The blog, as he notes, provides for greater flexibility than before and allows him to be a conversation facilitator.

[The blog] allows us to point to other voices and people who have said smart things and allows us to encourage conversation. None of us are as smart as all of us. I do personal finance writing, it's not like I am an oracle. The best thing I can do is make a few provocative points and raise a few ideas and have it out in the comments.

And the comments raise a bunch of things that we didn't have room for or just completely missed. It's not always a success, but with every smart point ... readers are engaged enough to deliver analysis that can add to the mix and that's something important.

As such, Lieber acknowledges the value that the community on the Bucks blog brings to the coverage he helps foster. He is guiding the coverage, but the commenters are themselves contributors to this conversation. They too can add to the experience of anyone coming to the Bucks blog.

Service Journalism as Community Journalism

Here, we have discussed two key concepts—the first the idea of service journalism as it is understood at *The New York Times* and the second, the idea of a many-to-many conversation facilitated through online platforms, some hosted by the *Times* and others hosted externally. These two points bring two advances to our understanding of what it means to do service journalism—especially in the digital age. The core of service journalism in a Web 2.0 era comes back to the idea of networked journalism, with journalists relying on a relationship with readers that is more easily facilitated through new Internet platforms.

This paper began by arguing that service journalism is considered by journalists who produce it to be a distinct form of journalism charged with helping people make decisions. They act as agents for people who would not ordinarily have access to people like executives. They can be the first testers for products, or provide information that ordinary people do not have time to research on their own. They are guides to the kind of information that directly affects people's lives. However, it is important to realize that these journalists do not see what they are doing as "fluff" journalism. Instead, they see how they approach service journalism as having the same rigor as how they might approach a "serious" story. But their work still holds up to the high standards of *The New York Times*, even if in the end these journalists are dispensing advice.

Second, at the *Times*, something new has evolved in the form of service journalism in both personal finance and personal technology journalism. These changes can best be described through the framework of networked journalism, whereby journalists and citizens/consumers of news are actively engaged in collaboratively creating news. We see how two platforms, one external to the *Times* (Twitter) and one internal to the *Times* (its blogging and commenting abilities), facilitate online conversations between journalists and their readers. Significantly, what some of these journalists observe is that a community coalesces around a shared interest in the content. In addition, this community provides insight not just to journalists but also to each other, particularly in the case of personal finance journalism. In short, we see the principles of collaborative storytelling, idea sharing, crowdsourcing, and all of the opportunities of a relationship that builds on a professional journalist steering the ship but an audience that is actively participating and following.

This change is one that is legions away from audiences writing in through letters— audiences who could have never before connected with each other. Now the audience invested in the content is aware of others invested in the content, and can work together to (generally) build common conversation. This is a change from the past; and service journalism in turn helps community, led in part by the journalists and how they use platforms to enable them to facilitate this community.

NOTE

1.   This later became NYTimes digital, and then NYTimes.com.

REFERENCES

BECKETT, CHARLIE (2008a) SuperMedia: the future as 'networked journalism', Open Democracy, 10 June, http://www.opendemocracy.net/article/supermedia-the-networked-journalism-future, accessed 10 January 2010.

BECKETT, CHARLIE (2008b) *SuperMedia: saving journalism so it can save the world*, Malden, MA: Blackwell.

BECKETT, CHARLIE and MANSELL, ROBIN (2008) "Crossing Boundaries: new media and networked journalism", *Communication, Culture and Critique* 1(1), pp. 92–104.

BENKLER, YOCHAI (2006) *The Wealth of Networks: how social production transforms markets and freedom*, New Haven, CT: Yale University Press.

BROOKS, ROBERT and GRAY, J. BRIAN (2004) "History of the Forecasters: naïve forecasters are better than the WSJ", *Journal of Portfolio Management Fall*, pp. 113–7.

CHERNOMAS, ROBERT and HUDSON, IAN (2011) *The Gatekeeper: 60 years of economics according to The New York Times*, Boulder, CO: Paradigm Press.

DEWEY, JOHN (1954 [1927]) *The Public and Its Problems*, New York: Swallow Press.

EIDE, MARTIN and KNIGHT, GRAHAM (1999) "Public/Private Service: service journalism and the problems of everyday life", *European Journal of Communication* 14(4), pp. 525–47.

EPSTEIN, EDWARD J. (1973) *News from Nowhere: television and the news*, New York: Random House.

FISHMAN, MARK (1980) *Manufacturing the News*, Austin: University of Texas Press.

GANS, HERBERT (1979) *Deciding What's News: a study of CBS Evening News, NBC Nightly News, Newsweek and Time*, New York: Vintage Books.

GANS, HERBERT (2010) "News and New Media in the Digital Age: implications for democracy", *Daedalus* 139(2), pp. 8–17.

GUDELUNAS, DAVID (2007) *Confidential to America: newspaper advice columns and sexual education*, New York: Transaction Press.

HANITZSCH, THOMAS, LÖFFELHOLZ, MARTIN and WEAVER, DAVID (2005) "Building a Home for the Study of Journalism: ICA creates a Journalism Studies interest group", *Journalism* 6(1), pp. 107–15.

HARTLEY, JOHN (2000) "Communicative Democracy in a Redactional Society: the future of journalism studies", *Journalism* 1(1), pp. 39–48.

JARVIS, JEFF (2006) "Networked Journalism", *Buzzmachine*, 5 July, http://www.buzzmachine.com/2006/07/05/networked-journalism, accessed 22 February 2011.

LUDWIG, MARK (2002) "Business Journalists Need Specialized Finance Training", *Newspaper Research Journal* 23(2/3), pp. 129–41.

MCELHENY, VICTOR (1977) "Computer Show: preview of more ingenious models", *The New York Times*, 16 June, p. 79. ProQuest Historical Newspapers, accessed 4 February 2011.

MNOOKIN, SETH (2008) "The New York Times' Lonely War", *Vanity Fair*, December, http://www.vanityfair.com/politics/features/2008/12/nytimes200812, accessed 10 January 2011.

QUIRT, JOHN (1993) *The Press and the World of Money: how the news media cover business and finance, panic and prosperity and the pursuit of the American dream*, Byron, CA: Anton/California-Courier.

ROUSH, CHRIS (2006) "The Need for More Business Education in Mass Communication Schools", *Journalism & Mass Communication Quarterly* 61(2), pp. 196–204.

SAPORITO, BILL (1999) "The Business Century: how the economy became hot news in the last 100 years", *Columbia Journalism Review* 37(6), pp. 47–52.

THE NEW YORK TIMES (1919) "Household Budget", 2 March, p. 35. Proquest Historical Newspapers, accessed 2 February 2011.

THE NEW YORK TIMES (1927) "Women Now Investing Millions; housewives big stock buyers", 16 February, p. 29. ProQuest Historical Newspapers, accessed 10 January 2011.

THE NEW YORK TIMES (1938) "Food News of the Week", 25 March, p. 13. ProQuest Historical Newspapers, accessed 10 January 2010.

TUCHMAN, GAYE (1980) *Making News: a study in the construction of reality*, New York: Free Press.

USHER, NIKKI (2011) "Professional Journalists, Hands Off! Citizen journalism as civic responsibility", in: Robert McChesney and Pickard Victor (Eds), *Will the Last Reporter Please Turn Out the Lights*, New York: New Press, pp. 264–77.

WILLIAMS, ANDY, WARDLE, CLAIRE and WAHL-JORGENSON, KARIN (2011) "Have They Got News for Us? *Journalism Practice* 5(1), pp. 85–99.

A NEW GENERATION OF LIFESTYLE MAGAZINE JOURNALISM IN CHINA
The professional approach

Shuang Li

This study examines the new approach and working standards of Chinese journalists who are working in international consumer magazines in China. In the past 15 years, Chinese lifestyle journalists have reoriented their multiple functions to present their social role as an "information vehicle", "serving the rising class", with "independence from media ownership and commercial forces" and "contributing consumerism to culture and traditional society". The elements involved in this new genre of journalism include financial and operational autonomy from the State and editorial independence from their international parent magazine companies. This professional approach also utilizes a working strategy that lays bare each individual's unique journalistic identity. The professionalization of these lifestyle magazine journalists is the result of a global and local media cultural collision; a product of the reconciliation of commercialism and professionalism.

Introduction

Using an overview of the development and current state of the Chinese lifestyle magazine industry, the purpose of this study is to discuss the new approach of Chinese consumer journalists in the context of journalistic professional development. Contributing to Chinese lifestyle magazines since the 1990s, these consumer journalists have become an increasingly professionalized section of the media during China's era of social transition. This study will examine the different elements of and roles played by these lifestyle magazine journalists in regard to their professional autonomy and ethics. The emergence of an ideology of "self-regulation" and "self-identity" among young journalists is an as yet undiscovered issue and can be viewed as a new trend in the modern Chinese media industry.

In China today, international lifestyle magazines are regarded as the cutting edge of the consumer magazine market. Conscious of the emergence of a middle class[1] eager for what they consider a "Western lifestyle" over the past decade, these magazines have attempted to provide content which reflects their readership's social aspirations in a bid to generate profits for their overseas investors. During the development of the Chinese lifestyle[2] magazine industry, journalists working in this area were dramatically rejuvenated. This study addresses the sea changes that are taking place in the practice and ideology of Chinese magazine journalists: the conflict between factionalism and pragmatism, and between journalistic ideals and practical realities. In particular, the study attempts to address the following four questions:

1) What are the working processes and consequent achievements of Chinese consumer magazines with regard to their journalistic culture?
2) Is a new generation of realistic magazine journalists emerging?
3) Is professionalization a new achievement for journalists working in the Chinese lifestyle magazine industry?
4) What new characteristics in journalism have magazine journalists contributing to "professionalism" in China created?

In order to find the answers to these questions, the author hypothesizes that the practices of Chinese lifestyle magazine journalists exist on three levels: the global level of systems, such as media globalization cultures, the national level of society as numerous consumerist cultures, and the micro level of individuals as pragmatic cultures. By analyzing these three levels, the author intends to discover how each could affect the possible direction of the entire hypothesis.

Since the 1980s, globalization has enabled foreign media firms to gain entry into the Chinese media system. Not only have they become an economic force in the marketplace, contributing new cultural content, but they have also had a major influence on Chinese political ideology by exporting the Western ideal of capitalism. The involvement of foreign media conglomerates in the Chinese media industry has resulted in the creation of a new commercial journalism, which is expressed in different types of news reporting, balancing content to attract both readers and advertisers. However, it is vital for the ideals of journalistic objectivity and public service to be rediscovered and restored among consumer journalists. Consumerism not only brings a new lifestyle to, and social stratification of, the Chinese metropolitan elites, but also causes China's new generation of journalists to reflect on their career beliefs and daily practices.

The Rise of Lifestyle Magazines

In 2009, there were 62 Chinese editions of foreign consumer magazines (Hong, 2009). Foreign publishers enthusiastically began entering the Chinese market after China's accession to the World Trade Organization in 2001. This was achieved either through publishing a Chinese-language edition of a parent magazine, or through the licensing of a brand and content to their Chinese counterparts. With their new access to the experience and resources of foreign magazine partners, including training programs for magazine professionals, which have in turn led to an awareness of mature overseas business models, Chinese magazines are rapidly improving the quality of their publications.

The launch of a new wave of magazine titles in China has led to a vastly expanded market. In 1985, Hachette Filipacchi with the Shanghai Translation Publishing House published a Chinese version of *Elle*, which became the first international fashion magazine on the Chinese mainland. *Rayli*, a Japanese fashion magazine, arrived in 1993 in a black and white version, and in 1998 *Cosmopolitan* was licensed by Hearst Magazines to Trends Media Group, the top Chinese lifestyle magazine firm. The newest permission granted by the Chinese government is *GQ* magazine, licensed by Condé Nast International, which issued its first Chinese edition on the mainland in October 2009.

These international lifestyle magazines represent the highest standards of Chinese media production and professionalism, making them comparable to their international parent magazines. This change marks a significant step for domestic magazines in China.

As a consequence, the journalists who have worked or are working on these international lifestyle magazines have a very distinctive approach to journalistic professionalism.

The Concept of Professionalism in the Chinese Context

Throughout the history of journalism studies, it has been argued that commercialization has destroyed the foundations of journalism worldwide, forcing journalists to focus their attention on chasing the lucrative market for sensational stories instead of reporting "serious news". As Christopher Meyers (in Pinson, 2010) criticized: "The business of journalism... [is] under a greater business threat. This has made it harder for fundamentally ethical journalism." In the present journalistic climate, consumer journalists are obliged to adopt the same practices required of other professional journalists, both in China and the West. The role of the consumer journalist with regard to professional development is still highly complex and little investigated. Compared to other models in different countries, "media transformation in China has not followed the classical path of liberal modernization exhibited in Great Britain and the United States... nor did it follow either a Scandinavian model or an interest-group conspiracy model" (Lin, 2006, p. 80). This factor should be considered when investigating the professional processes of Chinese consumer journalists.

As Ma (2000, p. 21) has highlighted, the enormous changes that have occurred in the Chinese media industry have meant that "the most distinguishable characteristic of the Chinese media in the 1990s is the tension between rapid commercialization and continued ideological control". Thus, the rise of professional knowledge-based control by the journalistic community is massively expanding, as opposed to market control and political control. This is occurring alongside the trend of a "democratization of political communication in China" (Zhao, 1998, p. 10). Furthermore, "gaining freedom with self-discipline can offer more flexibility for China's journalism" (Chen, 2005). However, consumer journalists are facing a new challenge: domestic and global capital forces command an ever greater influence on and control over their daily work.

In practice, the concepts of professional journalism, including both normative and situational factors, are shaped and reshaped. Journalists' decisions are made on the basis of market requirements, together with the prevailing values of their profession and society (Pasti, 2005). Nevertheless, academic research is critical of the idea of journalism as a profession (Zelizer, 2004). Schiller (1992) and Soloski (2008) argued that the concept of professionalism is being used as a safeguard for contemporary journalists. However, for most media critics the primary concern about news production in the twenty-first century is the tendency to produce "soft news" and "infotainment". McChesney (2004, p. 87) criticized this trend, claiming that it "pushed journalists to make content directed at demographics considered desirable by media owners and big ticket advertisers".

Scholars have thoroughly investigated the concept of "professionalism" in Chinese journalism. Many of them have stated that it is the most important norm of the news profession; stressing that Western journalists have scrupulously maintained this standard since the last century (Huang, 2005; Lee, 2003; Pan, 2000; Pan and Chan, 2003; Zhao, 2004). The essence of the concept of professionalism has two sides. While objectivity is the primary one, a combination of the independence and uniqueness of the media and journalists' positions make up the other. Professionalism, the objectivity of journalism and the independence of media are all concepts that point to the highest ideal: to spread the truth. Furthermore, comparative media research on journalists across national boundaries and cultures is becoming increasingly popular, as media scholars try to draw a general picture of journalism in global transition and trans-national environments. Analysis of the changing dynamics of journalism in global terms has indicated that "three political themes have been particularly salient over recent years: ecology, human rights, and democracy" (Volkmer, 2011, p. 309). These themes have been legitimized in the national and international codes of journalistic ethics, which in the 1970s typically emphasized the universal values of "peace, democracy, human rights, social progress and national liberation" (Nordenstreng, 1989, p. 282). The discussion about journalistic professionalism is often blurred by a simplification or homogenization of the view on professional journalism (Ruusunoksa, 2006).

One of the fundamental issues in the debate over ethical journalism in China is whether the professional environment for journalism can be improved without party control. "The kernel of the professional spirit of journalism is the self-control of journalists. Gaining freedom with self-discipline can offer more flexibility for China's journalism" (Chen, 2005).

Lifestyle magazines in China are still under the control of the political system and therefore remain a channel for propaganda. The intriguing issue is how professional lifestyle journalists are able to effectively perform their role in the commercial marketplace in competition with their Chinese colleagues working on international magazines, while simultaneously obeying party regulations and ideologies. An additional issue is whether these professional journalists pursue the same career patterns as their Western counterparts, and furthermore, how the professionalism of Chinese lifestyle magazine journalists should be measured.

Methods

This paper examines data collected during a number of in-depth interviews with Chinese lifestyle journalists. Interviewees were chosen on the basis of their employers. This restricted the sample to those working for lifestyle magazines, most of which were at least indirectly owned by an international media company. In each magazine, the choice of participants was based on three levels of the office hierarchy: junior-, middle- and senior-level editors. Specific research instruments were developed for each of these levels. On the individual level, an open-ended questionnaire was produced and group discussions were conducted with a sample of journalists who had at least five years work experience in print media. Four journalists were chosen from each of 10 media organizations selected. One journalist was selected from the lowest level of the editorial hierarchy (non-decision-makers: Feature Reporters, Editors, Art Designers, etc.). Two journalists were chosen from the highest level (strategic leadership: Editors-in-Chief, Publishers, etc.), and a further journalist was selected from the middle level of the editorial hierarchy (operational decision-makers: Editor-Directors, Senior Reporters, Advertising Managers, etc.).

Most of the interviewees worked, or had previously worked, for one of four international magazine groups: Hachette Filipacchi Media, Hearst, Condé Nast and G&J. A few also worked for domestic lifestyle magazines groups, such as Trends Media Group, SEEC and others. However, Trends Media Group and SEEC also have copyright agreements with two or more international magazine companies. Furthermore, in order to gain an overall perspective of Chinese lifestyle magazine journalists, the author chose a small number of people working for competitive domestic lifestyle magazine publishers as interviewees. These publishers were veterans of the Chinese consumer industry, which meant they had worked in their positions for at least 10 years and had come from a wide range of famous Chinese brands in China including *Readers*, *Story Time*, *The Finance*, *Business Week* and *South Windy Window*.

A total of 64 Chinese magazine professionals were interviewed in Beijing between April 2006 and August 2008. Interviews were either recorded with notes taken (43) or unrecorded with notes (21). Additional data, such as publications and magazine content, were collected from March 2007 to September 2009. In order to avoid personal over-interpretation, the author also used additional data to verify findings.

Chinese Consumer Journalism's Self-identity

Chinese magazine professionals' occupations can be categorized into journalists and media managers.[3] Of the 64 respondents in this study, 20 (31 per cent) were classified as journalists, while 44 (69 per cent) were media managers. One issue that needs to be clarified here is that the positions of Editor-in-Chief and Editor-Director are counted as "managers" for the purpose of this study. This is because in China the role of both Editor-in-Chief and Editor-Director usually demands responsibility not only for content issues, but also for overseeing staff recruitment and training, as well as brand promotion. Both positions also involve liaising with other advertising and distribution departments.

In terms of some basic demographic backgrounds, a number of issues emerge (Table 1).

Just over half (51 per cent) of the magazine journalists and managers were born in the 1970s, which represents the biggest proportion of those participating. This percentage reflects the fact that young magazine professionals are an important generation for consumer magazines. According to the results, 13 of the 20 interviewed journalists were born in the 1970s, accounting for 65 per cent of the total number of journalists. At the same time, 20 out of 44 interviewees working at managerial level were born in the 1970s, which is more than 45 per cent of the total managers. However, the second largest proportion of magazine managers (14 out of 44) were born in the 1960s. The majority of them have attained the highest position in their respective organization, such as Editor-in-Chief or Publisher. In contrast, most of the managers born in the 1970s are in middle positions at magazines, such as Editor-Director or Advertising-Director. The table shows that seven out of 20 of the interviewed journalists were born in the 1980s and nine out of 44 managers were born in the 1950s. Although this is the smallest amount in total, the

TABLE 1
Interviewee age (magazine professionals, $N=64$)

Decade of birth	Journalist ($N=20$)	Manager ($N=44$)	Total	%
1950s	0	9	9	14
1960s	0	14	14	23
1970s	13	20	33	51
1980s	7	1	8	12

former shows the future of journalism, while the latter shows that there are still some older senior journalists and government officials working at some of the transitional magazine firms.

Thus, magazine professionals born in the 1960s and 1970s form 47 out of 64 (73 per cent) respondents. This means that these two age groups (covering the "baby boom" generation from the 1960s and early 1970s, to the "first generation of only-children" in the later 1970s) are the core workers of consumer magazines in China. From a sociological perspective, the "baby boom" generation and the "first generation of only-children" have some common characteristics. Both groups were born between the older generation and the new younger generation in China and during their childhood and youth had very few material possessions and no spiritual life. Both were bravely trying new things in work and life, but always abided by the communist party line (Wang Feng, personal communication, December 22, 2006). These characteristics have certainly been evident in the interviewees' careers. Their experiences during the period of reform in China have led both of these generations to use traditional concepts of journalistic ethics and repackage them with techniques from the Western concept of professionalism. This subtle approach allowed them to achieve their aims during the economic reform and shows that by still holding on to a certain rule of belief in China, new innovations can be realized.

During the interviews, one specific question was posed to all the participants: "Which occupation do you think you belong to?" As the author used face-to-face in-depth interviews rather than a structured questionnaire in the field work, some of the respondents did not answer every question as required. Therefore, Table 2 shows types of self-identity, but does not include all of the participants.

Overall, only 28 per cent of respondents said they saw themselves as journalists. Younger respondents were less likely to identify themselves as a journalist, with only two out of 20, or 10 per cent of non-managers describing themselves thus. By contrast, 16 of the senior magazine workers (36 per cent) preferred to call themselves journalists. This suggests that younger magazine professionals may be less required to play a traditionally journalism-oriented role while carrying out their daily routines.

In contrast to their older colleagues, young or junior magazine journalists tend to describe their occupational situation as "worker", with 12 out of 20 (66 per cent) using this title. In comparison, only seven out of 44 magazine managers, or less than 16 per cent, called themselves "workers". Moreover, those that did, used the term more in self-mockery than in seriousness. However, the overall number of respondents viewing themselves as "workers" exceeds "journalists", and represents the highest percentage overall. This

TABLE 2
Self-identity of journalists ($N = 64$)

	Journalist ($N = 20$)	Manager ($N = 44$)	Total	%
Journalist	2	16	18	28
Businessman	0	4	4	6.1
Cultural trader	0	5	5	7.8
Publisher	0	2	2	3
Worker	12	7	19	29.6
Cannot label	4	2	6	9
Did not answer	2	8	10	15.6

indicates that there has been a loss of belief in traditional perceptions of the journalistic role among the new generation of Chinese magazine professionals.

As the data in Table 2 were collected from interview information rather than a questionnaire, the interviewees were not provided with a fixed list of possible answers to select from, but instead described their occupational orientation. Therefore their answers should be interpreted as having embedded meaning involving their situation at the time. Thus, "businessman", "cultural trader" and "publisher" could be classed as having the same meaning as "non-journalist" when the interviewees were asked to choose a label which they believed best expressed their self-identity. Adding the three figures together, 11 of 44 magazine managers identified themselves as working in a commercialized environment. This is a new trend that Chinese journalists face during media transition and reform in China. As well as having to contend with the increasing financial pressures in their profession, journalists now have to operate in an environment that has become wholly part of a commercialized media world. Even if media professionals are able to keep their personal integrity and do not become "red-envelope" journalists, they will still be expected to do everything possible to make a profit for their media organizations, although the managers obviously have more duties and responsibility than junior journalists.

However, this new commercially driven self-identity has not eroded all media professionals' journalistic beliefs. Two respondents claimed during several conversations that a person's life was more important than other issues; not regarding the new commercial imperatives of their trade as a hindrance, but rather viewing their position as an opportunity to better themselves: "we are alive, we have better chances than others, so we may have a chance to do the work we wish to do now and in the future." In terms of their goals, interviewee Xu Fang—the founder of *Lifestyle*,[4] the most popular shopping guide newspaper in Beijing—wanted to establish a *Guardian*-style newspaper for Chinese intellectuals. However, he maintained that this would only be possible if there was greater media freedom in China. Yang Lang, the vice-president of SEEC Media Group,[5] one of the large consumer media groups in China, plans to establish a Chinese version of *Time* magazine. Xu Fang and Yang Lang see their respective current media formats as the direct result of China's media reforms, and they both aim to survive in the existing media system.

Nevertheless, six of the 64 respondents did not label their occupations, and 10 of them failed to answer the question. One reason for this may be because some interviewees were not familiar with the author and felt no necessity to answer this question, while others may have thought "a job is a job"—a means to make a living.

The New Occupational Choices of Senior Journalists

Chinese lifestyle magazines started to develop in the late 1980s, at which time media commercialization had also begun to establish its own roots in China. Some serious pioneering news journalists adjusted their positions in line with their profession's increasing commercialization; taking the new occupational roles of publishers and media managers.

Thus, many media practitioners made new occupational choices through the late 1980s to 1990s and changed their career paths from political reporting to information gathering. In addition, Chinese media professionals attempted to introduce more new consumer media titles in order to extend their careers. Of the 64 media professionals interviewed, at least 28 fitted into this occupational change category. These 28 interviewees were also all over 30 years old.[6] This means that 28 of the 59 respondents (47 per cent) who joined the media industry in the 1990s changed the focus of their journalistic practice. This is a relatively high percentage.

When examining these 28 interviewees more closely, it is clear that most reached their current positions in consumer magazines via two paths. Some media professionals had been appointed as Publishers or Chief Editors by the Chinese Communist Party (CCP) or government institutions, and consequently became official delegates in the 1990s. Examples include the Editors-in-Chief of *Family*, *Readers* and *Story Time*, and the publishers of Trends Media Group and Guangdong Publishing House. However, an increasing number of participants could be classed as having volunteered, and this second group actually outnumbers those who were appointed. These media professionals now occupy posts such as Editor-Director, Editor-in-Chief, Advertising Director, International Copyright Director, Senior Editor and Syndication Coordinator. All have solid work experience and hold principal positions in a variety of magazines.

During the in-depth interviews, most interviewees ranked social responsibility as the most valuable ethic in their working standard. From 1993 to 1998, Wang Feng was a Senior Reporter for *Sanlian Life Weekly*, the most popular news magazine read by Chinese intellectuals. In 2003 he joined Trends' *Men's Health* as an editor, becoming the editor of Trends' *Esquire* in 2005.[7] He is acknowledged as the journalist who has done the most to bring the news concept and ideal to fashion magazines in China. "I never think *Esquire* . . . is as simple as a magazine full of materials. We have to add our own voice to society and our own influence as well (in *Esquire*); it could not be by simple materialism" (Wang, in Gao, 2006).

In order to obtain and maintain this influence, Wang Feng emphasized "news value" as the foundation of his magazine. Wang did not believe that "news value" would make *Esquire* any different from other fashion magazines as he thought "fashion is not a concept of material, rather, its values and lifestyle" (Gao, 2006). Therefore, he required his team to insist that "real consumption and luxury are spirit and emotion", and this was the "core value and belief" of *Esquire* (Wang Feng, personal communication, December 22, 2006). Some media critics (Zhang Xiaoqiang, personal communication, February 5, 2007; Yin Wei, personal communication, January 29, 2007) argued that the concept of "news value", which Wang emphasized, was used only as a means to market *Esquire*. Critics also maintained that this idea of "news value" generated a considerable amount of hype for the magazine, necessitated by the joint pressures of advertising, circulation and a joint-venture organization. In short, *Esquire* could not escape materialism (Wu, 2007). Furthermore, as the Chinese consumer magazine industry is still in its infancy, business success is more dependent on foreign brand co-operative models and international consumer advertisements. *Esquire* certainly takes advantage of this business model and it has enabled its editor to unleash some personal choices such as "news value" and a "journalistic ideal" to bring value to *Esquire*'s brand in China. In addition, Wang Feng clearly recognized that in order to add weight to his new position, he would need to be seen to uphold these professional standards. Being a former news journalist, he knew that he would have to justify his career change to maintain his stature in the journalism community and not lose the respect of his former colleagues and friends. His success in this endeavor was underlined in the testimonial of one senior journalist who introduced

Wang Feng to the author. He evaluated him as "one of the magazine professionals who has not lost his journalistic ideal", so "he's worth interviewing". From this perspective, Wang Feng is still treated as a journalist in the community. This is simply because he upholds the ideals of the journalism profession, and is not categorized as a "cultural businessman" or "marketer" like other staff working for consumer magazines.

However, being an assistant publisher of Trends Media Group, Wang Feng is not alone in his career ideal. Xu Wei is another example of a journalist who holds journalistic ideals in fashion reporting. Xu graduated in 1994 from the Journalism Department at Renmin University, the oldest and most highly respected institution that teaches journalism in China. She joined *Sanlian Life Weekly* after graduating, and then became an editor at Trends' *Cosmopolitan* a year later. Xu Wei has been a vocal critic of her profession, claiming that "for such a long time, this job has had no meaning for me, as I think that only political, economic and social news are the real meaning of news. Can luxuries, like a lipstick or clothes make any change in our society, can they save a human life? I doubt it" (Xu, 2007a). However, Xu also provided answers to her questions:

> More than a decade ago, when I had just joined the media, a journalistic expert told me something that was meaningful to me, something about the passionate desire for an insight into the world through news: "In fact, the press should be concerned about human nature. And the nature of human sex, love, death, joy, money is an eternal theme of the press". (Xu, 2007b)

The conclusion that can be drawn here is that Xu and other consumer magazine professionals have extended the boundaries and significance of news from "pure" news to "consumer" news. The former is usually translated as "news that deals with serious topics or events", while the latter contains "less quality" and is filled with supposedly unimportant topics in people's lives.

Wang Feng and Xu Wei's descriptions of their professional self-discipline, together with their career aims, show that they believe that journalistic practice holds a high level of social responsibility and that one of journalism's core aims should be to serve the people and society. Although upholding this principle is not as vital as ensuring that the profession remains a "keystone to democracy" (which journalists should always bear in mind during their day-to-day practice), journalism's role is to serve the modern citizen living in the consumer society. Moreover, it is a part of that society.

Although some senior journalists have a choice in regard to which news values they hold, others have less freedom because of the particular area of journalism they work in. Another interviewee, Li Ergang (personal communication, December 26, 2006) discussed this issue further: "Most of the fashion magazines have no reputation concerning their journalistic beliefs, because they only work for foreign bosses, profits and advertising, with very much less attention paid to their social responsibility and media justice."

The issue Li Ergang raises here is that commercialization has brought fierce competition to the Chinese consumer magazine market. Although magazine professionals initially tried to hold on to their original beliefs and values, enormous commercial pressures over the past 10 years have finally destroyed any vestige of their former consciences and moral obligations. Other interviewees such as Yi Wei (personal communication, January 29, 2007) and Xu Lei (personal communication, May 14, 2007) agreed that some of the magazine professionals used "journalistic belief" as an adornment to attract credulous readers, and also to trick themselves.

When fieldwork was conducted for this study, "news values" were found to be highly prized, or acknowledged as a major principle of journalistic practice by all the very senior interviewees, such as Editors or Editors-in-Chief. In contrast, none of the lower-level journalists used "social responsibility" to explain their daily working beliefs or career aims.

There are two reasons for this: firstly, people in senior positions in lifestyle magazines realize that if they wish to gain promotion, be awarded pay rises and generally survive in the media market and the organizations they work for, commercial imperatives have to take precedence over any thoughts of social responsibility in their working practices. Therefore senior management have, to a great extent, separated their career aspirations from reality. It seems that there is no visible connection between reality and belief. Secondly, people working in current fashion magazines are normally young, with the majority of them aged less than 30 years old. Critics argue that unlike more contented senior media professionals, the younger generation demonstrates a social dissatisfaction that is mirrored in the trivial content of the Chinese consumer magazines they produce; engaging merely with commercialism and customer service.

The author believes that this overriding influence has meant that "news value" and "social responsibility" remain the two core principles that form the "self-image" of these magazine professionals. These values were reinforced when they voiced their journalistic belief in the press during interviews conducted with them between 2004 and 2008. Therefore, despite the tense commercial competition among Chinese consumer magazines, these testimonies suggest that a voice of media credibility has appeared. However, other journalists that were interviewed did not show any evidence of holding any strong beliefs or ethics. Although some magazine journalists define their idealized role as being a public servant, most still need to inherit journalistic ethics and reconcile themselves with their profession's civically-minded attributes in China. This is a new trend in the community of Chinese journalists.

From this point of view, the challenge facing Chinese consumer magazine professionals is how to use conventional journalistic techniques and achieve and maintain a level of performance that is on a par with serious media.

Comparing Magazine and News Journalists

In 2002, Lu and Yu (2003) conducted a survey of journalists in Shanghai that examined their occupational status during the process of social transformation. The following section attempts to compare the results of that survey with the findings from this study of lifestyle magazine journalists.

The Age Factor

Two surveys conducted within the past decade provide particularly fine details of the demography of Chinese journalists. They are Lu and Yu's (2003) survey in Shanghai as well as a survey carried out by the combined Media Research Institute (MRI) at Renmin University of China with the Domestic Affairs Department of the National Journalists' Association in 1997 (Yu, 1998). According to Lu and Yu (2003), the average age of news professionals in Shanghai was 34.7 years. Yu's (1998) survey focused on 2002 media staff selected from 183 media institutions, both at central and local levels, and found that the average age of journalists in China was 37.4 years, with 24.6 per cent being under 29 years of age. As this paper established that more than 51 per cent of consumer magazine journalists and managers were born in the 1970s, it is clear that these young professionals represent the largest age group of consumer magazine journalists in China. It also indicates that people are entering the journalism profession at an increasingly younger age in China.

The conclusion that can be drawn here is that consumer magazine journalists are younger than professionals in other areas of the media. The age factor highlights a significant difference between lifestyle magazine journalists and other media professionals.

Overseas Experience

According to Lu and Yu's (2003) survey, 30 per cent of the professionals in Shanghai had visited overseas media institutions. This figure does not include those who had had collaborative experience with their colleagues from overseas (15.6 per cent); short- or long-term vocational training programs (12.8 per cent) and internships in overseas institutions (5.2 per cent). All four groups combined amount to over half the sample. This is a great improvement compared with Yu's (1998) earlier survey which had found that almost 90 per cent of the respondents had never or seldom communicated with foreign journalists or foreign visitors. In addition, more than two-thirds of journalists had never, or seldom, had the opportunity to take vocational training courses.

However, when comparing the above findings to the results presented here in regard to lifestyle magazine journalists, all the participants working in different magazines mentioned that they had benefited from international training or overseas media connections. Therefore, access to overseas professional training remains a key difference between these lifestyle magazine journalists and other traditional journalists.

Commercial Pressure

According to the survey in Shanghai (Lu and Yu, 2003), the concept of competitiveness causes the most stress among media professionals. Competitiveness occurs in three forms: the most dominant, which affects 82.3 per cent of media professionals, is competition at work. This is followed by competitive pressures from colleagues, and finally competition from online and overseas media. Although the respondents of this study were paid a higher than average salary in comparison to other Shanghai industries, and had more opportunities to take training programs in foreign countries, they still did not have a high level of self-esteem. Most of them were greatly affected by pressures from work, with 35 out of 64 (55 per cent) complaining that their work environments suffered from endless role-related and promotion pressure. However, the pressure on lifestyle magazine journalists stems more from commercial forces such as advertisers, investors and publishers rather than their domestic competitors or colleagues. This also differentiates them from their newspaper colleagues, as the latter have more domestic competitors.

Job Satisfaction

The survey in Shanghai in 2002 (Lu and Yu, 2003), and the nationwide survey conducted in 1997 (Yu, 1998), found that all the participants had a low degree of satisfaction in regard to their salary, welfare bonus and promotion potential. Generally speaking, the average career span for media professionals in Shanghai is 10 years, although some have had careers of up to 38 years in the media field. The majority of media staff (74.6 per cent) who have worked solely in the media industry remained with their first employer.

However, in this study, of the 41 magazine managers who were born in the 1970s and 1980s, 38 (92 per cent) had spent less than five years at the same magazine. The reason behind this is the aggressive competition between older magazine organizations and newly established magazine houses. Therefore, compared to their colleagues in other media organizations, consumer magazine journalists have more opportunities to move from job to job.

Conclusion

Based on an empirical study of lifestyle journalists in China, this paper proposes that, influenced by the three forces of capitalism, professionalism and the political role, current journalists in China hold three values, which relate to: (1) employees' journalistic orientation; (2) the extent of professionalization; and (3) the level to which they see themselves as a mouthpiece for the community. The most prominent value voiced by respondents was employee orientation, with "mouthpiece" ranking last. This research has shown that, among consumer magazine journalists, employee orientation is a significant factor. Journalists working in lifestyle magazines, particularly co-operative ones, have merged the Chinese model with the West's, and increasingly place greater emphasis on the latter's template as they perceive it to be ideal. Although we may describe consumer magazine journalists as profit-driven or market-driven, they have nevertheless tried to preserve traditional journalistic values, such as editorial autonomy and societal service within this new paradigm. They have also attempted to remain consumer-oriented journalists rather than pure profit-seekers. Nevertheless, the motivation model of employee orientation in the consumer magazine industry has also given these magazine journalists more career choices.

Furthermore, consumerism is reflected in the media industry and becomes news-consumerism. It can be simply summarized as having the following two aspects: firstly, the media maximizes its own information resources to reach the greatest possible share of its target audience and achieve the maximization of commercial interests. Secondly, the media, through news reports on material consumption or the importance of consumer culture, creates a "consumer society" atmosphere that stimulates public consumption both materially and spiritually. A significant effect of this news consumerism in China is the strengthening of the media's obligation to fulfill its social responsibilities, despite the likelihood that it solely strives to generate more profit. It also introduces the professional concept of "public service". Taking into consideration the current environment and the media discourse taking place, the contradiction between traditional political factionalism and outside professionalism appears to be playing out in the conflict that is occurring in Chinese news and media reform. This needs to be addressed (Shi, 2006). However, Chinese magazine journalists have actively investigated the different business and cultural systems in China and their magazines' parent countries, such as Japan, France and the United States, in order to explore and experiment with a unique "Chinese experience". The restructuring of the social role and function of the media and its journalists has induced consumer journalists to use and ultimately rely on the symbolism of professionalization for their social status and respect more than other types of journalists do. The professionalization of these consumer magazine journalists is a result of a global and local media cultural collision; a consequence of the reconciliation of commercialism and professionalism.

By investigating the daily practices of consumer magazine journalism in China and the ideology and ethics behind its practices, and by discussing the original relationship between consumer journalism and other more "serious" forms of journalism in China, this study has found that consumer journalists actually share the same journalism ethics and ideology as their "serious" counterparts. To avoid political retribution and commercial pressure, consumer journalists reorient the multiple functions of journalism as an "information vehicle" in the "service of the rising class", "independent from media ownership and commercial forces", and "contributing consumerism to culture and traditional society". Journalism is therefore viewed as playing an important social role. This new challenge means that lifestyle magazine journalism involves more elements in the professional ideological and practical paradigm than other forms of journalism in China.

I argue that the genre of "lifestyle journalism" is rising in China. The definition of "lifestyle journalism" refers to the journalists who use cultural instruments, commercial technologies, globalized networks and knowledge. More importantly, this form of journalism exhibits an individualized creativity and socialized independence inherent throughout the consumer and lifestyle magazine industry. As a consequence, lifestyle magazine journalism in China has reached an international standard. Moreover, a more commercial behavioral change has occurred that is linked to the profession's understanding of media commercialization and informationalization.

Just as the strengths of this study are clear, so too are the weaknesses. For instance, according to journalism practice, examining the journalistic procedures of all consumer magazines would be necessary in order to produce the most representative data. This is because lifestyle magazines, particularly international brand magazines, only form the top tier of the consumer magazine industry. In China, international involvement in the consumer magazine sector consists of no more than 100 titles, but according to the state's records, there were more than 3000 in total in 2009. Although these 100 titles represent an advanced paradigm of magazine journalism, in order to produce a complete picture of contemporary magazine journalism in China, it would be necessary to carry out a wider study. Therefore, further research should investigate the professional process of the entire corps of journalists in the consumer magazine industry.

NOTES

1. "Middle class" is still a controversial and unclear concept in Chinese sociology. However, most glossy consumer magazines still use this concept to describe their target audience. For that reason, the author borrows this concept as one that is universally understood within academic theory and industrial practice.
2. Within a Chinese context, the definition of "lifestyle" means a fashionable or desirable attitude and consumer behavior, and a higher standard of living, taste and pursuit, which distinguishes a person from the ordinary population.
3. In China, all the people working in media organizations are categorized as journalists and supervised by the Central Propaganda Department of the Chinese Communist Party.

However, in every organization, "journalist" refers to the junior level of editorial hierarchy, including all non-decision-making workers: reporters, editors and so on. All of the middle- and senior-level staff are given the title of "manager".

4.   *Lifestyle* is a weekly tabloid-size light glossy newspaper in Beijing, which was founded in 1993 by *Chinese Business*, the broadsheet financial newspaper. Xu Fang was the founder and president of *Lifestyle* from 1993 to 2006 and also Chief-Editor of *Chinese Business* from 1988 to 1993.

5.   SEEC Media Group is a media company based in mainland China. It is listed on the Hong Kong stock market and publishes *Caijing*, *Better Homes and Gardens* and *Sports Illustrated* and several co-operated magazines and domestic magazines, such as *The Finance* and *The Stock Weekly*, etc. Yang Lang is a senior journalist who worked for Xinhua News agency, *China Youth* (broadsheet newspaper), *Sanlian Life Weekly* and *The Finance* (financial weekly magazine), from Reporter to Editor-in-Chief.

6.   Chinese youth are accounted on the age of over 22 years old when they secure their first job after graduating from university. If you count the year of this research as 2008, the eligible media participants will be at least 30 years old now if they joined the media industry in the 1990s.

7.   After working for six years in Trends Media Group, Wang Feng became Editor-in-Chief of *GQ* (China) to launch *GQ* (China) in August 2008. *GQ* (China) officially launched in 2009, a year later.

REFERENCES

CHEN, LIDAN (2005) "Self-improvement Upon Journalists' Professional Spirit and Operating Criteria", 28 November, http://academic.mediachina.net/article.php?id=4477, accessed 11 November 2010.

GAO, LUYING (2006) "Shishang Xiansheng De Yingshishang—Shishang Xiansheng Zhubian Wangfeng Zhuanfang" ["The Hard Fashion of Trends' *Esquire*—interview with Editor of *Esquire* Wang Feng"], 23 December, http://women.sohu.com/20061223/n247216680.shtml, accessed 16 November 2010.

HONG, YUHUA (2009) "Tanxun Zhongwai Qikan Banquan Hezuo Chenggong Zhidao" ["The Success of Co-operation Models Between Chinese Magazines and Their Foreign Partners"], 24 August, http://www.chinaxwcb.com/index/2009-08/24/content_178799.htm, accessed 10 August 2011.

HUANG, DAN (2005) *Xinwen Zhuanye Zhuyi De Jiangou Yu Xiaojie* [*The Image of Communicators: the construction and deconstruction of journalistic professionalism*], Fudan: Fudan Publishing House.

LEE, CHIN-CHUAN (2003) *Chinese Media, Global Contexts*, London: Routledge.

LIN, FEN (2006) "Dancing Beautifully, But with Hands Cuffed? A historical review of journalism formation during media commercialization in China", *Perspectives* 7(2), pp. 79–98.

LU, YE and YU, WEIDONG (2003) "Shehui Zhuanxing Guocheng Zhong Chuanmeiren ZHiye Zhuangkuang—2002 Shanghai Xinwen Congyezhe Diaocha Baogao Zhi Yi" ["The Occupational Status of Journalists During the Progress of Social Transformation—an interview report on Shanghai journalism in 2002"], *Journalism Monthly* 3, http://law.eastday.com/epublish/gb/paper159/200301/class015900002/hwz595969.htm, accessed 17 November 2010.

MA, ERIC KAT-WAI (2000) "Rethinking Media Studies, the Case of China", in: James Curran and Myung-Jin Park (Eds), *De-westernizing Media Studies*, London: Routledge, pp. 21–34.

MCCHESNEY, ROBERT, W. (2004) *The Problem of the Media: U.S. communication politics in the twenty-first century*, New York: Monthly Review Press.

NORDENSTRENG, KAARLE (1989) "Professionalism in Transition: Journalistic Ethics", in: Thomas Cooper (Ed.), *Communication Ethics and Global Change*, New York: Longman, pp. 277–83.

PAN, ZHONGDANG (2000) "Improvising Reform Activities: the changing reality of journalistic practice in China", in: Chin-Chuan Lee (Ed.), *Power, Money, and Media: communication patterns and bureaucratic control in cultural China*, Evanston, IL: Northwestern University Press, pp. 68–111.

PAN, ZHONGDANG and CHAN, JOSEPH M. (2003) "Shifting Journalistic Paradigms: how China's Journalists Assess Media Exemplars", *Communication Research* 30(6), pp. 649–73.

PASTI, SVETLANA (2005) "Concepts of Professional Journalism", paper presented to the International Conference Democratization of Media and Information Societies—Potential and Reality, Euromedia Research Group, Zurich, June.

PINSON, LISA (2010) "In Digital Age, Journalism Ethics Are More Vital than Ever", *Bakersfield Express*, 3 March, http://bakersfieldexpress.org/2010/03/03/in-digital-age-journalism-ethics-are-more-vital-than-ever/, accessed 3 March 2010.

RUUSUNOKSA, LAURA (2006) "Public Journalism and Professional Culture: local, regional and national public spheres as contexts of professionalism", *Javnost—The Public* 13(4), pp. 81–98.

SCHILLER, HERBERT (1992) *Mass Communications and American Empire*, Boulder, CO: Westview Press.

SHI, ANBIN (2006) "DangDai ZhongGuo MeiTi ShengTai De BianQian Yu XinWen ZhuanYe ZhuYi De ChongGou" ["The Change of Ecology on Chinese Media and Restructure on Journalism Professionalism"], *QuanQiu ChuanMei BaoGao* [*Global Communication Report*], 15 March, http://xiaosanzi.blog.hexun.com/6737720_d.html, accessed 21 November 2010.

SOLOSKI, JOHN (2008) "News Reporting and Professionalism: some constraints on the reporting of news", in: Howard Tumber (Ed.), *Journalism: critical concepts in media and cultural studies*, Vol. 3, New York: Routledge, pp. 53–69.

VOLKMER, INGRID (2011) "Journalism and the Political Crises in the Global Network Society", in: Barbie Zelizer and Stuart Allan (Eds), *Journalism After September 11*, London: Routledge, pp. 308–18.

WU, JUNJUN (2007) "Shishang Zazhi de Dushihua Shengcun Celue" ["The Metropolitan Strategy of Fashion Magazine"], http://people.cnad.com/html/Article/2007/0530/20070530150457297.shtml, accessed 16 November 2010.

XU, WEI (2007a) "Xiang Ai Shechipin Yiyang Ai Ziji" ["Love Yourself Like You Love Luxury"], http://space.yoka.com/blog/1263, accessed 16 November 2010.

XU, WEI (2007b) "Caifu Yu Kuaile Diaocha De Qishi" ["The Enlightenment of Survey of Happiness and Fortune"], 30 April, http://blog.sina.com.cn/s/blog_486478d40100ag8x.html, accessed 1 March 2011.

YU, GUOMING (1998) "Chinese Journalism, the Survey of Professional Ethics and Professional Awareness on Chinese Media Professionals", http://www.66wen.com/05wx/xinwen/xinwen/20061102/25268_2.html, accessed 17 November 2010.

ZELIZER, BARBIE (2004) *Taking Journalism Seriously: news and the academy*, Thousand Oaks, CA: Sage.

ZHAO, YUEZHI (1998) *Media, Market, and Democracy in China: between the party line and the bottom line*, Urbana: University of Illinois Press.

ZHAO, YUEZHI (2004) "Underdogs, Lapdogs, and Watchdogs: journalists and the public sphere problematic in reformed China", in: Edward Gu and Merle Goldman (Eds), *Chinese Intellectuals Between the State and the Market*, London: Routledge, pp. 43–74.

Index

Page numbers in **bold** type refer to figures
Page numbers in *italic* type refer to tables
Page number followed by 'n' refer to notes

acta diurnal populi Romani 5
Adventure, Travel and Ecotourism World
   Congress 45
advertising 43
advice 13
Afar 52–3
agents 43; covert induced 43
Amsterdam, Treaty (1997) 78
Andrews, L. 111
Anholt, S. 43
Another 98
anti-homosexuality laws: Tasmania 45–53
App Smart 113
Appadurai, A. 60–3
Arena 92
Arvidsson, A. 43
Ashley, Y.: and Duffy, A. 7, 58–73
Attacks on the Press in 2004 (Committee to
   Protect Journalists) 61
Australia: High Court 45, *see also* Tasmania
authenticity 14

Bakhtin, M. 94
Barnhurst, K.: and Nerone, J. 29
Barthes, R. 61–2, 92–4
Baudelaire, C. 97
Bauman, Z. 15, 95–6
Baumann, S.: and Johnston, J. 59, 62
BBC3 87
Beck, U. 44, 63
Beckett, C.: and Mansell, R. 107
Bedeviled Island (Greenwald) 52–3
Benhamou, R. 92
Benjamin, G. 68
Benkler, Y. 107
Bernadotteskolen school 32
Bernard, S. 113, 116–17
Billboard 20
Blair, J. 110
blogging: fashion 91–103; finance 111, 116–17
Bolter, J. 95; and Grusin, R. 92, 95–7, 100–3
Borrelli, L. 92
Boston Globe 20

boundaries and genres study 25–40
Bourdieu, P. 12, 93
Braga, F. 69
branding: Tasmania case study 45–53
British Broadcasting Corporation (BBC) 2–3;
   BBC3 87; Lifestyle Channel 76; *Wildlife
   Magazine* 47–8
British Fashion Design (McRobbie) 93
broadcasting: public service 75–88
Brown, D. 61
Brunsdon, C. 76
Bucks 111, 116–17
Busch, R. 46
Bush, V. 93–4
business news scholarship 108
Business Week 125

cafémode 99
capitalism 43, 122; contemporary 43; forces and
   values 132
Carlson, M. 99
Carolus, J. 5
Channel 4 television 87
China 8; Communist Party (CCP) 128; consumer
   journalism self-identity 125–7, *126*; journalist
   backgrounds/ages 125–7, *125*; lifestyle
   magazine journalism 121–36; news vs
   magazine journalist comparison 130–2;
   professionalism concept 123–4; Renmin
   University 129–30; senior journalist
   occupational choices 127–30; study method
   124–5
Chinese/Malay/Indian/Other (CMIO) 59–60
Chua, B. 59–60; and Kuo, E. 65; and Rajah, A.
   62, 68
Cicero 5
circuses 58
citizen journalism 99
citizenship 16
collective intelligence television 86
Comedy Central 3
commercialism 5, 26; media 7
common sociality 43

community journalism 106–20; foundations 107–8; and Twitter 114–18, *see also* service journalism
competition 79–80
Condé Nast International 122–4; *Traveller* 47
confessionals 13
consumer journalism self-identity: China 125–7, *126*
consumerism 6, 25–6, 122, 132–3; and New Economy 14–15, *see also* genre blending study
content: mapping 29; mills 15
Copenhagen: Fashion Week 36; Royal Veterinary and Agricultural University 31
corruption (of journalism) 26
Cosmopolitan 122, 129
cosmopolitanism 44–5; banal 44; cultural 44, 51; political 44, 47, 51
Counihan, C.: and Van Esterik, P. 58–61
Court of Europe 79
Croome, R. 51
cross-media production 77–8
Crouch, G.: and Dore, L. 41
cultural boundaries: Singapore 61–2
cultural journalism 7, 25–6; citizenship 16; critical 18; hard news 26–8; soft news 27–9; taste 12, *see also* genre blending study
culture: self-improvement 69–70

Daily Telegraph 48
Damstyle 98
Dazed Digital 98
Deleuze, G.: and Guattari, F. 95–6
Denmark 31, 36; (Danish) newspapers 28–39
Derrida, J. 94
Deuze, M. 15, 99
developmentalism 60
Dewey, J. 107
Discovery Channel 2, 75
Discovery Communication International 19
Diva 93
Dixon, J. 102
Do-It-Yourself Citizenship 16
Domingo, D. 88
Dore, L.: and Crouch, G. 41
Dormoy, G. 99
Dowty, R. 47
Duffy, A.: and Ashley, Y. 7, 58–73

economy 27
editorial importance 34–5; competitive media landscape 34–5
Eickelkamp, A. 14
Eide, M. 27, 31; and Knight, G. 5–6, 76, 107
Ekstra Bladet 28–39
Eliot, A. 14

Elle 99; Chinese 122; Show Me Your Wardrobe section 102
Embarrassing Bodies (Channel 4) 87
empathy: social 17
entertainment 12
Entwistle, J.: and Rocamora, A. 93
Epstein, E. 109
ES Magazine 99
Esquire 128
ethical journalism 14, 123
Ethical Traveler 47
ethnic classification/separatism: Singapore 59–61
ethnic separatism: food 60–1
ethnocentrism 18
Ettrup, N. 36
European Union (EU) 77–9
Evans, C.: and Thornton, M. 100
everyday life 27–9; changing coverage 31–3, 36–7

Face, The 92
facehunter 101
Facehunter, The (Rodic) 103
factual programme changes 75–8
Fair, J. 47–9
Family 128
fashion 7–8, 28, 31–2, 35–6; blogs 97–103; changing coverage 31–2, 36–7; decentred 97–100; democratising effect 8; and flanerie 96–7; hypertextuality 92–5; magazines 97–103, 122; media study 92–3; remediation 100–3; rhizomatic 95–7; seasonal collections 96
Fashion System, The (Barthes) 92
Fashion Theory 93
fashionstreetlisboa 98
Fashiontoast 100
FBI (NRK consumer programme) 80, 84
Finance, The 125
Financial Times 47
Fishman, M. 109
Fiske, J. 11, 16
Flanagan, R. 46
flanerie: and fashion 96–7
Flinn, J. 49–51
Foley, B. 99
food 7, 12, 20, 29, 33–4; article categorisation 64–5; authenticity/creativity 62–4; changing coverage 33–4; ethnic separatism 60–1; experts and expats 65–6, 69; global culture and boundaries 15–16, 61–3; health/others 65–7, 70; politics influence 58–71; poverty and politics 65–6, 69–70; role in identity 63–71; Singapore media study 64–71; where and what to eat 65–9; writing 62–4
Foucault, M. 94
Franklin, B.: *et al* 4

freebies 41, 47, 51
From, U.: and Kristensen, N. 7, 25–40
Fuery, K. 91, 96, 99
Fürsich, E. 4, 7; and Kavoori, A. 3, 41

G&J magazine group 124
Gadgetwise (Pogue) 112
Gans, H. 109
gardening 16, 29
G'Day USA 50
gender analysis 16
genre blending study 25–40; blurring boundaries
   25–39; changing coverage and consumption
   29–34, *30*; Danish newspapers 28–39;
   everyday life 28, 32–3; fashion 31–2; food/
   travel/motoring 33–4; hard news and cultural
   journalism 26–8; living 31; media institution
   changes 26–39; production perspective 35–7;
   strategic trademarks/theoretical perspective
   37–9; study methodology 28
Gevinson, Tavi 94, 99
Giddens, A. 62
Giese, D. 35–6
Giffard, C.A. 5
Gill, A.A. 47
global sensibility 18–22
Go, F.: and Govers, R. 43
Golin, C.: and Cardoso, E. 27
Goode, J. 61
Govers, R.: and Go, F. 43
GQ 99, 122
Grazia 101–2
Great Depression 108, 110; Wall Street Crash
   110
Greenwald, J. 47; *Bedeviled Island* 52–3
Grisey, G. 98
Grobart, S. 112
Grusin, R.: and Bolter, J. 92, 95–7, 100–3
Guangdong Publishing House 128
Guardian 92
Guattari, F.: and Deleuze, G. 95–6
Gudelunas, D. 114
Gunns (wine/pulp mill) 46

Hachette Filipacchi Media 122, 124
Hahn, H. 93
Hanitzsch, T. 3; *et al* 107
Hanke, R. 61
Hannerz, U. 44
Hanusch, F. 1–10, 41
hard news: and cultural journalism 26–8
Hargreaves, J. 100
Harpers 99
Harper's Bazaar 100
Hartley, J. 3–4, 15, 75–6, 107
Haskins, J. 111

health reporting 7, 13, 75–6, 79–80; HIV/AIDS 76;
   and NRK 74–89; SARS 76; and wellness 27–9,
   see also Puls
Hearst Magazines 122–4
Heimstone 98
Hill, A. 77
HIV/AIDS 76
Hjarvard, S. 27, 38
Hömberg, W.: and Neuberger, C. 13–14
Hovden, J.: and Knapskog, K. 27
hypertextuality: fashion 92–5

i-D 101
identity 43; competitive 43
ideology: and politics 15–16
In Real Life (IRL) 97
infotainment 4, 75, 123
inter-coder reliability process 64–5
internet forums 13
Islands 47

James, A. 62–3
Janssen, S.: *et al* 27
Jansson, A. 26, 38
Jarvis, J. 107
Jazewitsch, A. 98
Jenkins, H. 77, 87
Jenkins, J. 99
Jenkins, M. 46
Jobling, P. 92
Johnson, R. 99
Johnston, J.: and Baumann, S. 59, 62
Jones, S.: and Taylor, B. 62
journalism: liquid 15
july-stars 100
Juvenal 58; *panem and circenses* 58
Jyllands-Posten 28–39

Karlascloset 100
Kavoori, A.: and Fürsich, E. 3, 41
King, G. 49–50; and King P. 52
kingdomofstyle 100
Kitch, C. 5
Klein, W. 100–1
Knapskog, K.: and Hovden, J. 27
Knight, G.: and Eide, M. 5–6, 76, 107
Korsmeyer, C. 61
Kristensen, N.: and From, U. 7, 25–40
Kristeva, J. 94
Kuo, E.: and Chua, B. 65

Laïdi, Z. 97
Landow, G. 94–5, 98
Lash, S.: and Lury, C. 45
Lau, S. 98–101
Law, G. 46
Lee Kuan Yew 60–1

leisure 12
Leong, W. 59
Levinsen, J. 37
Lewsi, R. 93
Li, E. 129
Li, S. 8, 121–36
Lieber, R. 113, 116–17
lifestyle 76
Lifestyle Channel (BBC) 76
lifestyle journalism 1–8; definition 2–4, 26–8,
    133n; dimensions 11–15; historical
    development 29
Lifestyle magazine (China) 127, 134n
lifestyle magazine journalism: China 121–36
liquid journalism 15
Lister, M.: et al 93
logging/forestry: Tasmania 48–54
London Fashion Week 93
Lonely Planet 19, 50
Los Angeles Times 20
Lowell Thomas Travel Journalism Awards 53
Lu, Y.: and Yu, W. 130–1
Lury, C. 42–3, 48; and Lash, S. 45

Ma, E. 123
McChesney, R. 123
McGaurr, L. 7, 41–57
McKenna, K. 111
McLuhan, M. 100
McNair, B. 3
McRobbie, A. 93
magazine journalism 8; in China 8
magazines 99; fashion 92–3, 97–103, 122; men's
    99, 122, 128
Makansutra (food guide) 71
Make My Body Younger (BBC3) 87
Manovich, L. 97
Mansell, R.: and Beckett, C. 107
market feedback 43
market-driven journalism 3–4
materialism 65–6
Mead, M. 61
media: commercialism 7; landscape 34–5; study
    (fashion) 92–3
Meijer, C. 11, 17, 20
Men's Health 128
men's magazines 99, 122, 128
Le Mercure 92
Merholz, P. 91
Metcalf, S. 46–7
metroXpress 28–39
Meyers, C. 123
Miles, P. 47
Miller, J. 110
mining: Tasmania 48–54
modernity: liquid 15
Moeran, B. 92–3

Le Monde 92
Mooney, N. 48–50
motor journalism 33–4
multiculturalism: and nation-building (Singapore)
    59–70, **66–7**
music reviews 20–2
Mythbusters 75

nation-building and multiculturalism (Singapore)
    59–70, **66–7**
National Geographic 75
National Geographic Traveler 46, 51–2; scorecard
    51–2
negotiation: social 12
Nelson, T. 93
Nerone, J.: and Barnhurst, K. 29
Nestlé 62
Neuberger, C.: and Hömberg, W. 13–14
New Economy: and consumerism 14–15
New York Times 2–3, 8, 20, 51, 106–18;
    CyberTimes 111; Electronic Media Company
    111; News of Food column 110; personal
    finance/technology 106, 110–14; and service/
    community journalism 106–18
New Yorker 61
Newman, O.: and De Zoysa, R. 59
news: business 108; hard and cultural journalism
    26–8; popular 11; soft and cultural journalism
    27–9; vs magazine journalist comparison
    (China) 130–2
newspapers: Danish 28–39
Nicholls, P. 50–1
nogoodforme 91
Norwegian Broadcasting Corporation (NRK) 7,
    74–89, 80, 84; adapting to competition 79–80;
    cross-media production 77–8; factual
    programme changes 75–8; and health
    reporting 74–89; lifestyle 76; online journalism
    88; and public service 75–88; reality and
    participation 77; reorganisation 79; study
    method 78, see also Puls

objectivity 14
occupational choices: senior journalist (China)
    127–30
Oftimica 98
online journalism 88
Othering strategies 19–21
Otterman, S. 51

People's Action Party (Singapore) 60
Perry, F. 36
personal technology 7
Philipsen, H. 77
Pliny the Elder 5
Pogue, D. 111–16; tweets 114–16, **115**
politics 27

Politiken 28–39
polygamy (of place) 44
Pop 99–100
popular news concept 11
Porter, S. 110
La Presse 93; *Courrier de Paris* section 93
problem solving 13–14; advice functions 13; and confessionals 13
production perspective 34–7
professionalism concept: China 123–4
public quality concept 11, 17–20
public relations practitioners (PRs) 41–3, 47–9
public role 11–24
public service broadcasting 75–88, *see also* BBC; NRK
Puijk, R. 74–90
Puls health program 7, 74–89; *Bedre* 78, 83–4, 87; cross media publishing 83–4; form and content (television) 80–2; health and lifestyle internet pages 84–5, *85*; independent web publishing 84–5, *85*; as multimedia production 83–6; and NRK 80–8; *Nye* 80, 85; as reality series 82–3; themes 81–3, *82*; user participation 85–6
punkyb (Grisey) 98
Purple 99–100

Quirt, J. 111

Rabine, L. 92
Rajah, A.: and Chua, B. 62, 68
rational/critical perspective 14
Rayli 122
Readers 125, 128
reality: and participation 77; series 82–3
Relation 5
relevance: productivity and public quality 16–18
remediation: fashion 100–3
Renmin University (China) 129–30; Media Research Institute (MRI) 130
research agenda 6–8
rhizomatic fashion 95–7
Ritchie, B. 51
Rocamora, A. 8, 91–105; and Entwistle, J. 93
Rodic, Y. 103
rojak (ethnic cuisine) 59–61
Rolling Stone 20
Rough Guide 19–20
Roush, C. 108
Royal Veterinary and Agricultural University (Copenhagen) 31
Rozin, P. 61
Rumi 100–1

San Francisco Chronicle 49–50
Sanlian Life Weekly 128–9
SARS 76

Sartorialist, The (Schuman) 101–3
Saussure, F. 92
Savage, D. 114
Schiller, H. 123
Schjonhaug, A.: and Slyngstad, E. 101
Schneider, V. 117
Schrödingers Katt 80
Schudson, M. 2, 5, 17
Schuman, S. 101–3
SEEC Media Group 124, 127, 134n
Seetoh, K. 71
self-improvement culture 69–70
senior journalist occupational choices: China 127–30
service journalism 14, 27, 76; business news scholarship 108; as community experience 106–18; community foundations 107–8; networked 107; and *New York Times* 106–18; personal finance/technology 106, 110–14; study method 109–10
Sex and the City 32, 36
Shanghai Translation Publishing House 122
Shugart, H. 61
signed accounts 42
Singapore 7; Chinese/Malay/Indian/Other (CMIO) 59–60; cultural boundaries 61–2; ethnic classification/separatism 59–61; food/politics influences 58–71; media study 64–71; nation-building and multiculturalism 59–70, **66–7**; People's Action Party 60, *see also* food
Slyngstad, E.: and Schjonhaug, A. 101
social empathy 17
sociality: common 43
Society of American Travel Writers (SATW) 53
soft news: and cultural journalism 27–9
Soloski, J. 123
South Windy Window 125
sports journalism 2
Stauth, G. 59
Stephens, M. 5
Story Time 125, 128
Straits Times 58, 64–70
study: justification 4–6; method 78
stylefromtokyo 98
Sundvor, E. 27
survivalism 60
Szerszynski, B. 44

tabloidization 26
Tasmania 7, 41–2, 45–53; anti-homosexuality laws 50–1; destination brand study 45–53; Devil Appeal 49–52; environment movement 47–53; Franklin River High Court 45; logging/forestry and mining 48–54; Wilderness Society 46–7; Wilderness World Heritage Area 45
taste 12
Tavi (fashion blogger) 94, 99

INDEX

Taylor, B.: and Jones, S. 62
technology: personal 7
Tedeschi, R. 113
television 2, 75; Channel 4 87; collective
    intelligence 86, *see also* British Broadcasting
    Corporation (BBC)
thesartorialist 101
thestreethearts 101
thestylerookie 94
Thornton, M.: and Evans, C. 100
Thousand Plateaus, A (Deleuze and Guattari) 95
Times 47
Titz, K.: *et al* 64
Tomlinson, J. 96, 101–2
tourism 43–52; marketing 43
Tourism Concern 47
Tourism Tasmania 45–52
Tourtellot, J. 52
Travel + Leisure 46
travel journalism 4–6, 12–14, 19–22, 28, 33–4;
    branding/destination 42–4; changing coverage
    33–4; as cosmopolitan project 44–5; Tasmania
    as case study 45–53
Travelers 19
Trends Media Group 122–4, 128–9
Tuchman, G. 109
Tvilum, P. 34–5
Twitter 114–18

Urry, J. 44
Usher, N. 8, 106–20

Van Esterik, P.: and Counihan, C. 58–61
Velayutham, S. 60

Village Voice 20
Violent Femmes 51
Virilio, P. 96
visiting journalist programs (VJPs) 41–2, 46–8,
    51–2
Vogue 92–3, 99–100; Point of View section 92

Wall Street Journal 108
Walsh, P. 99
Walterlin, U. 48
Wang, F. 128–9, 134n
wellness: and health reporting 27–9
Wheeler, M. 50
Whitt, J. 5
Wilderness Society (Tasmania) 46–7
World Trade Organization (WTO) 122
World War II (1939–45) 110
WWD 99

Xu, F. 127
Xu, L. 129
Xu, W. 129

Yang, L. 127
Yi, W. 129
Yu, W.: and Lu, Y. 130–1

Zelizer, B. 2–3
Zoysa, R. De: and Newman, O. 59

JOURNALISM PRACTICE

Volume 5 Number 6 December 2011

JOURNALISM PRACTICE

Editor: **Bob Franklin**, *Cardiff University, UK*

Journalism Practice provides opportunities for reflective, critical and research-based studies focused on the professional practice of journalism. *Journalism Practice*'s primary concern is to analyse and explore issues of practice and professional relevance. The journal aims to complement current trends to expansion in the teaching and analysis of journalism practice within the academy, reflection on the emergence of a reflective curriculum and thereby help to consolidate journalism as an intellectual discipline within the landscape of higher education.

Journalism Practice is devoted to: the study and analysis of significant issues arising from journalism as a field of professional practice; relevant developments in journalism training and education, as well as the construction of a reflective curriculum for journalism; analysis of journalism practice across the distinctive but converging media platforms of magazines, newspapers, online, radio and television; and the provision of a public space for practice-led, scholarly contributions from journalists as well as academics.

www.tandfonline.com/rjop

Routledge
Taylor & Francis Group

Related titles from Routledge

ROUTLEDGE

Explorations in Global Media Ethics

Edited by Muhammad Ayish and Shakuntala Rao

Studies of global media and journalism have repeatedly returned to discussions of ethics. This book highlights the difficulty that journalists encounter when establishing appropriate ethical practices and marks the pressing importance of global media ethics as a subject of current debate. A wide range of contributors – both scholars and practitioners of journalism – identify how changes in journalism practice, developments in new media technologies, legal regulations, and shifting patterns of ownership all play a role in creating ethical tensions for journalists, with some chapters in the book suggesting practical solutions to this pertinent issue. The growing need to faithfully represent other diverse cultural groups is also considered.

Explorations in Global Media Ethics recognises that, with the escalation of globalisation and a public striving for honest quality media, journalists around the world face an increasing pressure to comply with and simultaneously satisfy diverse ethical practices at both a local and a global level. The book sympathises with the position of the journalist and calls for greater consideration of his ambiguous role.

This book was originally published as a special issue of *Journalism Studies*.

May 2012: 246 x 174: 124 pp
Hb: 978-0-415-62285-1
£85 / $135

Available from all good bookshops